Medical Doctors
of
Maryland
in the C.S.A.

by
Daniel D. Hartzler

HERITAGE BOOKS
2007

HERITAGE BOOKS
AN IMPRINT OF HERITAGE BOOKS, INC.

Books, CDs, and more—Worldwide

For our listing of thousands of titles see our website
at
www.HeritageBooks.com

Published 2007 by
HERITAGE BOOKS, INC.
Publishing Division
65 East Main Street
Westminster, Maryland 21157-5026

Copyright © 1979 Daniel D. Hartzler

Other books by the author:
A Band of Brothers: Photographic Epilogue to Marylanders in the Confederacy
Carroll County, Maryland Baseball: Men's Amateur and Semi-Pro Baseball, 1850-1999
Marylanders in the Confederacy

All rights reserved. No part of this book may be reproduced or transmitted in any form or by any means, electronic or mechanical, including photocopying, recording or by any information storage and retrieval system without written permission from the author, except for the inclusion of brief quotations in a review.

International Standard Book Number: 978-0-7884-3150-0

DEDICATION

This work is dedicated to those who have the confidence to enter into an endeavor with complete determination in absolute devotion to their Creator.

PREFACE

No other event in American history has produced so many volumes from so many individual sources as the War Between the States. The tremendous impact of this gigantic conflict between Americans in this borderland where physicians had been practicing in relative peace caused chaos. The object of this work is to establish in a durable form, a record of the exciting, romantic careers of those practitioners who made the supreme Southern commitment. Due to the scarcity of documentary material these sketches are written in a cavalry gallop. I have made no attempt to dwell on the many activities of their brilliant genius other than to mention their feats. Neither has much distinction been made between Maryland's native medical sons or her adopted ones of whom there were eight who did not reside in the state until after the war. These patriots went to war that freedom and independence might continue to live in America as handed down by their fathers' fathers. I have tried to show the causes for their action by incorporating the developments in the state as they unfolded.

Western Maryland was a predominantly Unionist stronghold but there was not a town or village that could not boast of or scorn a soldier in the Confederacy, depending upon their political views. Allegany County gave three doctors to the cause, Washington eight and Frederick an unbelievable eighteen.

Eight of these physicians had seen previous service in the army and eight in the navy as medical officers in the past or had resigned before accepting commissions in the C.S.A. These were the very few doctors who had in any way experienced the environment surrounding combat casualties. One was a West Point graduate, one served in the state militia as a major general, five as elected company officers and ten were in Maryland's surgical corps.

The great majority of the physicians of this volume entered the Southern service as privates in the rank and file. Fifteen continued to wear everything from the butternut of an enlisted man to the wreath of a brigadier general. They were conspicuous warriors as line and staff officers, in the ordinance, engineer, signal, and quartermaster corps. The majority of these doctors entered the medical corps because of the dire need. As medics many practiced as contract physicians employed by the Confederacy before receiving commissions, while eight contract doctors never did enter the corps. In the medical department of the two hundred and eight doctors included in these biographies, one was surgeon-general of Virginia, one became surgeon-general of Florida and another surgeon-general of North Carolina, while sixty-five gained the rank of surgeon. Dentists are also mentioned with the recognition of five D.D.S.'s who served in our nation's first dental corps and two M.D.'s were also dentists. Of the eighteen naval physicians, two were surgeons, four passed assistant surgeons, eleven assistant surgeons, and one was an acting assistant surgeon.

The surgeon tendered his affection and compassion while his ears were pierced by the heavy cannonade, the clash of sabers and many times he felt the splinters of minnie balls, then came the horrifying groans and shrieks, the bitter sobs and heavy sighs. His eyes fell upon the dismal look of despair upon the faces of the young warriors, the dreadful sight of shattered and mangled forms of God's most refined creation. His hands labored incessantly in life and death procedures for which civilian training had not prepared him. His nose could smell the hideous odor of burned flesh and he could almost taste the gangrenous effluvia. Finally darkness hid the dreadful scene but as he tried to sleep his brain was pierced by the never forgotten piteous cries and maniacal ravings of those he was unable to relieve.

Of these heroic doctors many were wounded while attending their brothers in arms on the field of battle; one lost an arm, others received psychological scars of their souls, while seven were killed in action or died as a result of the insidious diseases that they were combatting.

The Southern soldiers accepted the results of the contest and laid down their arms in good faith but when asked like a whipped child to say they were wrong and sorry for what they did, it was asking too much. They felt they were right in 1861 and they knew they were right in 1865. Perhaps the cleverist cliche written by a Marylander after the war was over was, "We were not whipped but wore ourselves out thrashing them." As time elapsed after the war more and more of our state's sons returned to their homes; hundreds of sons and daughters of other Southern states, escaping from the persecution of reconstruction, came to the old land of sanctuary, as Maryland was known in the early days of the colony. They were destitute, having lost everything except the honor and glory they deservingly earned on the battlefield. Peace and prosperity of the country was now what they had at heart. They grew to realize that God never intended America to be broken into two countries and the question had been permanently settled by the sword. The Confederate flag which they hallowed did not affect the love for the Stars and Stripes any more than the admiration for a loving wife affected the love of the God they served. Their memory is enshrined in the hearts of all our countrymen who believe in the wonderful heritage we are privileged to enjoy.

I have endeavored to produce an authentic picture of the Southern feeling in Maryland, the medical procedures and treatment of the time. I have been fortunate in tapping the resources of national agencies, federal and private libraries, medical institutions along with both published and private manuscripts. I am not only in debt to the many resourceful and accommodating professional staffs of the above but also the wonderful generosity of the following:

William A. Albaugh III	Father Paul P. Iaia
Benjamin F. Allen	Robert K. Krick
Ms. Rose Bowman	Miss Rose Latzo
Carroll Brice	Miss Susan Anne Lucy
William L. Brown III	Dave Mar
G. Craig Caba	Dr. Gilcin F. Meadors
Miss Virginia Carmichael	Ms. Mary Bess Miller
Mrs. Janet Colburn	Reuben H. Morningstar, III
Erick Davis	Star Pictures
Dr. E. A. Dettbarn	Stuart Mullendore
Mrs. Mary D. Dudderar	Harry Wright Newman
Donald & Jeanne Elliott	Daniel C. Toomey
Gardner P. H. Foley	Bill Turner
Ms. Gerry Garren	Miss Mary Ringgold Trippe
Dr. John & Marian Goettee	Bradley Yohe

FOREWARD

There have been wars almost since the beginning of mankind. Each war has had its share of heroes. Some were those who gave commands, and some were those who followed commands. There were those who gave support to the troops, providing supplies or delivering communications. Also, there were those brave people who bore no arms but risked their lives in the midst of battle to provide services to their men. They were the men of the cloth who gave spiritual assistance. They were the dedicated nurses tending to the needs of their patients. Finally, there were the doctors using whatever skills they had, whatever medicines were available, attempting to repair the terrible wounds of battle or treat the ravaging diseases which seem to be a part of every war.

The author has chosen to relate the names and biographies of a particular group of doctors who rendered service during the Civil War, 1861-1865. After seven years of research he has compiled a vast list of Marylanders in the Southern army, navy and marines. From this tremendous assembled mass he has extracted the doctors of this state who served as surgeons for the Confederacy and by further exploration has uncovered a wealth of information. Such a collection is unique in that Maryland was not one of the Confederate States, however, being a borderline state, there were those who chose to serve the cause of the Confederacy. What was surprising to the author, and should be to the reader, is the large number of doctors who made this choice, total of two hundred and eight in all.

Every known source was used in writing this book, but it must be understood that there may be some inadvertent omissions. No historical source book claimed to have compiled a perfect record. Therefore, the author cannot be held accountable for any errors or omissions. However, he must be credited for having uncovered some heretofore little known facts about Maryland physicians who joined the Confederacy. This book, the only one of its kind on this subject material, should become a most valuable resource book for historians, as well as for the descendants of the doctors listed.

A dedicated physician treats the human body without regard to race, color or creed, nor to the type clothing or uniform his patient is wearing. His primary concern is only for treating the wounded or sick body. Why then did these men choose to join the Confederacy? Why did they risk alienation by their colleagues who were sympathizers with the union? Let them tell you their stories on the following pages.

Ernest A. Dettbarn, M.D.
Walkersville, Maryland

ILLUSTRATIONS

Page
13 Secession Badge
15 Secession Badge
16 Secession Badge
17 Patriotic Envelope
18 Secession Badge
19 Patriotic Envelope
20 Secession Badge
21 Lt. Col. James Brethed
24 Secession Badge
26 Chloroform Inhaler
27 Militia Hat Badge
28 Secession Badge
31 Secession Cockade
32 Assistant Surgeon Harry Woodward Dorsey, Jr. Frockcoat
33 Amputation Kit
34 Assistant Surgeon Richard Emory
45 Patriotic Envelope
48 Medical Canteen
54 Apothecary Medicine Chest
55 Patriotic Envelope
56 Surgeon Charles MacGill
57 Maryland Cross and Cross Of Honor
60 Apothecary Scale
63 Medicine Bottles
65 Surgeon John Randolph Page
67 Surgeon's Pocket Kit
69 Maple Medical Chest (side view)
70 Maple Medical Chest (top view)
72 Dental Surgeon's Kit
75 Mortar and Pestle
76 Surgeon William Frederick Stewart
78 Surgeon's Amputation Kit
80 Dental Case
81 Dental Operating Kit
84 Cranium Operating Kit
85 Surgeon Thomas H. Williams
86 Surgeon's Leather Bag
88 Pocket Watch "Dr. J. B. Wortham"
90 Assistant Surgeon William Proby Young
91 Assistant Surgeon John Forney Zacharias
92 Surgeon's Kit—Dr. J. F. Zacharias

EDWARD T. ADAMS

Crisical issues faced a rapidly growing nation in 1860 as Edward T. Adams realized Maryland was the most important of the border states because of her geographical position. There were two forces at work which influenced her loyalty: the new industrial manufactures with semi-skilled workers and the traditional plantation colony of the agriculture system, which was still the dominant factor that led to close Southern association. The conflict of opinions and sentiment existed in every city, town and village between merchant and customer, employer and employee, neighbor and friend, father and son. Thus the state tottered on the brink of civil war, the greatest American tragedy, in which Marylander would soon fight against Marylander, brother against brother. Adams was a medical student at Georgetown University but being inflamed with the Southern ideals of independence, he postponed his schooling and following his impetuous youthful spirit he joined the Confederate Maryland Guerilla Zouaves which became Co. C Nelligan Louisiana Infantry. Soon he was detailed as a hospital steward, then as an apothecary in Chimborazo Hospital in Richmond. Passing the medical board in the late spring of 1864, he was commisioned an assistant surgeon on June 1 and assigned to the 25th Virginia Cavalry. At the end of four dreadful years, 600,000 American soldiers had died in the disastrous War Between The States. In terms of casualties this fraternal conflict was the costliest war our nation ever faced. A surprising tragic feature of this war's statistics was that many more men were killed by sickness and disease than by bullet, shell, sabre or bayonet. Of the 360,000 deaths in the Union armies, only 110,000 were battlefield casualties. Of the 258,000 Confederate deaths, only 94,000 were combat inflicted. A fascinating note on Georgetown University shows of the 1,500 students and alumni of military age when the war began 1,141 actually donned uniforms, 216 in blue and 925 in gray.

W. JOHN ADDISON

Born in Prince George's County W. John Addison was practicing in Baltimore by 1850 and received a commission in the Southern navy as assistant surgeon in the early summer of 1861. South Carolina had seceded on the 20th of December, 1860, and by the 1st of February she had been joined by Mississippi, Florida, Alabama, Georgia, Louisiana, and Texas. Early in February, Jefferson Davis was elected president and the military build was under way. As the formal collision was rapidly approaching the newly established Navy Department, with its limited resources, endeavored to organize its sailors and to build and equip its ships. In these infant days assignments were made hurriedly for immediate necessity. Assistant Surgeon Addison served on the C.S.S. *Maurepas* and was commended for gallantry at St. Charles, Arkansas on June 17, 1862. Dr. Addison was then sent to Jackson Station that fall. By 1863, he was aboard the C.S.S. *Patrick Henry*. Being sent to the Red River defenses he was on the ram *W. H. Webb* when she ran the gauntlet from Shreveport to below New Orleans in the last naval action on the Mississippi. The vessel was run ashore and burned on April 24, 1865. Surgeon Addison was captured and sent to New York, then to Boston harbor arriving at Fort Warren on May 10. He was confined until released when he took the oath on June 13 and returned to Prince George's County.

SAMUEL ANNAN 1800-1868

Born in Philadelphia Samuel Annan received his medical education at Edinburgh University in the Class of 1820. He practiced in Emmitsburg with his half brother, Andrew Annan, where on April 5, 1822, he performed the first tracheotomy in the state of Maryland. In 1826, he came to Baltimore where from 1827 to 1834 Dr. Annan was professor of anatomy at the Washington Medical College in Baltimore which he founded. In 1835 he was assistant commissioner of the Board of Health. From 1838 to 1845 he was the attending physician at the Alms House. In 1846 he secured a position at Transylvania University in Kentucky where he taught obstetrics and after three years was professor of practice. From 1853 to 1857 Dr. Annan was superintendent of Western Lunatic Asylum at Hopkinsville. He then became surgeon of a ship line that went from this country to Liverpool. The nucleus of the Confederate Medical Corps was composed of former personnel in the Federal Army. The need for many more medical officers coincided with the assemblying of armies as large scale epidemics of measles, malaria, typhoid fever and other camp diseases broke out early in the war. It was at this time that Dr. Annan volunteered his services and was commissioned on August 16, 1862, from the state of Maryland. He was working in Lynchburg General Hospital No. 1 until November 12 when he was assigned to duty on the board of examiners for furloughs and discharges. In August of 1863 Dr. Annan was at the hospital at Buchanan, then in October he was transferred to St. Mary's Hospital at West Point, Mississippi. On February 8, -865, he was on field duty with the Army of Tennessee. He was paroled at Macon, Georgia, and stated that he was returning to Baltimore.

GEORGE W. ARCHER 1824-1907

This son of Dr. Robert Harris Archer, Sr. of Harford County completed his medical training at the University of Pennsylvania in 1847 and became the third generation practitioner establishing his office at Churchville. Dr. Archer was appointed surgeon of the 42nd Regiment Maryland Militia on January 23, 1861. Agitated by the invasion of the Southland, he left his family and crossed the Potomac in the fall of 1861. On November 5, he appeared before the examining board and eight days later was appointed an assistant surgeon assigned to General Hospital No. 1 at Richmond. He joined two brothers already in the C.S.A., Robert Harris, Jr., a lieutenant colonel in the 55th Virginia Infantry and James, a private in Dardan's Mississippi Artillery. By January of 1863, assistant surgeon Archer was practicing his profession in Montgomery White Sulphur Springs Hospital. The medical corps was kept extremely busy. It must be remembered that the discoveries of Louis Pasteur, Joseph Lister and their associates, which completely revolutionized procedure and theory, were not known. The South mobilized more than 600,000 fighting men and it is conservatively estimated that, on the average, each one of these fell victim to disease and wounds approximately six times during the war. Such statistical data illustrates the gravity of medical problems that confronted the doctors under the stars and bars. By February of 1865, Assistant Surgeon Archer was at Montgomery, Alabama, in St. Mary's Hospital. After the inevitable happened, he returned to his native state near Belair where he was a distinguished physican and litterateur.

ARCHIBALD ATKINSON, JR. 1832-

Born in Virginia he attended medical lectures at the University of Virginia and was graduated from the University of Pennsylvania in 1854; he also studied at Dublin's Rotunda Hospital and the University of Paris before coming to Baltimore and hanging out his shingle in 1857. His sober conviction of right and justice lead him to the Southern side of this controversy. Dr. Atkinson was appointed assistant surgeon to Wise Legion when the first contingency of doctors was formally inducted on June 21, 1861. On August 16, 1862, he was placed with the 10th Virginia Cavalry for only a month when he was again transferred to the 31st Virginia Infantry. On September 26, 1862, he was promoted to surgeon. He was wounded at Opequon on September 19, 1864, in the Third Battle of Winchester, then captured near Harrisonburg. Both governments agreed in June of 1862, that if the enemy's chaplains, officers of the medical staff, apothecaries, hospital nurses and servants fell into the hands of either American army they were not prisoners of war unless the commander had reasons to retain them. This extremely significant development meant that when an army retreated after an engagement the understandable reluctance of previous times to stay with the wounded because of the dreaded captivity was overcome. But because of maladministration of subordinate officers and controversy of prior exchange of medical officers detention sometimes occurred for months. Surgeon Atkinson was exchanged on January 11, 1865, assigned to Walker's Brigade and surrendered at Appomattox on April 9. He received a professorship in materia medica and therapeutics at the College of Physicians and Surgeons in the Monumental City. Later he was associated with the Baltimore Medical College.

CALEB DORSEY BAER 1828-1863

Baer was born in Middletown Valley, son of Dr. Jacob Baer. Caleb and his older brother by one year, Charles J., were educated at the Frederick Academy, Baltimore City College, St. John's College and the University of Maryland Medical School. They became practitioners working in the beautiful valley between Catoctin and Blue Ridge Mountains. Jacob Baer was a surgeon's mate of the 16th Maryland Regiment of Infantry during the War of 1812. In the spring of 1861, he was an advocate of the unconstitutional conduct of the Federal Government and beseeched the immediate recognition of the independent new Confederacy. Yet, on July 28, 1861, he became examining doctor of this congressional district and was appointed surgeon of the 1st Regiment Potomac Home Brigade Infantry U.S.A. He held this position only four months before resigning and returning to private practice in Frederick. In the meantime Caleb Dorsey tendered his abilities to the C.S.A. and was commissioned an assistant surgeon on June 19, 1861, to the 2nd Missouri Infantry. Conflict of thoughts and opinions were so widely varied and intense excitements rose to such a pitch that some became so emphatic that the cherished unity of the family was shattered. Charles J. Baer stayed in Middletown Valley during the trying conflict and during the three major battles near his home he attended suffering men who wore both the blue and the gray. Caleb Dorsey Baer was promoted to surgeon and assigned to the 9th Missouri Infantry on March 22, 1863. Soon he was made senior surgeon of the 4th Brigade of Forrest Division. On June 9, an officer filed charges of neglect of duty against him. The accusations stemmed from a march on June 5 near Little Rock, Arkansas, when he neglected to furnish adequate ambulance transportation for the 9th Regiment wounded while the smaller Regiment of sharpshooters had the largest wagon. While at Helena in charge of the sick and wounded, Surgeon Baer was taken ill and died on August 30. After the war, his body was disinterred and returned to Frederick where it rests in the family plot at Mt. Olivet Cemetery which now contains the remains of all three doctors, thus physically the family circle was completed. The remembrance of his gracious deeds, his untiring devotion and his buoyant courage "Inspiratione ad altros" inspired others to emulate him.

JOSEPH ABELL BADEN 1833-1902

Born in St. Mary's County Baden attended the public schools and Charlotte Hall College, then was graduated from the University of Maryland Medical College in 1865 and practiced in his native county. The eastern shore was not conspicuous for its loyalty to the Federal Goverment. St. Mary's County was a hub of secession within a state known as America in Miniature and was dubbed the little South Carolina. Even in the first two months of 1861, the slogan of the populous was "The Union and The Constitutional rights of all the States, for the sake of the States, but under any circumstances, and under all circumstances, the Union of the South for the sake of the South." By the end of April all eleven militia units paraded under the banner of the Southern Republic. The County Commissioners authorized the procurement of $10,000.00 for arms; the citizenry almost to a man demanded the state to withdraw; frenzied excitement was at fever-pitch. Within the next few months practically every family in the county could boast of members in the Confederate service. Dr. Baden was commissioned an assistant surgeon on May 1, 1862, and was at Winder Hospital on Cary Street in the western outskirts of Richmond where many other physicians from the black and gold state were working. He remained there until ordered to Longstreet's corpsmen of the west and was transferred back to his old post in Winder Infirmary. In 1865 he was relieving the suffering at Jackson Hospital. Leaving with the evacuation of Richmond, Assistant Surgeon Baden was paroled on April 30 at Norfolk and gave his destination as Calvert County. He practiced after the iron clad oath was removed until 1876 in St. Mary's County when he came to Baltimore still in general practice. He became Supreme Commander, Order of the Golden Chain and Medical Examiner of Royal Arcanum.

JOSEPH A. BALDWIN 1816-

A Connecticut native, Baldwin was raised in St. Mary's County. During this period, the majority of the medical students received their training in the offices of old practitioners who served as preceptors, but an increasing number were seeking enrollment in medical schools. Dr. Baldwin came to this state's largest city, which was termed the Paris of the South, sometime in the latter 1840's. From 1850 to 1858, he was a member of the Baltimore Vaccine Society. The secession people of this state in 1861 felt that they could do nothing short of surrendering all their state rights and institutions in complete submission to satisfy the Northern factions. Secessionists lived by and held dear the glorious Constitution upon which this nation was constructed. They solemnly believed their liberties were assailed and that the war waged against them was of subjugation, and they were choosing love of liberty and right over love of the Union. Dr. Baldwin not only voiced his opposition to the threatened horrors of coercion but gave up his practice to go to the aid of the South. Being ordinated a surgeon he was the principal authority at the General Hospital at Lake City, Florida, by the summer of 1862. When the remorseable end came, Surgeon Baldwin was serving with O. G. Jones, Battery of Texas Light Artillery and was paroled in June of 1865 at Brownsville, Texas.

Cardboard secession badge
Erick Davis collection

THOMAS S. BALDWIN

He is listed in the Roster of the Society of the Army and Navy of the Confederate States in the State of Maryland. This register in the archives collection of the Maryland Historical Society in Baltimore has him on their rolls as a medical doctor who was a confederate veteran. The large collection of C.S.A. documents in the National Archives that have survived are far from complete.

CHARLES BARBER

Barber is listed as a confederate surgeon from Anne Arundel County by Carroll Brice who compiled Maryland C.S.A. Veterans, Dates and Cemeteries.

ARTHUR R. BARRY 1839-1903

Born and raised in Prince George's County on his father's plantation Barry was graduated from the University of Georgetown in 1861. He was among the first to enlist in April of 1861 as a private in Captain Francis B. Schaeffer's National Rifles. This unit of Marylanders and Washingtonians became Company F 1st Virginia Infantry. After the Battle of Manassas he was detailed to assist with the wounded and was sent with them to the hospital at Charlottesville as acting assistant surgeon. With very little or no training and experience in military medicine or surgery these officers endeavored to perform daily miracles. Medical officers in the field were faced with a vast amount of problems —the early epidemics of great numbers, treating the wounded during and after an engagement without proper supplies, and the continued struggle for camp sanitation. In the hospitals, because of the overcrowdedness, there was a considerable amount of confusion. The chief failure of hospital staffs was their inability to furnish the patients with a nourishing and palatable diet and the abandonment of the infirmary in the face of oncoming enemy troops. Many of the deficiencies were due to causes over which the medical men had little or no control. Dr. Barry was appointed an assistant surgeon on October 28, 1861, and was stationed successively at Chimborazo Hospital, the First Maryland Hospital also in Richmond and then at Statesville North Carolina Hospital. On September 22, 1862, he was assigned to the 61st Virginia Infantry. He was promoted to surgeon on March 16, 1863, serving again in the field with the 9th Virginia Infantry. The men of Company B of this regiment were brother free-staters and were known as the Baltimore Heavy Artillery. Surgeon Barry was with this command through the perilous battles from Gettysburg to the gloomy end at Appomattox. At Fortress Monroe he attempted to obtain transportation to Baltimore but due to the assassination of President Lincoln he was refused. Asking for passage to Mexico to join Maximillian, but being without funds, Dr. Barry stopped in Texas and taught school for six months before settling there at his chosen profession.

WILLIAM J. BARRY 1819-1890

Dr. Barry was a graduate of the University of Maryland Medical College in 1844. During the Mexican War Dr. Barry was appointed a surgeon from this state and served with the 11th Infantry from April 9, 1847, until discharged with the rank of a major on August 14, 1848. Returning to his native city of Baltimore he continued his work and was a member of the state Medical and Chirurgical Faculty. Most citizens of this state were disturbed with the results of the 1860 presidential election. The abolitionist's stand of Lincoln's Republican party polled only 2,294 votes out of 92,421. The dividing issues had been prevalent for a decade; the radical secessionists reached the boiling point but few in Maryland realized that the conflict was imminent. The cause of the South appealed so strongly to Dr. Barry's conceptions of the rights of the States and their people that he gave up all he had to stand with the Confederacy. On November 16, 1861, he was appointed an assistant surgeon and by December was serving with the 17th Georgia Infantry. On February 4, 1862, he was appointed to cavalry but during the Battle of Fredericksburg he was changed to Frobels Batteries. By the summer of 1863, he was administering to the 4th Alabama Infantry and with the coming of the new year he was transferred to Howard Grove General Hospital at Richmond. On October 1, 1864, he received a star on his collar of a major becoming a surgeon and was sent to the Army of the West. Surgeon Barry was president of the board of examiners for conscripts in the tenth Congressional District of Tennessee. At Columbus, Mississippi on May 16, 1865, he was honorably paroled. He entered the Maryland Line Confederate Soldiers Home at Pikesville on December 12, 1888.

ALEXANDER BEAR

As a student of medicine at the University of Maryland he was urged by the stirring events of the time to trade the book and the pen for the musket and the bayonet. The devotion to righteous principles led him to enroll in Company D, 4th Virginia Infantry, as a private on April 18, 1861. On July 17, he was given special duty at Winchester as a hospital steward. His unit was reorganized and he was elected 2nd lieutenant by his company on August 5. After his enlistment of one year was over, Lieutenant Bear was mustered out with the rest of the company. Receiving an appointment from the Secretary of War upon recommendation of the Surgeon General he became an ordained steward. Hospital stewards held the rank of sergeants; they were required to be skilled in pharmacy and were responsible for the cleanliness of the wards, patients, all articles in use, the matrons and all attendants. Apparently he was a successful candidate in passing the army medical board and became an officer of the medical corps. Assistant surgeon Bear can be found serving with the Virginia State Line and later he was in charge of the hospital at Marrion, Virginia.

SAMUEL BECK 1839-1896

He was born in Kent County and was graduated from Dickinson College at Carlisle. Espousing the fervor of the secessionists he left the campus of the University of Maryland Medical School without a diploma, demonstrating the sincere fidelity of his courageous actions. Like so many young Marylanders of the aristocratic families he entered upon the manly and arduous duties of a Confederate combatant. He received a 1st lieutenant's commission in artillery and, along with two others, attempted to raise Motley's Virginia Light Artillery. After two months the company had not completed its quota and was disbanded in August of 1862 with the enlisted men being absorbed into other units. Lieutenant Beck received a staff appointment under General John Henry Winder, who was also a refugee from Maryland. He served in the Department of Henrico until late in the war when he passed the examining procedure of the medical board and became an assistant surgeon in the provisional army. In the late 1860's Dr. Beck was practicing at Hainesville in Kent County until 1879 when he became Clerk of Court at Worton a position he held for twelve years. He was also a trustee of Washington College at Chestertown.

Cardboard Secession Badge
Erick Davis collection

ALEXANDER T. BELL 1826-1913

Bell was a physician who had practiced through the late Ante-Bellum era of inferior private medical schools that produced a considerable number of quacks. Numerous systems of medicine appeared and flourished, the alla-pathic, the homeopathic, and the hydropathic by means of chrono-thermalists, thompsonians, mesmerists, herbalists, Indian doctors, clairvoyants and spiritualists. The influence of French pathology and the independent outlook of genuine deliberators as Dr. Bell, with the increase use of the lancet and scalpel, brought progress on the eve of the tragic war. He was appointed an assistant surgeon

on July 19, 1861, and placed with the 9th Virginia Infantry. In January of 1863, he was assigned to the 3rd Virginia Cavalry but soon gained a transfer to General J.E.B. Stuart's Horse Artillery with assistance from a colleague, Dr. James Breathed. Dr. Breathed had exchanged his valise of medical instruments for the sword of a warrior and became adored. He recruited over one hundred Marylanders into his battery in August of 1862 and Dr. Bell no doubt was thrilled to become a part of this command which was idolized by the entire army. Being elevated in rank, Surgeon Bell in early 1865 became a member of the exemption board of Portmouth. Then he was assigned to the prison hospital at Libby, in Richmond. When the city was evacuated he stayed to attend the ailing Federals. He was paroled at the hospital on April 19, and was retained to continue his treatment. After several years he returned to his inherent state and by the 1890's was in Baltimore. He held membership in two Confederate Veteran Camps, Franklin Buchanan No. 747 and Isaac R. Trimble No. 1025. Dr. Bell entered the Maryland Line Confederate Home on October 5, 1910.

JAMES W. BELVIN

After receiving his education from the Washington Medical College, Belvin was appointed an assistant surgeon in the Southern Navy and his records state that he was born in Maryland and appointed from Maryland. The loss and destruction of naval records render it impossible to follow the assignments, the changes and the details that took place in the Confederate Naval Department. The surviving naval archives are almost non-existent so many gallant deeds of daring and superb enterprising ingenuity can only be found in contemporary accounts.

Cardboard Secession Badge
Erick Davis collection

The only data available reveals that in early 1862 Dr. Belvin was in Richmond — assigned to the gunboat *Hampton* which was under Captain William Harwar Parker, a fellow brother from the "land of pleasant living" who a year later would be commandant and form the Confederate States Naval Academy. In 1864, Assistant Surgeon Belvin would be aboard the steamer, *Beaufort*, in the James River Squadron. As the conclusion neared and the remaining ships were set to the torch, he joined the Naval Brigade in the Army of Tennessee and surrendered with General J. E. Johnston at Greensboro on April 26, 1865.

J. W. F BEST 1837-1901

Coming from Anne Arundel County Best was just ready to start his chosen profession when South Carolina had requested the possession of Fort Sumter. The Secretary of War in Washington promised that the garrison would be removed but Lincoln was moving to reinforce the fort. It had been skillfully conceived by the President and his artful advisors in Washington to force the new Confederacy to fire upon the fort. Although anticipated, Marylanders were aroused with mixed emotions by news of the attack on Sumter. On April 15, 1861, President Lincoln called for seventy-five thousand volunteers; Maryland was called to furnish four infantry regiments. This was first met in the "Old Line State" with mingled feeling of astonishment, dismay, and disapprobation; then the populous went wild, the cherished hope of neutrality in the struggle had ended. The state was not only expected to remain in the Union but to assist in the use of force to bring back the states adopting secession. Dr. Best departed from Anne Arundel County and enlisted as a private in Company I of the 40th Georgia Infantry. On May 19, 1862, he laid down his musket because he was appointed surgeon

Southern patriotic envelope
Daniel D. Hartzler collection

of his regiment. Later he was senior medical officer of the 40th Georgia and certainly came in contact and passed the army medical board at least once.

There were numerous complaints about the incompetence, drunkenness, and the knife-happy butchering of the surgical corps. The Surgeon General was required to have the medical board reexamine all doctors.

On May 30, 1864, Surgeon Best was dismissed and dropped from the rolls for failure to pass the boards.

POWHATAN BLEDSOE

Leaving his medical studies at the University of Maryland Bledsoe made his way through the Federal lines to Richmond. From 1858 through 1860 it now became clear that the aggressions and attacks of the North on Southern society were not to be confined to discussion and vituperation but were to be directed by physical force. Most Marylanders were utterly opposed to disunion as a remedy or relief but now her truest sons did not hesitate to go to the aid of the South. Dr. Bledsoe on August 16, 1862, joined the 32nd Virginia Infantry as their assistant surgeon. On January 14, 1863, he was assigned to General Hospital, No. 1, at Scottsville. By August of 1864, he was associated with the 36th North Carolina Infantry, then sent to the hospital at Fort Fisher, North Carolina. Fort Fisher was the controlling point of the port of Wilmington, and was under siege of the Federal fleet from December 20, 1864, to January 15, 1865. After exhausting all energy the fort was surrendered. The garrison lost about 500 men. Assistant Surgeon Bledsoe was operating when he was captured.

JOSEPH ADRIAN BOOTH

Listed as a Confederate surgeon in a compilation of Maryland C.S.A. Veterans, Dates and Cemeteries compiled by Carroll Brice, Dr. Booth was a brother of the "mad Marylander," John Wilkes Booth, who assassinated Abraham Lincoln. He went to Charleston for the Southern cause and saw Fort Sumter fall but did not enlist. Apparently he had changed his mind and going to Philadelphia to practice medicine he was ostracized by his family who were hot Southerners.

LEWIS A. BOSWELL

Dr. Boswelll was graduated in medicine from the Washington University Medical College in Baltimore. No state, neither border nor deep South, was torn apart so drastically in a process of violence and bloodshed more than Maryland during those tragic years of the early sixties. Illegally but actually the War Between The States was declared when Lincoln called for volunteers on the fatal April 15, 1861, with the proclamations of April 19 and 27 which launched a blockade of Southern ports. With events moving rapidly in the States both governments looked anxiously to the reaction of the European powers. These countries apparently did not comprehend the causes of the great crisis facing the American people. Proclamations of neutrality from the European continent left both governments competing with constant envoys. Boswell was passionately ambitious to the defense of the South and turned all his efforts in that direction as he became an acting assistant surgeon in Winder Hospital. Winder infirmary was located in the capital of the Confederacy and opened in April of 1862. This was a large institution that extended over one hundred and twenty-five acres and had a capacity of almost five thousand patients in its six divisions. The facilities included Russian steam, plunge and shower baths, water closets, a bakery, an icehouse, a sixteen-acre garden worked by convalescents and a dairy herd of sixty-nine cows. Two canal boats were used to obtain additional food for the inmates. In the spring and summer of 1863 he was working as an assistant surgeon in Howard Grove Infirmary or Hospital, the two terms being synonymous in the Confederacy. Assistant Surgeon Boswell was relieved on September 20 and assigned to the 17th Virginia Infantry until April 30, 1864, when he was transferred to Moseley Battalion of Reserve Artillery. By fall of 1864 he was with Pegram's Company of Light Artillery. As the gloom of despondency finally became a reality he was paroled on April 25, 1865, at the headquarters of the 2nd Division 6th Army Corps.

ROBERT H. E. BOTELER

After attending the Virginia Military Institute he was graduated from the Medical College of the University of Maryland in 1861. He settled in Adamstown where he was practicing when the shuddering plague of political turbulence shook the land. Frederick County was considered a strong Union County but the stars and stripes were not flown or saluted by five militia companies in the spring of 1861. One of these was the Minute Men of Adamstown of which Dr. Boteler was elected captain. This militia company was composed of three officers who were colleagues in the medical profession, 1st Lieutenant Jacob G. Thomas, 2nd Lieutenant William H. Johnson. The Minute Men planted a pole and hoisted a Southern banner on the lot adjoining the railroad where they rallied. Each night three men were selected for guard duty but by the third week in May things were getting pretty hot and the company was broken up. Dr. Boteler and many of the Minute Men left for the Confederacy and the struggle for which many gave up their lives. He first served with Major General Mansfield Lovell at New Orleans. General Lovell was the son of a distinguished Marylander who had been surgeon general of the United States Army. After the surrender of New Orleans he worked as a contract physician. When the conflict ended he was with another Marylander of flag rank, Brigadier General Allen Thomas, in Polignac's Division under Kirby Smith. After the war, Dr. Boteler was practicing medicine in Washington County at Keep Tryst. In 1872 Dr. James Garrard Wiltshire, who was a hospital steward before becoming a dashing trooper in Mosby's Rangers where he rose to the rank of a lieutenant during the war, formed a partnership with Dr. Boteler at Funkstown which only lasted several years.

JOHN MASON BOYD 1833-1907

A son of Judge Samuel B. Boyd, John Mason was born in Maryland and migrated to Knoxville, Tennessee, with his parents. After completing a course at East Tennessee University he entered the office of Dr. William J. Baker. From this tutelage he attended the medical department of the University of Louisville for a term and then went to the University of Pennsylvania where he graduated in 1856. Returning to Knoxville he was associated with his former preceptor and the following year assisted in a difficult operation, this being the third in medical history and for the first time was successful — that of a supravaginal hysterectomy. He enlisted as a private on October 18, 1862, in the 11th Tennessee Cavalry Company K and served until the next spring when he was detailed to hospital service. At the close of the war he went to New York and Philadelphia taking additional courses in medicine. Then he studied for a short time in France, England and Germany before resuming his residence in Knoxville. In 1875 he was joined in practice by his younger brother, Samuel Beckett Boyd, after attending medical school. Dr. Boyd was deeply active in civic affairs, serving as alderman for the city, president of the fire company, trustee of the University of Tennessee, Eastern State Hospital, Deaf and Dumb Asylum, and Knoxville General Hospital where he was chief of staff. After his death the women of the city erected a memorial to Dr. Boyd in the form of a marble archway at the entrance to the Court House lawn. It is inscribed " Our Beloved Physician — Dr. John Mason Boyd."

Satin secession badge
Erick Davis collection

THOMAS JACKSON BOYKIN 1828-1909

As a son of Brigadier General Thomas Boykin of the War of 1812 he was graduated in medicine from the University of Pennsylvania in 1851. Moving to Nebraska, Dr. Boykin was elected to the upper house of the legislature in 1859. Abandoning the political arena and his practice he recognized his faithful, intrepid duty as soon as news reached Omaha that Fort Sumter had surrendered and the war had begun. He was commissioned a surgeon on September 2, 1861, and became medical purveyor at Wilmington. Surgeon Boykin was then assigned o the 26th North Carolina Infantry and by virtue of seniority he was made brigade surgeon of Ransom's brigade. After the Seven Days fight around Richmond, he requested lighter duty and on August 24, 1862, he was returned to Cape Fear. Through his important post the Confederacy received the principal part of the medical supplies that were purchased in Europe. Numerous medicines were smuggled through the Free State but the majority were captured from the Yankees. By November 16, Medical Purveyor Boykin was in Raleigh. In April of 1863, he was in Wilmington and by November 12 at Petersburg. On February 23, 1864, he resigned and was sent by Governor Vance of North Carolina as State agent to Bermuda in charge of immense stores on the island. Dr. Boykin remained at this post until the end came. A year later he came to Baltimore and was engaged in the wholesale drug business. He was a member of Franklin Buchanan Camp of Confederate Veterans, then the Isaac R. Trimble Camp.

CORNELINS BOYLE 1817-

He was born in the "freedom loving state" and practiced medicine in Washington after completing his studies at Columbia Medical College in 1844. He was vice president of the Medical Society of the District of Columbia and was well known for his secession tendencies and in the early spring of 1861, Dr. Boyle was elected captain of the National Rifles, a militia company that grew to three hundred and sixty Southern-minded men. They drilled at Beach's great hall, many times in what was supposedly secret. The uniform adopted was of gray Kentucky jeans with jacket gleaming with Maryland state seal buttons. Dr. Boyle tried to obtain arms from the government's Inspector General but it was known to officials that these disguised rebels were preparing to seize the national capital at an opportune time. Dr. Boyle was sincere in his principles of enfranchisement by abandoning the home and joining the C.S.A. He did not pursue his profession of therapy in the second struggle for independence but was assigned to detached duty by General Beauregard in early 1861. General J. E. Johnston retained him and states that "he was a citizen of Washington and sacrificed a lucrative medical practice; his services as provost marshal

Southern patriotic envelope
Erick Davis collection

for the army appear to be essential." Dr. Boyle applied his medical knowledge when time permitted, during critical periods, from his provost marshal duties at Gordonsville. The Quarter Master General requested that he be transferred to this corps and it would have been done had it not been for a letter dated November 16, 1863, from Robert E. Lee. "Major Boyle was commissioned especially for the service on which he is now engaged. I know of no one who can take his place." Retaining the same capacity until the end came, he returned to the District of Columbia to find that his large valuable estate had been seized by the government. It was not returned to him until the fall of 1865.

TOMLIN BRAXTON

Braxton felt the strain of a border state that placed the population in a precarious position with embarassing attitudes. Maryland was allied to the Southern states by similarity of institutions, by close ties of blood, of trade and political sympathy. As the storm clouds gathered South Carolina had sent recruiting officers to Baltimore in December of 1860. Five hundred Marylanders were sent by ship in March of 1861 to the "Game Cock State." They were referred to as the "Baltimore Rebels" and were mustered into Company C, Lucas's South Carolina Artillery at Charleston Harbor, Rhett's 1st South Carolina Artillery

Cardboard secession badge
Erick Davis collection

Regulars at Castle Pinkney and Company G 1st South Carolina Infantry. Dr. Braxton was appointed by the governor of Virginia on May 16 to the 19th Virginia Infantry and was formally commissioned as an assistant surgeon on July 1. He was discovered within enemy lines, was arrested by the Union Army, and held until June 27, 1862, when released from Camp Chase Ohio. Ordered to Goldsborough, North Carolina, he was promoted to surgeon on October 5. He was transferred to the 30th Battalion Virginia Sharpshooters. One of their six companies, E, was composed of Maryland veterans; many had seen twelve months service with the 21st Virginia Infantry as Company B. Command of the battalion was bestowed upon J. Lyle Clarke, formerly of the Maryland Guard, to the elation of those from the "old liberty-loving state." Medical officer Braxton was made senior surgeon of Warton's Brigade on February 3, 1864. By March he was detailed to Jackson Hospital as administrator. He remained in Richmond working in Winder Hospital until the war closed.

Lieutenant Colonel James Breathed
courtesy of Miss Virginia Carmichael

JAMES BREATHED 1838-1870

Born at Breathedsville, James Breathed was educated at St. James College and the University of Maryland Medical College, then apprenticed under Dr. James Macgill at Hagerstown. Going to Missouri to practice his profession which he abandoned at the outbreak of war, Dr. Breathed returned to his father's home in Washington County to cast his fortunes with those of his state. On his journey east he had as a traveling companion J.E.B. Stuart. Finding the legislature very hesitant about the future course of Maryland, he could not wait for further deliberation and departed for deeper south where he joined Company B 1st Virginia Cavalry as a private. Stuart, recognizing young Breathed, of a few weeks previous, assigned him to detached service as a scout. On March 23, 1862, Dr. Breathed was selected 1st Lieutenant under Captain John Pelham in a battalion of horse artillery organized by General Stuart. On August 9, 1862, Dr. Breathed was promoted to captain when he recruited

well over a hundred Marylanders into Stuart's Horse Artillery. James Breathed had exchanged his valise of medical instruments for a scabbard which contained the powerful sword of a heroic warrior. The name of the intrepid, reckless, dashing Lieutenant Colonel Breathed will be handed down to generations yet to come. In battle he cut, slashed, and cannoned with grim relentlessness as long as it was necessary. The battle over, this physician then gave his skill as a surgeon to save even his enemy's pain. During the four years of combat the gallant doctor was wounded four times. After the war he quietly resumed his professional work choosing Hancock for his home. His field of practice extended across the Mason-Dixon Line where some objected to the "rebel" doctor coming. But soon they all loved him, some Pennsylvanians bestowed his name upon their children. His noble life ended at the age of thirty-two and his grave for years was annually decorated by survivors from the Union Army.

WILLIAM D. BRENGLE

Coming from Frederick, Brengle, like most people of this state, had kind feelings toward the South but he was concerned with the maintenance of the Union. The sixth Massachusetts Regiment was the first to march in obedience to the call of the President. In the procession down Broadway in New York wild enthusiasm was demonstrated; similar scenes occurred in New Jersey and Philadelphia. On April 19, 1861, while proceeding from President Street Station to Camden Street Station in Baltimore the troops were harassed by pro-southern citizens. Stones began to fly and a shot rang out. Whether fired deliberately or accidentally by soldier or civilian is unknown. The troops fired by orders of their untrained officers and the first blood of the war was shed. The majority of the conservative Marylanders were so influenced by the Pratt Street Massacre and their convictions were of such strength that they felt justified in reversing their allegiance. Dr. Brengle joined the C.S.A. and worked in the capacity to which he had devoted his occupation. On September 2, 1862, he was assigned Medical Director and Inspector of various hospitals in Virginia. He was ill and in the General Hospital at Staunton in December. Dr. Brengle's convalescence was slow and he was unfit for duty for six months. As he recuperated he began to serve the less fortunate and when he recovered he was stationed at this institution. He then became Medical Director of Wofford's Brigade; this is unusual because he was only an assistant surgeon. He was paroled on May 1, 1865, at Danville; returning to Frederick he took the oath on August 22.

CHARLES BREWER

A son of Dr. William Brewer of Anne Arundel County, Charles entered the U.S. Army as an assistant surgeon on August 29, 1856, after an internship with his father in Annapolis. He was sent west and that fall saw action against the Cheyennes. He removed a ball from the left breast of a young lieutenant named J.E.B. Stuart. Later he would be introduced to Stuart's sister and they became brothers-in-law. On April 19, 1775, the minutemen of Massachusetts attacked British soldiers at Lexington and sixty-six years later the patriots of Baltimore, unpremeditatedly in the same type moment of fury, assaulted an invader. Twelve citizens and four soldiers were killed, scores of citizens were wounded and thirty-six soldiers were casualties. When news of the slaughter reached Assistant Surgeon Brewer he resigned effective May 7, 1861. The majority of the officers from our state in the army and navy renounced their commissions. Seventeen days later he reached Richmond and was appointed the same rank in the Southern army. Dr. and Mrs. Brewer resided in Richmond. On May 11, 1864, after General Stuart was wounded at Yellow Tavern he was taken to the home of Dr. Brewer. The next day Stuart was visited by President Davis and in reply to the question, "How do you feel?" he replied, "Easy, but willing to die if God and my country think I have fulfilled my destiny and done my duty." He was told by his brother-in-law that it was not possible for him to survive the night. At twenty-two minutes before eight he said to Dr. Brewer, 'I am going fast now; I am resigned; God's will be done." When the end of hostilities came Surgeon Brewer was paroled at Richmond on April 18, 1865.

HENRY BRISCOE

Briscoe practiced the medical profession at Chaptico. With most Marylanders he held sacred the principles laid down in the Declaration of Independence and embodied in the Constitution, but now the vindictiveness and the hatred of the North was evidenced by the actuality of the government's lethal act. The population was infuriated that they were now one of what was a divided household, read yto stand shoulder to shoulder against the trespassing hordes. Dr. Briscoe crossed the Potomac and first saw service with the Wilmington City Guards until commissioned on November 24, 1862. As an assistant surgeon he became a member of the staff at General Hospital No. 2 at Richmond. He was then assigned to the 26th Virginia Infantry. On July 4, 1864 he was admitted to General Hospital No. 4 with a flesh wound of the thigh. Returning to his regiment he was again wounded on August 10. Assistant Surgeon Briscoe surrendered at Appomattox. Signing his parole on April 10, 1865, he states his destination as his former residence in St. Mary's County.

ARTHUR BROGDEN 1837-1875

He was working in Anne Arundel County when the Baltimore militia was ordered to assemble on April 20, 1861. After the aggression and now the physical attack, the militiamen of the Monumental City flew to muster and were anxious to repulse the encroachment - the First Rifle Regiment of six companies commanded by Colonel George Peters; First Regiment Artillery and Calvary of six companies, commanded by Colonel Joseph P. Warner; Fifth Infantry Regiment of ten companies, commanded by Colonel Augustus P. Shutt and the Fifty-Third Infantry Regiment of nine companies commanded by Colonel Benjamin Huger. Of these four militia commanders three would volunteer in the C.S.A. George Peters was Chief of Ambulance Corps as a colonel, Joseph P. Warner was a first lieutenant in Company D Chalmette Louisiana Regiment and Benjamin Huger rose to the rank of a major general. Dr. Brogden's appointment as assistant surgeon was signed on October 28, 1861, and he was sent to General Hospital No. 6 in Richmond. For a month he was detailed at Fredericksburg, then he returned to No. 6. On July 22, 1863, he was sent to King's 2nd Missouri Battery at Branden, Mississippi. He was reassigned on October 12 to Ballentine's Mississippi Calvary near Atlanta. On November 5, 1864, he became Surgeon Brogden and by the end of the month he was chief surgeon of Jackson's Cavalry Division. He was paroled in Alabama on May 4, 1865.

JOHN W. BROWN

Brown is listed as a Confederate surgeon from Anne Arundel County by Carroll Brice who compiled Maryland C.S.A. Veterans, Dates and Cemeteries.

JOHN DICKSON BRUNS 1836-

Born in New Orleans Dr. Bruns was graduated with honors from Charleston College in 1854 and from the South Carolina Medical College in 1857. Practicing in New Orleans he was editor of the Charleston Medical Journal and Review from January, 1858, to January 1861. From his family in Baltimore he learned that on the evening of April 19, 1861, Police Marshall G. P. Kane telegraphed to Captain Bradley Tyler Johnson of the Frederick Volunteers, "Streets red with Maryland blood. Send expresses over the mountains of Maryland and Virginia for the riflemen to come, without delay. Fresh hordes will be down on us tomorrow. We will fight them and whip them or die." By seven o'clock on the twentieth they took possession of a train and by eleven marched down Baltimore Street to Monument Square. Next came the Baltimore County Horse Guard and Wilson Carr Nicholas's Garrison Forrest Rangers. The Patapsco Light Dragoons from Anne Arundel County rode to city hall, where, after being addressed by the mayor, their bugler struck up Dixie amid cheers. Then came Captain George R. Gaither and the Howard County Dragoons, by the steamer *Pioneer* came Captain Aaron Bascom Hardcastle with two companies from Talbot County, the Easton Mounted Guard and the Home Guard. From Carroll County came the Carroll County Rangers and the Smallwood Infantry. The Union Rifles and the Cecil Guards from that county arrived along with the Harford Light Dragoons, Harford Riflemen and the Spesutia Mounted Rangers. Then the United Rifles under Captain Frank A. Bond and Captain Nicholas Snowden with the Vansville Rangers also of Prince George's arrived. All of the above mentioned militiamen had the fortitude of their noble convictions to join the Confederacy. George Proctor Kane became a colonel of the Maryland Line, Bradley Tyler Johnson a brigadier general, Wilson Carr Nicholas, Captain 1st Maryland Infantry Compand G, George Ridgely Gaither, lieutenant colonel 1st Virginia Cavalry, Aaron Bascom Hardcastle colonel 33rd Mississippi, Frank A. Bond, captain of staff as assistant adjutant general, Nicholas N. Snowden, lieutenant 1st Maryland Infantry Company D. Dr. Bruns was aide-de-camp on staff and field duty in the spring of 1861, was appointed assistant surgeon and sent to the South Carolina Hospital. On December 14, 1863, he was promoted to surgeon and transferred to Roper Hospital in Charleston. At the close of the war, he went to Europe and pursued his medical studies, then came to Baltimore. He returned to New Orleans as professor of practice and theory in Charity Hospital Medical College in 1874.

ARTHUR P. BURNS

After the Pratt Street fracas, the staunch Unionists of Maryland were in a catastrophic condition; never had so many weighty events occurred within such a short period to disturb their equilibrium. The violence of the mob in Baltimore against the passage of Federal troops had separated the conservative Unionist from the unconditional Unionist. The firm pacifists of the state had hoped amity was possible denouncing both secession and coercion but now they were aligned with the elevated pro-southern sentiment. The ardent Unionist sacrificed ties of friendship and in many cases the tenderest cords of kindredship were severed because they were first and foremost Americans and after that Marylanders. Dr. Burns was a genuine defender of liberty and justice offering his abilities to the Confederacy. On June 17, 1861, he was appointed assistant surgeon of the 7th Virginia Cavalry. Company G of this regiment was the first cavalry unit of completely Maryland personnel and was organized by Doctor and Captain J. Frank Mason. By December of 1862 Assistant Surgeon Burns was ordered to the New Market Congressional District to examine conscripts. On August 11, 1864, he resigned as surgeon chief of the medical board in the Eighth District and proceeded to Winchester Hospital to alleviate the suffering to the best of his God-given ability.

HARVEY LEONIDAS BYRD 1820-

Byrd was born in South Carolina, educated at Emory College in Georgia, receiving his M.D. at Pennsylvania Medical University in 1840. He commenced his profession at Salem, Georgetown, Savannah and then Baltimore. The entire state was aroused; the sacred soil upon which they had received their being, which gave them their livelihood and in which reposed the ashes of those who were most near and dear, was threatened. So many now felt the enthusiasm which had been steaming Southern hearts as their state was invaded. This was just the beginning, would their towns and homes be laid waste? Old Maryland was under attack, they must come to her defense for whoever came with hostile intent was an adversary and her enemies were theirs. Dr. Byrd was appointed an assistant surgeon on October 24, 1861, after seeing service on staff duty. He was sent to Brunswick, Georgia until the first of the year when he became surgeon of the 10th Georgia Cavalry Battalion. He was sent to Nott Hospital for duty at Mobile, Alabama, until February 27, 1864, when Surgeon Byrd was transferred to Macon in conscript service. From 1867 to 1872, he was professor of medicine, therapeutics, and obstetrics at the Washington Medical University in Baltimore. He was also one of the city's vaccine physicians in 1873 checking on small-pox virus. The next three years were spent at the College of Physicians and Surgeons; then he became one of the founders of the Baltimore Medical College in 1881. Dr. Byrd was editor of the Oglethrope Medical and Surgical Journal for three years followed by being co-editor of the *Independent Practitioner*, a monthly devoted to Medican and Dentistry. He held membership in the state Medical and Chirurgical Faculty, the Baltimore Medical Associates and was the first president of the Epidemiological Society of Maryland.

ALEXANDER MILLS CAMPBELL

Born in Campbell County, Virginia, he was already a licensed medical doctor when he enrolled in the Baltimore College of Dental Surgery receiving his D.D.S. in 1857 and he then practiced in Baltimore County. When the first lanyard was pulled that sent a cannon ball toward Fort Sumter he knew he would be in the war of secession and first went to Harper's Ferry where the troops gathered. The alumni of the dental department of the University of Maryland certainly were aligned to the South. Of the sixty-seven dentists who were soldiers during this conflict, eight saluted Old Glory while fifty-nine saluted the stars and bars. The teeth of Confederate veterans from careless habits, scanty diets, the absence of toothbrushes and dentifrices were deplorable. Of every one hundred men sent to the hospital or on the sick list, exclusive of those wounded, five could be traced directly to teeth. Physicians did little more than extract teeth or lance abscesses of the gums. The C.S.A. recognized and established a dental department. With the use of breastwork type of defense, rheumatic, broken teeth and neuralgic suffering was topped by face and mandible wounds. The usual method of treating broken jaws was to place a papier mache cast over the face but resultant infections

Silk Secession Badge
Erick Davis collection

under these casts often led to horrible disfigurement. James Baxter Bean, a Baltimore dentist, was employed by Brown and Hape during the first two war years in Atlanta, manufacturing dental materials. In the summer of 1864, the medical bureaus recognized that Dr. Bean's phenomenal rate of recovery in maxillo-facial surgery was due to the invention of an interdental splint. Wax impressions of the patient's uninjured and broken portion of the mandible were used to make a vulcanized India rubber splint. It had both horizontal surfaces and cup-shaped depressions that were sufficiently deep to engage the crown of the teeth; the teeth were placed in the corresponding indentations and held in position by an occipito-frontal bandage. The medical board in Richmond unanimously recommended the use of the splint and all jaw fractures were sent to Dr. Bean at Receiving and Way Hospital. Assistant Surgeon Campbell surrendered at Nonrico, Mississippi, with Nelson Light Artillery of the 7th Mississippi. A way of life was gone forever and with it many old cliches — a lady could have rough hands, a gentlemen would saddle his own horse and a medical doctor might admit that his patient needed a doctor of dentistry.

GEORGE HENRY CAPERTON 1828-1895

Caperton was born in Monroe County, now West Virginia. Graduating in the medical class of 1853 from University of Pennsylvania he set his practice up in Cumberland. Mass meetings were held all over the state since the April 19, 1861 clash in the Monumental City. In the western counties resolutions were adopted strongly protesting the use of coercion by the United States Government. They were in tune with the radical wrongs which the South was enduring but most felt that the Union should be preserved if that could be done with honor. However, this area was far from solvent; there was a definite partition and a surprising number of men from the piedmont region joined the C.S.A. Scarcely was there a town or village in Western Maryland that would not furnish a young rebel who would become famous for his courage and bravery. Dr. Caperton enlisted in the 24th Virginia Cavalry and was nominated as quartermaster sergeant. On June 11, 1862, he was appointed first lieutenant and aide-de-camp to the staff of General J. Echols. He was commissioned an assistant surgeon on March 2, 1863, and sent by medical director J. A. Hunter to south-west Virginia. On January 22, 1864, he was assigned to Montgomery Springs Hospital until June 1 when Assistant Surgeon Caperton became a member of the Examining Board. After being paroled he eventually settled in Baltimore, operating in Gundry Hospital and was a member of the Medical and Chirurgical Faculty.

THOMAS H. CARTER 1831-

Educated at the Virginia Military Institute completing his studies in 1849 and subsequently graduating in medicine at the University of Virginia, Carter then came to Baltimore. During the intense excitement of the last of April, 1861, the police barely maintained control so Dr. Edward Schwartz organized an auxiliary police corps. It looked as if the "Free State" had taken her stand with the South, the expression of Southern feeling was very emphatic. The strength of those for independence had immensely flourished and Union sentiment was withdrawn. On April 23, between three and four hundred of the most respectable black residents made a tender of their services to city authorities. Dr. Carter returned to the place of his birth and chose to use his military training over his medical discipline. On June 1 he was chosen captain of the King William Virginia Artillery. On returning to this state during the Antietam campaign he was wounded at Sharpsburg as his battery repulsed the heavy columns of Burnside's troops. On November 1, 1862, Dr. Carter was promoted to major and after several months was acting chief of artillery of D. H. Hill's Division. On April 4, 1863, he was made lieutenant colonel and under the reorganization of the army became colonel, commanding Cutshaw's Battalion. Again wounded at Winchester on September 19, 1864, he was chief of artillery of the 2nd Corps., and he was recommended for promotion by General J. A. Early. Subsequently with the army of Lee retreating to Appomattox his combat ceased. Finally going to Washington he became a member of the District of Columbia Confederate Veterans.

CHARLES WILLIAM CHANCELLOR 1833-

Chancellor attended Georgetown College receiving his A.B., 1849, University of Virginia A.M. 1851, Jefferson Medical College M.D., 1853. Located in Baltimore he experienced the critical, forceful encroachment and beheld the vigilance of the city's militia units as they were constantly on duty at their armories. The volunteer civilian militia displayed rigid discipline as they mustered at least once a day and drilled for several hours. The pervading spirit within the state military was convinced of the rightness of the Southern struggle for independence. Some could not stand to think of their muskets being used against those who marched behind Old Glory and resigned. Officers were quickly changed to reflect the unimpaired feelings of their own unit while some county companies were so diverse in sentiment they were disbanded immediately. New companies instantly sprang up through the counties as bellwethers of the Confederacy cried that the state had been cursed by conservatism, now the threat of the heroes of coercion was genuine. The time to fight had come and they were organizing to stand side by side under their great Constitution in the struggle against the Freemen Bureau in the uniform of blue. The leaders of the new loyalist companies preached the importance of Maryland's fidelity to the Government and the far reaching influence and effect they would have upon the struggle for national unity. Dr. Chancellor became assistant surgeon on July 1, 1861, of the 19th Virginia Infantry. On May 22, 1863, he was relieved and assigned to General Hospital No. 2 at Charlottesville, then as Medical Director of Pickett's Division. He was one of thirteen physicians working in this large institution and by the end of that summer until the war's end he was in charge. He went to Memphis and practiced a short time before returning to Baltimore. In 1868, Dr. Chancellor became associated with the Washington Medical University and in 1874 he was elected to the Baltimore City Council of which he became president in four years. He also served as secretary and president of the State Board of Health. Dr. Chancellor was editor of the *Sanitary Messenger* and late in life became consul to Havre, France, after which he resided in Washington, D.C.

JULIAN J. CHISOLM 1830-1903

Departing from the Medical College of South Carolina in 1850, Chisolm studied in London and Paris, then came to the "Free State" to practice. In 1858 he was back at his alma mater as professor of surgery. While in this state, he found that Maryland was devoted to the Union, only listening to the suggestions of disunion but refusing to join the misguided people of the Northern states in their assaults. In 1860 the Maryland House and Senate adopted and passed the following resolution: "To cling to the Union as long as its principles can be preserved and the blessing for which it was intended can be secured, but our deep and solemn convictions that the Union must be torn in fragments unless equal rights to all sections of the country are sacredly preserved. We also respectfully but earnestly desire to assure our brethren of South Carolina, that should the hour ever arrive when the Union must be dissolved, Maryland will cast her lot with her sister states to the South and abide their fortune to the fullest extent." Dr. Chisolm and Dr. F. Peyre Porcher operated a hospital for the treatment of Negroes in 1857. Just prior to the war he traveled again to Europe and observed the treatment of soldiers on the battle fields of Magenta and Solferino. Dr. Chisolm was at Fort Sumter as the action opened but had no wounded to treat. He was ordained a surgeon; the Surgeon General realized the lack of surgical texts in the South and behest by him he wrote a book entitled *Manual of Military Surgery* which became the official text for the Confederacy. He became medical purveyor but through his writing was known for giving recommendations on laxness in sanitary matters, boiling and filtering water, treatment of diseases, and gunshot operating technique. On April 13, 1864, Surgeon Chisolm was issued $850,254.57 while stationed at Columbia which was the largest warrant publication of funds to a medical purveyor by the Confederate States Treasury Department. He also took time to see patients at Wayside Hospital. After the war, he crossed the Atlantic and after a year in Europe, Dr. Chisolm became the head of eye and ear surgery and dean at the University of Maryland. He was among the first to use cocaine in eye surgery and his operative treatment of cataracts was well known. Presbyterian Eye and Ear Charity Hospital was established in December of 1871 under the direction of Dr. Chisolm who became executive surgeon. He was president of the Baltimore Academy of Medicine and vice-president of the American Medical Association in 1895 upon retiring.

JOSEPH EDWARD CLAGETT 1830-

Pleasant Valley in Washington County was his birthplace and as a pupil of his father, Dr. James Hawkins Clagett, Joseph attended courses in Winchester, Baltimore, Philadelphia, New York, Richmond and Charleston. In 1851, Dr. Clagett began to practice in Rohrersville, until 1855 when he went to Harper's Ferry in the drug business. With the President's fatal proclamation requisitioning troops, Virginia responded by passing the ordinance of secession on April 17, 1861, to be ratified by the people on May 24. Virginia troops, with whom were also Western Maryland militiamen, repossessed and occupied the armory at Harper's Ferry. This state's secessionists were led by Robert Milligan McLane and George W. Hughes who were distinguished patroits of the past but

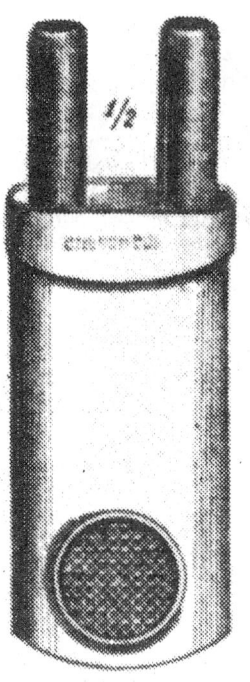

Metal chloroform inhaler invented by Surgeon Julian J. Chisolm during the war. Daniel D. Hartzler collection

they were old soldiers and not willing to plunge into conspiracy to overthrow the state government until the legislature sanctioned secession. Governor Thomas H. Hicks, although pressured, had declined to summons either house because they contained a substantial number of those favoring withdrawal. But Maryland could not act until Virginia and the referendum was completed, for she was not back to back or side to side as the other departed states were. There never had been an hour when she could have struck a blow for independence. Dr. Clagett was commissioned to the medical corps on December 4, 1862, and worked in Stuart, Louisiana and Camp Lee Hospitals in the capital. Assistant Surgeon Clagett was also employed in hospitals at Orange Court House, Warrenton, Hanover Junction, and Guinea Station. After being advanced to the rank of surgeon he held the position of chief surgeon in the Receiving and Forwarding Hospital. In 1866 he came to Baltimore to practice his profession and the following year taught Materia Medica at Washington Medical University, until 1873 when he was instructing in obstetrics. He was a member of Isaac R. Trimble Camp of Confederate Veterans. After 1878, Dr. Clagett spent most of his time traveling abroad.

POWHATAN CLARKE

Clarke was one of many who felt the youthful fire of domicile defense blaze with fury. The warm blood coursing in the veins of Baltimoreans flowed rapidly as the city called her sons. The mayor's call did not go unheeded as compatriots hastened to protect their hallowed homeland. Isaac Ridgeway Trimble formed three regiments of citizen militia: The Maryland Line Regiment of nine batallions, plus naval harbor marines and engineers under Colonel George W. Hughes and Major Samuel T. Walker; the Southern Guerilla Home Guard Regiment of two batallions commanded by Colonel John R. Johnston, and Lieutenant Colonel Leonard Grover, and Trimble's Un-Uniformed Volunteer Regiment of thirty-four companies under Colonel Trimble and Lieutenant Colonel William H. Hayward. Over fifteen thousand volunteers were enrolled for defense of the city and began to drill. These new citizen companies selected their own officers with headquarters in various localities. The fife and drum were heard in every section of the city. Dr. Clarke was commissioned a first lieutenant on June 8, 1861; preferring staff duty he did not use his medical training. Serving under a fellow "Free-stater," General Joseph Lancaster Brent, he was promoted to captain of artillery on March 9, 1864. Dr. Clarke was then assigned to ordnance duty and was acting chief of ordnance of the District of Western Louisiana and soon became a major. As the war drew to a close, he was lieutenant colonel on General C. J. Polignac's staff. The General was French-born and returned to France before the downfall of the Confederacy was finalized. Nothing more can be found of Dr. Clarke until several years later when he was practicing in Baltimore.

ALEXANDER F. CLENDENIN

Awarded a diploma in medicine from the University of Maryland in 1859, he was practicing in the Monumental City; on April 18, 1861, he wrote to President Jefferson Davis in Montgomery and requested an opportunity to appear before the C.S.A. medical board that he might become a medical officer. The very next day the patriots of Baltimore opposed the Northern invasion and Dr. Clendenin volunteered for the staff of militia surgical officers. After his service to the city he went to Virginia to continue his protest and on June 21 he was appointed a surgeon in Wise Legion. He was not happy in Virginia state service and on January 12, 1862, he again wrote to President Davis desiring to be in the regular Confederate service. Surgeon Clendenin was then ordered to the 5th Virginia Cavalry.

HENRY KING COCHRAN 1832-1903

Born in Charlottesville, Virginia, he studied medicine at the University of Virginia and at Jefferson College in Philadelphia. He was then a student of his uncle, Robert M. Cochran, in Baltimore before practicing in Bellevue Hospital in this city. During the pervading spirit of guardianship, railroad bridges were destroyed, the wires were all cut north of the city and communication by rail or telegraph between the capital and the Northern states was closed. City officials appropriated $5,000,000 for defense to drive back the hated invader. On April 21, 1861, Mayor George William Brown had gone to Washington on a special train to confer with the President and General W. Scott. They arrived at an understanding that the capital would be reinforced but no troops would go through Baltimore. The National flag was not to be seen in the city; the black and gold and Confederate banners were everywhere. Universal demand had grown for the Maryland secession blue cockade, boys cried vociferously through the streets from morning till night selling satin or pasteboard badges. Monument Square was packed, crammed with a mass of quivering, excited humanity ready to die for the state. Dr. Cochran was commissioned an assistant surgeon in the medical corps and stationed in a Richmond Hospital. On April 30, 1862, he was sent to Ashland; on July 17, he and Dr. Arthur R. Barry, also of this state, were sent to the camp of instruction at Greensboro. After serving in the western campaign and the siege of Corinth, Assistant Surgeon Cochran was transferred to Old Seabrook Hospital near Petersville. After many months he was assigned to Wilmington where he contracted chills from which he never wholly recovered. His parole was signed at Greensboro on April 26, 1865, and he located in Smythe County, Virginia, where he practiced. He was proud that he never took the oath of allegiance and grew to be a stronger Confederate as the years advanced.

1861 silk militia physician's hat badge
Erick Davis collection

WILLIAM H. COLE 1837-1886

Baltimore was the birthplace of Dr. Cole and he adopted his early life to the study of law. At the age of twenty he was admitted to the bar and proceeding to Kansas to take part in the fierce struggle of 1857-58, he was chosen a member of its territorial Legislature. In 1860 he graduated in medicines at the University of Louisiana and saw his native state, as did most of the country, as a Southern border state that stood for neutrality. She denied the Federal troops the right to pass through her territory without her consent to strike other sister states. When in defiance of this right Massachusetts troops were marched through the streets of the state's largest city and her populace shot down in cold blood, excitement was intense. The citizen militia by far outnumbered military weapons. Major Edward Hitchcock McDonald, a former Baltimorean in Virginia service, on April 23, 1861, arrived with one thousand arms requested by General George H. Stewart, Sr., commanding the militia. The Virginia Advisory Council agreed to loan this state five thousand more arms from the Lexington arsenal but this did not materialize. Gun shops in the city were broken into and lost most of their guns and munitions. The citizen militia units were armed with everything from hunting rifles, shotguns and pistols to dress swords, Bowie knives and pikes. Young medical doctor Cole was one of the first to enlist in the National Volunteers, a militia unit from Washington composed of mostly Marylanders which became Company E 1st Virginia Infantry. By October 13, this private was on detached service serving with the medical department. In March, 1862, he was appointed a hospital steward at Hotel Hospital at Manassas. By April 19, he had passed some of the medical board and was acting assistant surgeon to the 8th Georgia Infantry. By August 20, 1864, he was acting assistant surgeon at Howard Grove Hospital in Richmond. Dr. Cole was working under a private contract at Raleigh and he was paroled on April 8, 1865, when the drums had ceased to throb and the flag was furled. Not able to return to his state he sought a residence in Texas and for the first time associated himself with the press. Soon returning to the place of his nativity and forsaking his two accomplished professions, Dr. Cole won distinctions in journalism. After being reading clerk of the Maryland House of Delegates for four successive terms he was elected to the United States House of the Forty-ninth Congress in 1884.

JOHN SUMMERFIELD CONRAD 1839-1896

Conrad was born at Fairfax Court House, but came to Baltimore in 1853 and was educated at Newton and Union Academies in Baltimore. His father failed in business and in 1857 he was obligated to leave school to support himself. He had a taste for the study of medicine and entered the drug store of Elisha Perkins, M.D. where he remained for three years with the stipulation that he should be permitted to attend two full courses of lectures. In 1860 he graduated from the Maryland College of Pharmacy after which he engaged in teaching as the assistant of his brother who was principal of an academy in Georgetown. He taught a few hours each day, devoting the rest of his time at the medical school of Columbia University in Washington. He graduated from the University in March 1862 and immediately went South where, in April, Dr. Conrad was an acting assistant surgeon in the C.S.A. The dissolution of the Union was

Satin secession badge
Confederate Museum collection

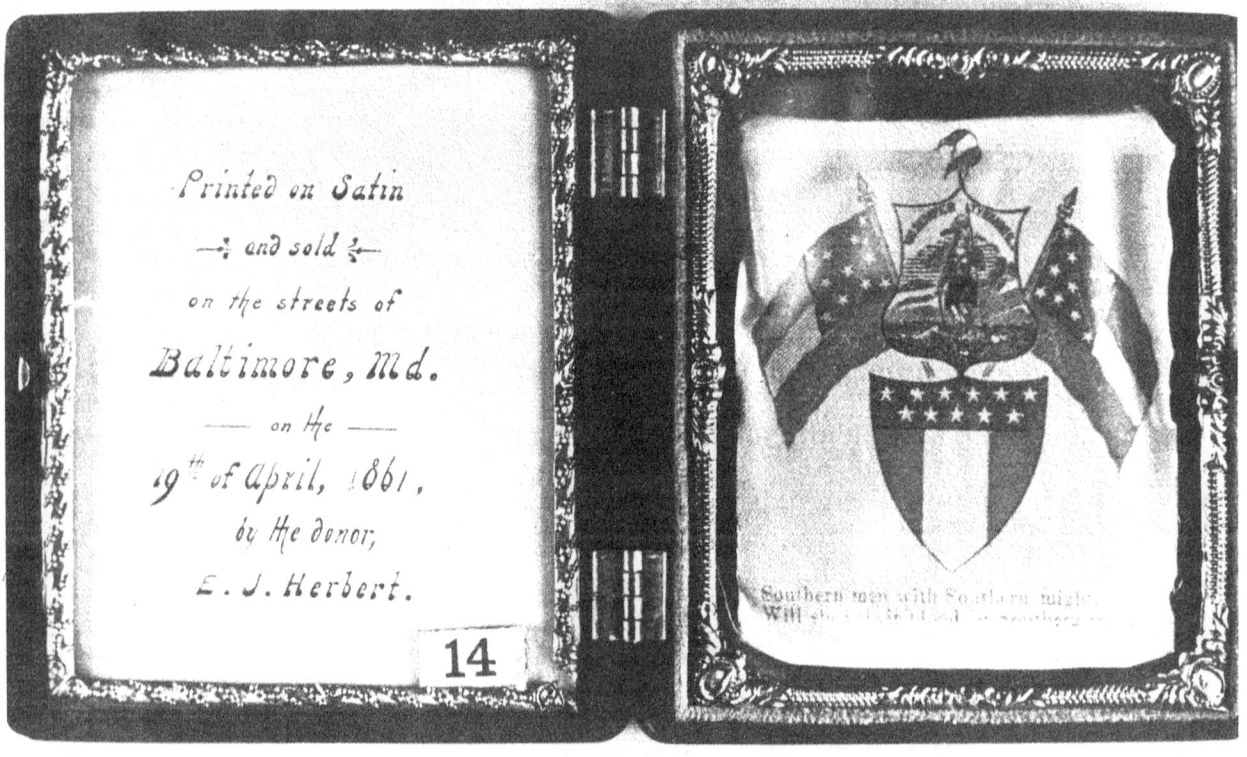

not what he wanted. The establishment of the Southern Confederacy was created because of the North's violent crimes and the war was caused by devious, political trickery. Both were secondary to the preservation of the supreme and sacred right of self-government that was put forth eighty-four years before. He was appointed an assistant surgeon on July 19 and in December was in the General Hospital at Camp Winder which became Winder Hospital. On June 24, 1864, Dr. Conrad was assigned to duty with the 59th Georgia Infantry in Tennessee. By September 27, he was transferred to the 1st Regiment Engineer Troops. Assistant Surgeon Conrad surrendered on April 9, 1865, with the Engineers Corps of the Army of Northern Virginia. Returning to Baltimore he was resident physician at the Baltimore Infirmary, which was to become University Hospital. In 1867, Dr. Conrad became Superintendent of the State Insane Asylum which would become Spring Grove State Hospital. After three years he opened Matley Hall and was proprietor of this private mental institution at Relay Station in the county. In 1872 he was appointed a professor's chair in Theory and Practice at the Washington Medical University in this city.

JAMES PHILIP COOKE

Hailing from St. Mary's County he completed his medical training at the University of Maryland in 1858. There were five schools that comprised the University of Maryland; the medical, dental, pharmacy and undergraduate were located in Baltimore and the agricultural college was located in Prince George's County. When the rumble of war began the college resembled the state itself. They possessed vitality but lacked unity; they were advanced in the profession but lagged in classical culture. They strangely combined a practical democracy with a social aristocracy with neither seeming to quite come to terms with itself. The slaveholding planters controlled the Agricultural College and the fashionable Baltimoreans influenced the professional schools, all being socially prominent and well-bred in their Southern allegiances. Leaving the oppressive and tyrannical power of the Federal military he left his practice at Chaptico and followed the hallowed banner. In the Confederacy Dr. Cooke was on the staff of a friend from the neighboring county of Charles, Brigadier General Joseph Lancaster Brent, before becoming a contract surgeon. As a contract doctor he was usually under the instructions of an assistant surgeon, but when they were busy or under-staffed the contract surgeons were placed in charge of wards.

JOHN WILLIAM CORRELL 1825-1900

Correll was born at Winchester, educated at Winchester Acedemy, then attended lectures at Winchester Medical College and was a pupil of Dr. H. McGuire. He began his practice in Virginia in 1847. Since the bloodshed in Baltimore, renewed pressure was brought to bear upon Governor Hicks to call a special session of the General Assembly. On the twenty-second of April the Governor finally announced that the special session would convene at Annapolis on the twenty-sixth. On the twenty-fourth Hicks issued a proclamation changing the place of the meeting of the Legislature to Frederick. Later the Governor declared that he had given the order to meet in Frederick because of the well-known strength of the Union sentiment of the town. Most "Free Staters" believed that the Nation would be divided irredeemably, yet there would still be marked hesitation. More people urged for instant secession though the majority of people in the state believed that of the two divisions, which seemed inevitable, that Maryland would go with the Southerners. Dr. Correll was appointed assistant surgeon on June 11, 1861, but no other records can be found. In 1866, he came to Baltimore to continue his practice and was a member of the Medical and Chirurgical Faculty of Maryland in 1875.

ISAAC THOMAS COSTEN 1832-1931

Educated in the public schools of Worcester County and Washington Academy in Princess Anne, he received his degree from Gettysburg College and went to the medical school at the University of Pennsylvania finishing in 1857. Dr. Costen opened his office in Pocomoke City. During the Civil War he ran the blockade with medical supplies for the Southern army, returning the mail for the families that were anxiously waiting to hear from their relatives in the Confederate service. While running the blockade with a considerable amount of money from the Pocomoke River to the Rappahannock the craft was spotted and pursued by a Union barge. The *Fairfield*, a forty-footer with the main mast forward, was being overtaken so she was beached; Dr. Costen and the captain made their escape into the treacherous marshland below Wagram Creek going to Accomack County. Because of the capture of the craft their identity became known so they could not return to their homes. He became a contract surgeon who were physicians privately employed by the government. They were hired to fill a vacancy that the overworked and under-staffed medical corps could not accomplish. Contract surgeons could be employed on a part-time or full-time basis. Their consecutive contracts could be several weeks or many months. After the war he returned to his home which at that time was called New Town and before long Dr .Costen could be seen on horseback calling on patients. In 1881 he was elected to the lower house in the state General Assembly and in 1888 he was chosen the first mayor of Pocomoke City. He was elected to the mayoralty for three more terms in 1890, 1908, and 1910. He descended from a slave-owning family and believed that as an institution slavery was wrong, but he vigorously opposed the Emancipation Proclamation, feeling that the matter was a moral one and not political.

EDWARD NAPOLEON COVEY 1829-1869

Bozman Point, an estate near St. Michaels, was his birthplace and he attended the academic school at that place. Going to Baltimore, he attended the school of medicine at the University of Maryland and studied under Nathan R. Smith. Going to Paris for three years, he continued to study, then returned to this country and received a position in the surgical department of the army in August of 1855. While serving in the West, Dr. Covey received information that the war had broken out at home. He, in company with his commander Albert Sidney Johnston, made his way to San Francisco and then by steamer to New Orleans. There they resigned their commissions on June 1, 1861, and offered their swords to the Confederacy. They were directed to report to Richmond where Dr. Covey was appointed an assistant surgeon on August 27. He accompanied General H. H. Sibley to Texas where he was appointed Medical Director and Purveyor of the general's brigade and was promoted to surgeon on January 31, 1862. In the spring of 1862, he was captured in New Mexico. Exchanged by that fall, he became Medical Purveyor at San Antonio. On March 11, 1863, until September 15, Surgeon Covey was ordered to Raleigh where he became Medical Director of the General Hospitals of North Carolina. Dr. Covey was so impressed with the treatment of fractured wounds by dentists using an interdental splint that he started dentists doing all facial surgery rather than physicians. On October 19 he proceeded to Columbia as Assistant Medical Inspector. He was then ordered to Richmond as Medical Inspector effective November 2 until August 1864 when he was sent to inspect and report on the hospital accommodations for prisoners at Andersonville. By that fall he was Medical Inspector in the field for Virginia, Tennessee, and Georgia while also being Superintendent of Vaccination of the armies in these states. After the surrender he and Secretary of State Benjamin went to London for several years before returning to his old home in Talbot County. In 1896, an epidemic of yellow fever in the South caused a call for volunteer doctors and nurses. Dr. Covey answered the call and was sent to Houston, Texas, where again he faithfully served his fellow Southerners. He was overcome with the fever and died the next day.

BENJAMIN MELLICAMP CROMWELL

Dr. Cromwell was healing people at Eckhart Mines in Allegany County when the beleaguered Legislature met in the Court House at Frederick. Governor Hicks was possessed with the idea, which was very prevalent in this border state, that they could stay in the Union yet refuse to take part in the war, remaining in the Federal Union, without rendering assistance. The Legislature showed itself at every step entirely out of sympathy with the policy of Lincoln. Wide divergence of opinions existed among its members; many resolutions offered time after time became buried in the Committee of Federal Relations. The same temporizing policy that had previously paralyzed the state still prevailed as the citizens anxiously awaited some formal statement. Even the proposal to allow the people to decide by means of an election of members to a state convention had been declared unfeasible. The conservatives advocated a passive course; if the state should decide to withdraw it was best to wait until the war was over when such action could be taken without placing the property and lives of the citizens of the state in jeopardy. Dr. Cromwell had the faith of his belief as he crossed the Potomac and was commissioned on May 26, 1862. He was assistant surgeon of the 3rd Louisiana Battalion until sent to Richmond Infirmary on December 5 for treatment of a serious wound. Returning to field duty he was captured on November 28, 1864, at New Market. On January 25, 1865, Assistant Surgeon Cromwell was exchanged as a prisoner of war.

ROBERT WOOD DAILEY 1821-

Dailey was born in Romney, now West Virginia. He was orphaned at an early age; moving to Winchester he was schooled at the Winchester Academy and graduated in medicine from University of Pennsylvania at Philadelphia in 1842. Dr. Dailey practiced at Romney until 1852 when he moved to Cumberland. He was occupied in this profession as a healer until June of 1861 when he proceeded to Richmond and was appointed a surgeon and assigned to Taliaferro's brigade. He soon became brigade surgeon and served in this capacity two years accompanying his command in the field through Jackson's campaign in the valley, the Seven Day's Battle before Richmond and at Cedar Run and Fredericksburg. Two of his sons left Cumberland and joined their father in the Southern army. Benjamin became affiliated with General T. Rosser's command as a courier during the Antietam Campaign and James united with Stuart's Horse Artillery during the Gettysburg Campaign. Subsequently Surgeon Dailey was surgeon-in-chief of the General Hospital at Lexington for a year until the infirmary was closed. He was then appointed senior surgeon of a conscript medical examining board with headquarters at Lexington. Here he continued to serve in this department of recruiting until the close of the fighting. He returned to Cumberland, but being unable to practice, reverted back to Romney where he was active in the deaf, mute and blind school.

JOHN S. DANIEL 1837-

A medical student at the University of Maryland, graduating in 1860 and serving an internship, Daniel learned that on May 6, 1861, Iiaac R. Trimble issued an order disbanding the civilian volunteer soldiers. Most of the county militia had returned home after about a week. The final orders were given to the Baltimore militia on May 12, as their weapons were quietly removed from the armories to individual homes. Many were taken South and put in good service there, while some, no doubt remained hidden away and forgotten. The next morning not a fancy militia uniform was seen on the streets which they had made so picturesque. Young medic Daniel enlisted in the Company G of the 3rd Virginia Cavalry as a private on June 12, 1861, at Ashland. On September 20, 1862, he was serving as a nurse and was detailed to the surgeon general. In September of 1863 he can be found as a hospital attendant at Farmville working in the capacity of a hospital steward. Because of vision problems he was unable to obtain a medical commission. His records show he had a permanent disability of amaurosis of the left eye and impaired vision of the right. Finally on November 21, 1864, he was accepted by the medical board and was appointed acting assistant surgeon. Dr. Daniel apparently remained at Farmville Hospital and appears on the list of Confederate prisoners of war paroled at Farmville on April 11, 1865.

JEREMIAH YELLOTT DASHIELL 1804-1888

Born in Baltimore, he went to school in Newark, Delaware and received his medical training at the University of Maryland in 1824. He then studied under his uncle, Dr. William Handy, in Baltimore and went into private practice in this city. On July 2, 1846, he was appointed a paymaster in the army and served throughout the Mexican War. Dr. Dashiell forsook his medical experience, and staying in the service, he was promoted to majority on March 2, 1849. He was a paymaster until dismissed from the service on July 10, 1858, after which he settled in Texas. With the election of the so-called "Black Republican" in the Federal government the "Lone Star State" considered the ordinance of secession. Dr. Dashiell secured an appointment under ex-lieutenant governor, Frank R. Lublock, who became adjutant general of the state. When the disruption came he kept looking toward his family and native state, wondering which direction they would go. Maryland was a Southern state, with all the institutions and past way of life, she was as fervent as any in the sunny climate. It appeared that Maryland would take her stand with those for Southern independence. The first United States flag displayed in Baltimore for some time was hoisted at the cusom house on May 1 where the Union convention was adjourned because of a lack of members. With the separation of the Commonwealth, Maryland would no doubt soon pass the ordinance and stand back to back with Virginia. Dashiell became assistant adjutant general obtaining the rank of colonel and spent most of the war in Austin.

Secession cockade — referred to as the Maryland blue cockade, with an "Extra Quality" state cuff button. Daniel D. Hartzler collection

JOHN J. DAVIS

His heart was broken when, during a thunder strom the night of May 13, General Benjamin Butler entered Baltimore, seized Federal Hill which commanded the city, and fortified it with fifty heavy cannon. Immediately Butler established liaison with the Fort McHenry garrison, ordering it to open its cannon on Monument Square if he was attacked. The next day he published a proclamation forbidding the display of banners and all devices representing the Confederate States, while seizing arms and hauling them to Fort McHenry. On May 14 after a month of hesitation the governor issued a call for the four regiments to make up the state quota as fixed by the President's fatal declaration. Hicks still preached the idea that the state could hold a neutral position, declaring that the President promised that troops would not be sent outside of Maryland or the district. Dr. Davis was employed by Surgeon Lafayette Guild in the summer of 1862 until April of 1863. On May 23, he was appointed an assistant surgeon from Maryland and assigned to General J. B. Hood. He applied for a transfer on December 20, 1863, and was sent to the 6th North Carolina Infantry. On January 22, 1865, Assistant Surgeon Davis was ordered to report to the 15th Alabama Regiment.

HARRY WOODWARD DORSEY, JR. 1831-1903

Glenmont at New Market was home to Dorsey and he was graduated in 1857 as a physician from the University of Pennsylvania. Some of the most emphatic men of Southern conviction had already departed for Montgomery and were present at the fall of Fort Sumter. Just after the Baltimore slaughter and the appearance of Federal troops detachments and squads of inflamed patriots started a steady stream as gallant youth poured into the Confederacy. Marylanders holding civil offices in the National Government started to resign. Many military men, restlessly awaiting the course the state would follow, began to tender their resignations, believing it was time to return to their native state. Dr. Dorsey was one of forty-three of that family lineage in this state who rendered their services to the South in the second struggle for independence. He joined the Confederate Army in September of 1862 at Frederick, just prior to the South Mountain Campaign. He received appointment as assistant surgeon under Dr. Wilbur R. McKnew in the 1st Maryland Cavalry in which his younger brother Ignatius Waters Dorsey was captain and quartermaster. Assistant Surgeon Dorsey was captured at Winchester on September 19, 1864, and sent to work in the wards of the West's Buildings Hospital at Baltimore. Being sent to the military prison camp at Hamilton he was exchanged on January 6, 1865, and returned to the 1st Maryland Battalion. Nobly riding with this devoted cavalry in April they made the last charge of the Army of Northern Virginia as this little command hurled themselves on the advancing foe and drove him back. Not surrendering at Appomattox they rode to Lynchburg where, after twenty days and all hope gone, they were paroled individually. Dr. Dorsey went to North Carolina. Upon returning to Maryland, he reported to the provost marshal of Frederick in August. After the iron clad oath was removed, he practiced at New Market, then moved to Hyattsville in the 1880's.

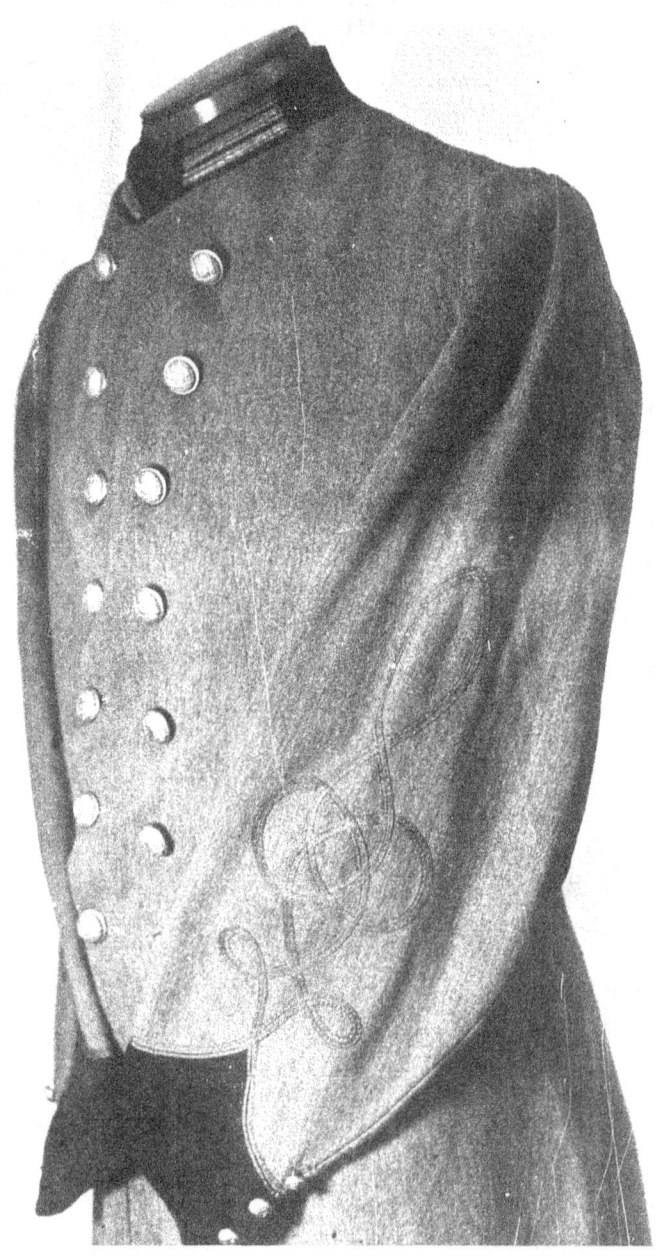

Confederate gray frock coat of Assistant Surgeon Harry Woodward Dorsey, Jr. with large Maryland state seal buttons on the double breasted front "Waterbury Button Co. *Extra*" The left sleeve has small Maryland buttons, one "Extra* Quality*" and two "Canfield Bro. & Co." The right sleeve has only one which is "Extra* Quality*". The back of the coat is also adorned with four large Maryland buttons the same as above. The breast lining is quilted cotton which may have been made from a bed spread.

Bill Turner collection

ROBERT H. DRYDEN 1833-1880

He was born and raised in Baltimore, then practiced in the county. In January of 1861, he was appointed an assistant surgeon in the U.S. Army, only holding this post for four months before resigning. The majority of Marylanders who were career officers in the military resigned their commissions. The great calamity of their state's fraternal blood and the grip of the Federal army with the flagrant violation of the Constitution would surely cause the Legislature to join the cotton states. Many enlisted at once in the C.S.A. while others such as Dr. Dryden waited for the general assembly to act. By mid-summer he was in Richmond and contracted with the government on August 13. By the early months of 1862 he was an assistant surgeon sent to the District of Indiana Territory. In November of 1863, he was transferred to the Mississippi Department. After several months, Assistant Surgeon Dryden was assigned to the District of Texas. Serving in New Mexico and Arizona until the flag was tearfully saluted for the last time, he later settled in Texas.

PHILIP BARTON DUVALL 1836-1863

Crownsville was the place of his birth and as a graduate of Anne Arundel Academy he then completed his medical studies at the University of Maryland in 1859. The State Legislature was composed of brave, high-minded, patriotic men but they were dominated by the spirit of conservatism. Not understanding that they were in the midst of a revolution, they stood by constitutional rights, holding on to the established guarantees — to habeas corpus, to trial by jury, to free speech, to law, until they and their constitutional guarantees landed in military prisons. They stood by their faith and never ceased from protest, but without warrant, charges or bail they were imprisoned. Thirty-two members of the House and Senate of which there were three M.D.'s, Mayor Brown, Marshall Kane and all the police commissioners became political prisoners for fourteen months. These were the States Rights leaders who were eager for secession. President Lincoln knew that without their presence the state would not withdraw. Dr. Duvall was awake to the despotism, desiring to drive every northerner from his state and his only option was to join the C.S.A. to deliver her from her oppressors. On June 30, 1861, he enlisted as a private in the 1st Maryland Artillery and was one of nine Duvalls from Anne Arundel County to fight for the South. Both he and Washington M. Hilliary were M.D.'s but served in the "Flying Artillery" as enlisted men. Dr. Hilliary had yielded up his life at Mechanicsville while faithfully serving his piece in battle. At Chancellorsville Sedgwick's foot soldiers got at such close range the Maryland Flying Artillery had to limber up and were driven from Mayre's Heights. The cannon were massed near Telegraph Road where they were concealed when the enemy came suddenly upon them. They opened with twenty pieces at such short range it shattered their ranks, thus starting their disastrous defeat. It was at this time on May 3, 1863, that Dr. Duvall was instantly killed at Hamilton Crossing while fighting with gunners of the rank and file. What survives is his noble memory upon the hearts of his comrades and his family and friends that mourn in Maryland. Upon the altar of Confederate cause was another sacrifice, "siste viator, heroa calcas," there he rests in peace.

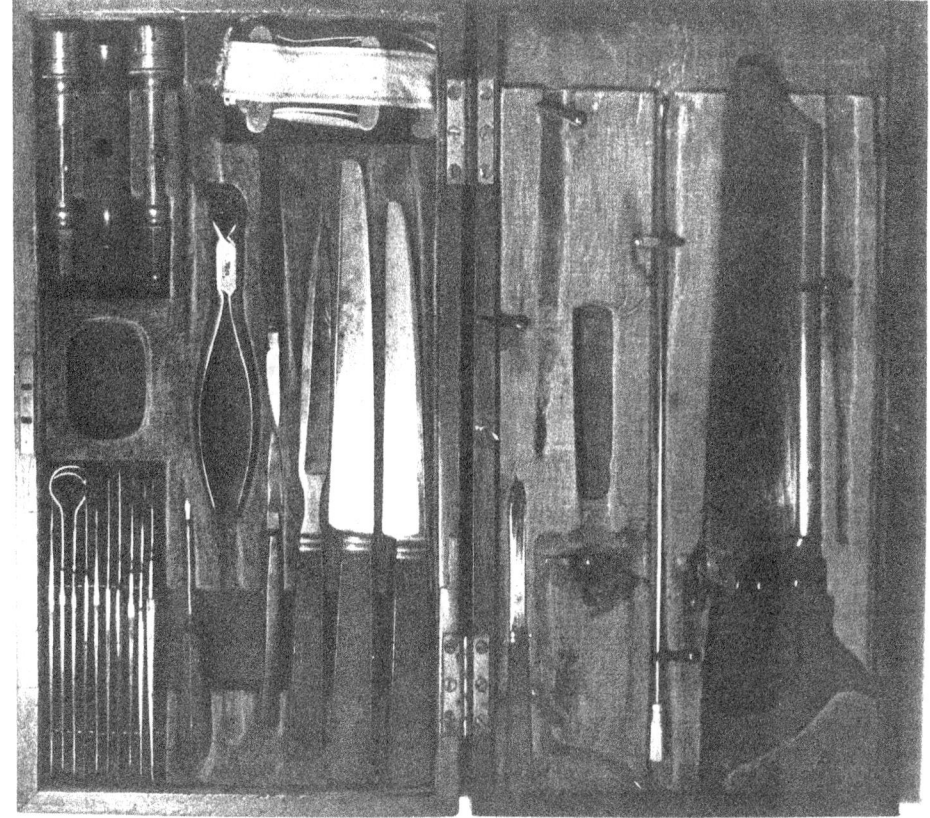

White velvet interior of an all encompassing 16½" x 9" brass bound walnut case containing twenty-three "Samuel Jackson Baltimore" marked instruments. Bone saw, bullet probe, gouge, tourniquet, three amputation knives, two scalpels, bone forceps, trow car, two trephins and handle, and aneurism hooks and needles.
Baltimore College of Dental Surgery Museum

J. H. EDWARDS

Departing from his business in Frederick County he went voluntarily into exile in order to protest the action of the Federal government. Only two Confederate memorandums can be located about him. Dr. Edwards was at Charleston, South Carolina, in the Provisional Army of the Confederate States and on August 10, 1863, was referred to as an assistant surgeon in the Eastern District of Florida.

TALCOTT ELIASON

Raised at Sabin Hill near Upperco, Virginia and attending Jefferson Medical College, he returned to his native area to practice until the country was eviscerated into war. The ingredient which brought to a head the adoption of the ordinance of secession by the "cotton states" was the outcome of the sectional presidential election. Lincoln and Hamlin received 180 electoral votes from eighteen states, all lying north of the Mason-Dixon Line. Breckin-

Assistant surgeon Richard Emory on the right with a beard, assistant surgeon Bodisco Williams of Washington, D.C. on the left, both served in Winder Hospital in Richmond.
Dave Mark collection

ridge and Lane secured 72 votes, all from Southern states; Bell and Everett received 39 in number while Douglas and Johnson obtained 12. Lincoln was declared elected, as he had a majority of the electoral college but in reality he received only 1,857,610 votes of the people, while 2,804,560 were cast against him. Dr. Eliason was appointed assistant surgeon on August 29, 1861 and assigned to the office of Medical Director T. H. Williams. On November 18, he was sent to field duty with the 1st Virginia Cavalry and on April 17, 1862 he was advanced to a surgeon. Serving with General J.E.B. Stuart's Cavalry he was a senior surgeon and referred to as division surgeon but on June 1, 1863 he was officially recognized as such. On July 7, 1864, he was relieved and four days later assigned to the 3rd Division of Howard Grove Hospital. Apparently this was not to his liking, for he resigned on July 15. After the crusade had ended he came to Washington County and doctored at Hancock.

RICHARD EMORY 1839-1895

Born at Taylor in Baltimore County he attended Rev. R. Gibson's school. He read medicine under Dr. N. R. Smith and graduated from the University of Maryland with an M.D. in 1861, after volunteering his services to the Baltimore Militia for twenty-two days after the invasion. He began his profession at Manor Glen as thousands of ardent volunteers left their families, homes and affluent occupations to go to the aid of their Southern friends. As they crossed the Potomac they selected their associates and comrades from contiguity, from friendship, from relationship or nearly joined the first unit they came to. Men of Maryland descent were scattered all over the Confederacy and thousands of young men who got through the lines sought out kinsmen, so nearly every regiment of the army had "Free Staters" in their ranks. The state militia units had been the training grounds for many of the new recruits. The Maryland Guard Batallion was the exotic, elite military organization of the day and the members were young men of prominent Baltimore families. The roster of Company G's sixty-eight men shows that no less than fifty-six joined the C.S.A. Dr. Emory left the sanctuary of his home in the summer of 1862 and was employed under contract. On September 26 Assistant Surgeon Emory was assigned to Winder Hospital in Richmond. He also served at General Hospital No. 13 on Twentieth Street between Main and Franklin which was known as the prison hospital. Early in 1865 he was detailed to the Nitre and Mining Bureau. In 1866 he resumed his practice in Baltimore County near Phoenix, then to Saint James at the family's old colonial house called Manor Glen.

THOMAS HALL EMORY, SR.

An alumnus of the Virginia Military Institute, Emory then received his M.D. from the University of Maryland, class of 1827. He returned to his native county of Queen Anne's to begin his learned occupation. In the spring of 1861, there were seventeen militia companies in this county parading under the secession banner, being avowedly for the state and local defense against Northern aggression. In June a unit known as the Maryland Zouaves was organized and was the only distinctive Union Company. They were armed by the Federal government and the local paper wrote, "This fine organization will carry no other banner than the Stars and Stripes. Have we not patriotic ladies enough to see that they shall soon have a standard to carry which shall once more gladden our eyes?" Dr. Emory received a commission as assistant surgeon in the Southern Navy on March 14, 1862, and was assigned to the C.S. steamer *Louisiana*. His next duty was aboard the C.S.S. *Bienville*, then he was ordered to the New Orleans and later Jackson stations. Assistant Surgeon Emory then saw service on the C.S.S. *Georgia* in the Savannah Squadron until the summer of 1863 when he was transferred to the cruiser *Florida*, under the command of Captain Joseph N. Barney. This prominent sailor from the "Black and Gold State" was seized with illness and had to relinquish command on February 12, 1864. On October 7 at 3:00 a.m., while nearly half the ship's crew was on leave in Bahia Brazil, a neutral port, the *Florida* was rammed and fired upon. The eighty remaining crew replied with small arms but they were soon overpowered. Some of the defenseless crew jumped overboard and Assistant Surgeon Emory was captured as he attempted to escape. On November 15, he was incarcerated in Maryland's Point Lookout prison until exchanged on February 1, 1865. He was in Richmond until the evacuation and the end. He returned to the eastern shore of our state until the 1870's when he moved to Baltimore County.

WILLIAM B. EVERETT 1837-1923

Coming to Baltimore from his birthplace in Kent County he was a medical student there when the invaders were assaulted. This patriotic pupil volunteered in the militia to stop the Northern hordes, serving with the military surgical staff. He saw many of these courageous fellows go to the aid of the South while he returned to complete his future declaration. Fortifications on Federal Hill were strengthened while Fort Marshall, just east of Patterson Park, and Fort Washington, northeast of the present Johns Hopkins Hospital, were established. Near Mt. Clare, on the confiscated estate of General George H. Steuart, Sr., who was in the Confederate lines for the duration, Jarvis Hospital grew in his mansion under the protection of an extensive works known as Fort No. 1. Ringing the city were other designated sites, some fortified briefly, others permanently with their cannon frowning down on the seiged city. Shortly after graduation, Dr. Everett returned to his ancestral home and with several others crossed the Chesapeake Bay in an open boat on St. Patrick's eve in 1862. Going before the medical board he was accepted into the medical corps. Assistant Surgeon Everett was sent to Pate's Battalion 5th Virginia Cavalry. On July 14 he proceeded to North Carolina where he was reassigned to the Tarheel forces at forts below Wilmington, then to Asheville at Fort St. Phillip Hospital. Desiring service at a combatant with his own kinsmen he resigned his commission in fall of 1864 and came to the Shenandoah Valley to enlist as a trooper in the 1st Maryland Cavalry. Returning from the Chambersburg, Pennsylvania raid the Maryland Cavalry Battalion was disastrously surprised by the enemy at Moorefield. The 2nd Maryland lost over fifty while the 1st lost still more heavily. Dr. Everett was persuaded to join Marquis's Virginia Battery as acting assistant surgeon. He was captured at Waynesboro in March of 1865 and exchanged; later he was paroled at Staunton on May 1 as acting assistant surgeon of the Virginia Reserve Forces. Dr. Everett returned to the Maryland Eastern Shore to practice medicine. Not only was he a physician of man's physical needs but more importantly man's spiritual needs as an ordained minister in the Protestant Episcopal Church. As a full-time clergyman, Reverend Everett filled the diocese of Easton, Richmond and then Washington. He was a member of the United Confederate Veterans Camp No. 171 in the District.

GEORGE G. FARNANDIS

Completing his studies at Mount St. Mary's College in Emmitsburg, he turned to the medical course at the University of Maryland. Graduating in 1852, he began his chosen occupation in his native city of Baltimore. He was resident physician at the Alms House from 1856 to 1859 and was demonstrator of anatomy at the University of Maryland in 1860. Dr. Farnandis was one of the many volunteers who came by Southern Maryland to Richmond in the late spring of 1861. J. Alden Weston, a former Baltimore militia colonel, with other fervent exiled city militia officers formed four companies under Major Weston. They were composed of many members of the Baltimore volunteer companies; these men were indeed the aristocracy. They were the nobility, well bred, well educated, well mannered, well traveled, well instructed; they had no trouble maintaining their reputation. The secretary of war began to shift companies into regiments as troops were needed. Each man of Weston's Infantry Battalion signed an individual petition which was sent to Jefferson Davis requesting that the battalion not be separated. On June 21, Company A, Weston Guard was ordered to join the 1st Maryland Infantry becoming Company C; Company B, Maryland Guard was assigned to the 21st Virginia Infantry as Company B; Company C Southern Marylanders guarded prisoners at Richmond until August 1 when they became Company I of the 1st Maryland Infantry; Company D, Maryland Guard was also sent to the 1st Maryland Regiment on June 1. Dr. Farnandis was on the staff of General Kirby Smith until April 4, 1863, when he was appointed to the Medical Corps. This assistant surgeon received an appointment to the Army Medical Examining Board. During the last year of the war, he was serving in the Trans-Mississippi Department. Returning to the Monumental City Dr. Farnandis was instructor of surgery at the Washington Medical University 1871 to 1873. He soon retired from medicine, residing on his farm in Harford County.

ARTHUR L. FOREMAN

Dr. Foreman was working in the medical profession and answered the call for doctors to serve in the Baltimore municipal civilian forces after the attack of Northern soldiers against the Pratt Street populace. He joined thirty-six colleagues who responded to the city's plea. The Baltimore Volunteer Militia Surgical Staff was composed of the following under Edward Warren who was appointed surgeon-in-chief, J. P. Adams, John W. Beard, Charles H. Bradford, J. S. Bradford, Horace A. Brooks, Richard Wilson Carr, Samuel C. Chew, Dr. Church, Alexander F. Clendenin, C. W. Coechling, Theodore Cooke, John N. Coonan, Richard Emory, Augustus F. Erich, William B. Everett, Arthur L. Foreman, Robert J. Freeman, Richard C. Lee, John C. Mackenzie, Thomas G. Mackenzie, Felix R. McManus, Gerald E. Morgan, H. C. Nelson, Charles E. V. Nickerson, William H. Norris, Abram H. Price, Samuel A. Raborg, Thomas Sappington, Allen P. Smith, Milton N. Taylor, John Hanson Thomas, Ignatius Davis Thompson, William Tyler, John Whitridge, Dr. Wilson and Dr. Yellott. This distinguished group of doctors included one Fredericktonian, William Tyler, who came all the way to the city to serve and eight were senior medical students who were about to graduate from the University of Maryland. Their headquarters were on Holliday Street near City Hall; they were completely separate from the surgeons of the already established militia units and were organized for the volunteer civilian corps. Dr. Foreman was one of ten of these practitioners whose chivalrous courage was conspicuous on the South's bloody battlefields. He was officially commissioned an assistant surgeon on June 2, 1863, in the C.S.A. He had been previously appointed by the Secretary of War; his commission was to be retroactive from September 29, 1862 and he had passed the medical board on December 8. Assistant Surgeon Foreman was ordered to the Army of Tennessee in hospital duty. This medical officer then saw field duty with the 25th Louisiana Regiment and after the war settled in Kentucky.

JOEL W. FRANKLIN

Francis J. Thomas was appointed adjutant general of brother Maryland volunteers on May 17, 1861, in the state of Virginia. On May 22 he reported "there are in all about 2,800 reported to me but only fourteen companies organized. I have been unwilling to bring more into Virginia until steps are taken to properly organize and arm them as they come." Colonel Thomas proposed that three infantry regiments be formed, at Richmond, Point of Rocks and Harper's Ferry and that cavalry and artillery battalions be organized to be filled by the numerous new arrivals. On June 8, Governor Letcher transferred the forces of the state of Virginia to the Confederacy. Thomas accepted a position on the staff of General J. E. Johnston and was killed at Manassas. Had Colonel Thomas's original proposal of organizing several regiments of the three branches of service materialized, thousands of newly arriving Maryland sons could have been easily funneled into these commands. Instead of being scattered throughout the entire Southern Army brigades of Marylanders could have been formed and fought together under the black and gold flag for the Confederacy. Dr. Franklin, a Virginian by birth, was appointed assistant surgeon of the 3rd Maryland Artillery and mustered into service with them on January 14, 1862, at Richmond. This battery was destined to a renowned fate west of the Allegheny mountains and was never privileged to fire their cannon within their cherished state. On July 11, 1863, Assistant Surgeon Franklin was transferred to the 56th Georgia Infantry. He was with Cumming's Brigade until September 16, 1864, when he was ill and in the hospital near Lovejoy's Station. Franklin served at Madison in Asylum Hospital in Georgia, then at the hospital in Cambria, Alabama until relieved on March 10, 1865.

ROBERT J. FREEMAN

Hailing from Somerset County, he was a volunteer physician on the surgical staff of the militia just after the Pratt Street massacre. He answered the cry of the Southland by being commissioned an assistant surgeon in the Confederate navy on August 20, 1861. At his home it wasn't until 1862 that the Federal authorities began to move in the Eastern Shore. Because of its comparative isolation these counties were under little supervision and control until this time which consequently afforded Confederate agents opportunities to establish lines for transmitting vast numbers of men and supplies to the South. In February the Union troops were busy disarming the militia companies and arresting secessionists. In the fall of 1862 Assistant Surgeon Freeman was ordered from the infirmary at Jackson, Mississippi to the hospital at Yazoo. His first sea service was on the ram *Atlanta*, after being promoted to passed assistant surgeon. He was one of the one hundred ninety-three sailors captured on board this vessel on June 17, 1863 at Warsaw Sound off Georgia. Passed Assistant Surgeon Freeman, after caring for the wounded, was conveyed to Fort Lafayette prison in New York harbor until exchanged on December 7. His next sea assignment was as medical officer on the *Palmetto States*.

EDWIN SAMUEL GAILLARD 1827-1885

Born in Charleston and educated in medicine at the Medical College of South Carolina, he was graduated with first honors in 1854. Settling in Florida until March, 1857, when he moved to New York, the following August he went to Europe and returned the following November. After the 1861 new year, he came to Baltimore until May when he joined the Southern army. As Marylanders went to the aid of the South, those coming over land by the western route rendezvoused at Point of Rocks and on the opposite side of the Potomac at Harper's Ferry. They were under the command of Thomas Jackson and were to be fed by Turner Ashby. Eight companies of five hundred men were collected at these two locations, electing their officers and busily drilling and establishing camp. They had refused to recognize the Virginia authorities because Virginia was not a part of the Confederacy. They believed that Maryland ought to be represented in the army by men bearing arms and her flag. It was impossible for her to be represented in the political department of the government; therefore, it was of vital importance that the flag of Maryland be upheld in the armies of the Confederacy. Their application was sent up through regular channels to President Davis and on May 21 the 1st Maryland Infantry Regiment was mustered into the Confederate State Army. Among the number of medical men at Point of Rocks was Dr. Gaillard who was commissioned assistant surgeon of the 1st Maryland Infantry. They had an overabundance of medical personnel so he was reassigned on June 24. By September 9 he was promoted surgeon and by December 7 detailed to the army medical board at Manassas. At the Battle of Fair Oaks, shortly after attending a wound suffered by General W. Hampton, Surgeon Gaillard's right arm was wounded and mangled so badly that it had to be amputated. On August 30, 1862, he was announced as Medical Director of General G. W. Smith's command. By April 29, 1863, he became Surgical and Medical Inspector of Richmond, with offices in the northeast corner of Main and Eleventh Streets. Medical Inspector Gaillard's last military duty was at Andersonville. After the surrender, he was granted a professorship of principles and practice of medical and general pathology at the Medical College of Virginia. His second marriage was to a daughter of Dr. Charles Bell Gibson, a war colleague. In 1868, he went to Louisville as Dean of the Kentucky Medical School. In 1880 he was in New York, but Dr. Gaillard is best remembered for his vigorous editing of the *Richmond Medical Journal* which he founded in 1866, the *Richmond and Louisville Medical Journal*, the *American Medical Weekly* and the *Gaillard Medical Journal*.

JOHN MUTIUS GAINES 1837-1915

Gaines was born at Locust Hill, Culpeper County, Virginia. His first collegiate education was in chemistry at the University of Virginia, class of 1858. He then pursued the medical course the following semester and attended the Jefferson Medical College in 1860 and worked at Alexandria. Not far away at Harper's Ferry the 1st Maryland Infantry was in a quandary. Company A was armed with Hall's breechloading carbines that they brought with them from Frederick. The three companies transferred from Weston's Battalion were armed with Springfields but the rest of the regiment had no weapons. They had rushed off from home and fired by enthusiasm they stole rides or walked to Harper's Ferry. Around them were warm-hearted comrades who shared their blankets and rations but they had no clothes, tents, bedding, cooking utensils — nothing that soldiers needed and must have to be of service. They had no government to appeal for arms, they were outlaws from their own state but they were too proud to go back, they had come to fight and stay they would. At this crisis, Mrs. Claudia Saunders Johnson, wife of Bradley T. Johnson, had left her comfortable home in Frederick with her five-year-old son to follow her husband, voluntarily going to North Carolina and applying for arms and equipment. This elegant daughter of a member of the North Carolina Congress secured five hundred Mississippi rifles, ten thousand cartridges, substantial money for camp supplies and uniforms totaling ten thousand dollars. Assistant Surgeon Gaines was received into the C.S.A. on July 17, 1861, at Culpeper Hospital. He was then sent to the Dea's Maryland Artillery. This unit enlisted for the war as light artillery for the Maryland Line but through the spring and summer of 1862 were used independently. With the approach of winter and the dwindling of combat they expected to join the Maryland Line but on November 3 they were ordered to Battery 8 Richmond Defenses being Company C 19th Virginia Heavy Artillery. After the Battle of Sharpsburg he was left in charge of the wounded at Boonsboro for six weeks. By November 6 his orders were addressed as Surgeon Gaines. After the retreat from Gettysburg he was left to administer to the wounded at Williamsport, then moved to Hagerstown where he remained for several months. He was then sent to Chester, Pennsylvania, with his patients until being exchanged in December, at which time he went to Petersburg and was assigned to the 8th Virginia Infantry until the combat ended. Dr. Gaines spent a year in Alexandria, then returned to Boonsboro and married a girl whom he had met during his stay after the Antietam Campaign. He went into medical practice with his father-in-law, Otho J. Smith, at Boonsboro until 1893 when he moved to Hagerstown and soon retired.

FRANK GALE

As a medical student at the University of Maryland he decided to sacrifice his studies for the cause of the South. At Fredericksburg and Richmond one hundred and forty-four orphans born under the black and gold flag were mustered into the 1st Maryland Artillery in June, 1861. Two guns for the battery had been completed when the Washington Artillery from New Orleans arrived at Richmond completely equipped with the exception of two guns. These cannon were turned over to the Louisianians but it was sometime until they were supplied with four napoleons and four parrotts. Frank Gale enlisted as a private on July 16 for the war at Richmond. No battery of Confederates won more distinction during this crusade than would the Maryland Flying Artillery, as they were familiarly known. They were imbued with a spirit of patriotism that overcame all sense of fear, and made them invincible upon the field of battle. It was one of the very few batteries in the Army of Northern Virginia that never lost a gun and no battery in the army saw more hard fighting or lost more men. On June 25, 1862, Section Company B was temporarily attached to Hampton Legion of which, now corporal Gale was gunner. At the old battle field at Manassas on August 28, the Flying Artillery fired the first shot. The next day as the enemy pressed on in overwhelming numbers they would limber their pieces to the rear for a hundred yards, halt and renew the fight and at Bristoe Station he became a casualty. Recovering from his wound he assisted around the hospital and then went before the medical examiners. On June 11, 1863, he was appointed to the medical corps. It cannot be established where Assistant Surgeon Gale pursued his doctoring but he does appear on the register of the Medical Director's Office as a practitioner in the Army of Northern Virginia. He did not return to the Flying Artillery and it's interesting to note that the 4th Maryland Battery of light artillery did have M.D.'s serving in the ranks but there were no medical officers serving as surgeons. Their main concern were the veterinarians and the care of the precious horses that enabled them to rapidly move.

CARY BRECKINRIDGE GAMBLE 1827-

Receiving his schooling at Washington College, the University of Virginia and in 1846 the University of Maryland Medical College, he, at the early age of nineteen, began the medical profession in Baltimore. In 1849, Dr. Gamble moved to Tallahassee. On May 17, 1861, he was commissioned a surgeon and was appointed surgeon general of Florida. From past knowledge of Marylanders he knew they were as devoted to the Southern way of life as much as their brothers and and sisters of the sunny Gulf States. That banner of the Southern Cross was studded with the stars of God's heaven, like Old Glory itself when it was stainless. They had drunk of freedom's milk and knew the entire nation was not allowed to commune. These Marylanders would spring from the loins of freemen to follow the banner of liberty, for their revolutionary sires were not inspired by a more intense devotion to freedom than they were. Preferring field duty he was with the 1st Florida Infantry and soon became brigade surgeon of Anderson's Brigade. On April 7, 1862, he was captured at Shiloh and exchanged on May 13 when he became post surgeon at Macon. On April 21, 1864, he was announced as Chief Surgeon Gamble on the staff of General P. Anderson commanding the district of Florida, then in the same capacity with General J. K. Jackson. By the fall of this year, he was again in Macon as senior surgeon in charge of the hospital. In 1866 Dr. Gamble returned to Baltimore where he cherished his service to the South with membership in the Franklin Buchanan Veterans Camp and the Society of the Army and Navy of the Confederate States in the State of Maryland.

FREDERICK GARRETSON 1837-1887

Born in Gloucester County, Virginia, and coming to this state with his parents at an early age, he was educated at St. James College, Hagerstown, interned under Dr. W. C. VanBibber in Baltimore and was graduated from the University of Maryland Medical College in 1857. His uncle with whom he apprenticed was one of the editors of the *Maryland and Virginia Medical Journal*. Collaborating with the editor were two physicians who would become surgeons in the Confederacy, Levin S. Joynes and Charles Bell Gibson. On May 23, 1857, he was appointed an assistant surgeon in the U. S. Navy. The greatest number of naval officers resigning from their former allegiances in the spring of 1861 were from our state. Their resignations were not accepted but they proceeded to Charleston, Montgomery and Richmond; later their names were stricken from the rolls as dismissed. As they joined the C.S.A. Navy, the Marine Corps was led by Commandant Colonel Lloyd James Beall, Colonel Algernon Sidney Taylor, Major Richard Taylor Allison, one captain and four lieutenants. The Provisional Navy was also led by sons of Maryland. Rear Admiral Raphael Semmes, and Admiral Franklin Buchanan, two commodores, nine captains, five commanders, twenty-two lieutenants, five surgeons, three passed assistant surgeons, nine assistant surgeons, four paymasters, six passed midshipmen, and nine midshipmen. Dr. Frederick Garretson VanBibber resigned and was classified as dismissed on May 6; upon entering the Confederate Navy he had his last name changed to his mother's maiden name. On June 10, he was made an assistant surgeon and by September 13, 1862, he was promoted to passed assistant surgeon. The first of the Confederate steam cruisers built in England was the *Florida*. She was fully fitted out at Mobile and on the night of January 15, 1863, she made her escape from the blockading fleet and set to sea. Her medical officer was Dr. Garretson and in the next seventeen months they captured or destroyed thirty-seven Federal vessels. By that summer Passed Assistant Surgeon Garretson was transferred to a naval station and was relieved by Assistant Surgeon Thomas Hall Emory, Sr. Passed Assistant Surgeon Garretson was paroled on May 17, 1865, at Augusta, Georgia, returned to Baltimore never again using the VanBibber name.

ELI GEDDINGS 1799-1878

He was born in Newberry District of South Carolina. Attending Abbeyville Academy he was licensed to practice in 1820. In the next five years, Dr. Gedding attended lectures at the University of Pennsylvania and the Medical College of South Carolina. In 1825, he became demonstrator of anatomy at the Medical College of South Carolina for a year, then for the next two years he was in Paris and London. Returning to America, he was Clinical Lecturer at Charleston Alms House until 1831 when he received a chair at the University of Maryland Medical College as professor of anatomy and physiology. He was editor of the *Baltimore Medical Journal* from 1833 to 1835 and the next two years the *North American Archives of Medical and Surgical Science Journal*. In 1837, Dr. Gedding returned to his alma mater of South Carolina where he taught until the war. Several sons of his former pupils rode with Company G 7th Virginia Cavalry. This was the first cavalry unit of completely Maryland personnel formed by J. Frank Mason, a physician. They started picket duty opposite Point of Rocks and followed their leader, Turner Ashby, along the upper Potomac forming the frontier line. Mason's company was the heart from which future Maryland cavalry units would draw their captains. Three celebrated lieutenant colonels, Harry W. Gilmor, Elijah V. White and T. Sturgis Davis, would also emerge from Company G and form heroic battalions of Maryland cavaliers. Dr. Geddings was ordained a surgeon on February 5, 1862. He became a member of the Army Medical Board at Charleston and was elected president. On May 1, 1863, he was performing clinical duties in General Hospital at Tallahassee until February 7, 1865, when Surgeon Geddings was assigned to the Army Medical Board at Charleston. After the struggle, he remained in this city. During the Federal occupation of Charleston Dr. Geddings was in charge of the property of the medical college which had been subjected to many depredations. After they were relieved of the foreign occupants he worked to revive the college where he lectured until retiring in 1873.

ROBERT R. GIBBES 1836-1877

Dr. Gibbes was born in South Carolina and appointed an assistant surgeon in the Confederate Navy. In coastal duty during the summer of 1862 his diary speaks of one continued season of fever, severe dysentery and rice-field dropsies. According to the classification of disease of the Confederate Naval Medical Department fevers were first on the list. Fluxes were classified as acute diarrhea— where frequent stools are unaccompanied by marked tenesmus, acute dysentery—with tenesmus, chronic dysentery— chronic with or without tenesmus, tubercular diarrhea— with tubercular ulceration. Diet, venesection and medication were used in the treatment of fluxes. Drugs recommended as remedies were: emetics, purgatives, diaphoretics, diuretics, opium, anodynes, hypnotics, astringents, vegetable tonics, turpentine, bromine, iodine and antiseptics. Assistant Surgeon Gibbes was captured off Warsaw Sound on June 17, 1863, on board the steamer *Atlanta*, being incarcerated in Fort Lafayette and then Fort Warren until exchanged on December 7. He was then assigned to the C. S. *Savannah* and in August of 1864 he writes in his diary, "Up to this date the time for me has passed drearily and wearily. Nothing but one uninterrupted season of disease and death and were I more fully to condense this diagram of my existence—two words would express my occupation and portray the picture of my past two months vividly—viz. Blood and Physic. The fevers have been of the most malignant type ever hitherto written of or noticed in this latitude. Bilious, remittent, congestive, intermittent and typhoid are everywhere . . . The majority of cases of bilious remittent fevers have terminated fatally owing to the above deficiency of stamina in material and add to this fact that almost every case has been admittted only after several days of prior complaint and sickness and the mortality is with reason for the most part apparent. Twenty-seven had died since July 1, 1864, and most of them of bilious congestive fever. I have performed several operations, three resections, five minor amputations and some few others." He was paroled on April 28, 1865, at Greensboro and after several years he came to Baltimore until the yellow fever outbreak in 1870 when Dr. Gibbes went to Governor's Island New York. He afterwards accompanied expeditions of government employees to the West as a medical officer.

CHARLES BELL GIBSON 1816-1865

Receiving his medical schooling at the University of Pennsylvania in 1836, he was a resident physician to the Philadelphia Hospital in 1838. Returning to the city of his birth Dr. Gibson became professor of surgery at the Washington Medical University in Baltimore from 1842 until 1848. Going to Hampden Sydney College he taught surgery and surgical anatomy. He not only held offices in the state medical society but also the American Medical Association and was known as the state's leading surgeon. On April 24, 1861, the Virginia Convention passed the ordinance organizing the military forces of the state. A medical department with a surgeon general, ten surgeons and ten assistant surgeons was provided and Dr. Gibson received the appointment as surgeon general. In early June when all Virginia staff officers were transferred from the state to the Confederacy he made a mere assistant surgeon. At the same time at Canary Island a group from the "Free State" was endeavoring to enroll their transient fellow statemen into an artillery company known as the Baltimore Artillery. Under Captain John D. Myrick they were mustered in on June 5 and assigned to the 9th Virginia Infantry as Company B. By June 11 he was Surgeon Gibson and established one of the earliest Richmond institutions known as General Hospital No. 1 at the city's Alms House. He was administrator of this facility until September 9, 1863, when he was appointed on the board of consulting surgeons for all the Richmond hospitals. By 1864 Dr. Gibson was employed as a contract surgeon in Richmond where he died suddenly. His life devoted to his fellow man was as bright as the keen blade of his scalpel and his "Servore plenitudo sine limitationes" bountiful service was encompassed by no boundaries.

PETER GOOLRICK

Goolrick of Baltimore experienced the stirring scenes in the city and heard the resounding cry for vengeance to burn the rebellious city by the North. The people of the state, without distinction of party, were one unit in prevailing sentiment. But the occupation of the state was extended, railroad bridges and canal locks were under permanent Union guard. Pickets patrolled vital turnpike points; every bridge and ford across the Potomac River, along the entire shore line, were constantly watched. The barrier of bayonets could not keep back the current of sympathy that day and night flowed to the South. All over the state the women irrepressibly flaunted the Confederate red and white in the face of the enemy of occupation. Babies wore red and white socks, girls red and white ribbons with red and white bouquets at their girdles and on their hearts, the young lads red and white cravats. The larger boys were sent South by their mothers, sisters and sweethearts. As they donned the gray, bade farewell to home and with a family's prayers and benedictions, went to a right and just cause. Maryland was silenced and bound to the North by force; thousands of her sons, believing that they were free to act as individuals according to their own convictions, voluntarily exiled themselves from home to serve the Confederacy. It is true that Southern blood is naturally warm and Southern brains impetuous, but Dr. Goolrick waited until the spring of 1862 before committing himself. By October 13, he was ordered to Medical Director Edwin S. Gillard and sent to General G. W. Smith's command. On April 4, 1863, he was appointed assistant surgeon and sent to the 49th Virginia Infantry. By June 1, he was advanced in the rank to surgeon. In the winter he was in Stark's Battalion of Artillery; then Surgeon Goolrick was administering to patients in the General Hospital at Staunton. He was one of the incorporators of the College of Physicians and Surgeons of Baltimore in 1872 and taught medical juris-prudence and toxicology.

RODNEY GLISAN

Glisan is registered on an index card as an assistant surgeon in the C.S.A. in the card file of Maryland Confederates compiled by Harry Wright Newman. Dr. Glisan is shown as an assistant surgeon in the U.S. Army resigning on June 7, 1861.

THEODORE W. GLOCKER 1841-1894

Graduating in 1859 from Baltimore City College and in 1861 from the University of Maryland Medical School, he practiced in the Monumental City where he was born, while his two brothers followed the battle flags of the South. The only one known to the author is a younger brother, Albert Campbell Glocker, who left school and met Captain George R. Gaither who brought to Virginia a part of Company B Howard Dragoons. These Howard County militiamen came to the service of the South with horses, arms, and accoutrements and mustered into the 1st Virginia Cavalry as Company M at Leesburg on May 14. So distinguished were these Marylanders that the company was changed to K and they assumed the conspicuous position on the right. In February of 1863, Dr. Glocker could stay inactive no longer; coming into the Confederacy he enlisted as a private in Company C 2nd Maryland Cavalry. After several months service of riding with the gallant band of Gilmor's Battalion of partisan rangers he was assigned to the General Hospital at Danville. On June 11, 1863, he was accepted into the Medical Corps as an officer. In February of 1864, he was relieved and ordered to report to the General Hospital No. 2 at the corner of Twenty-fifth and Clay Streets in Richmond which had a staff of seven surgeons and eighteen assistant and acting assistant surgeons. In August of 1864, Assistant Surgeon Glocker was working in the Staunton General Hospital until December 21 when he was transferred to Harrisonburg General Hospital. With the C.S.A. future shrouded in gloom after the surrenders, he returned to Baltimore to treat the ill and was a member of the state Medical and Chirurgical Faculty.

EDMUND K. GOLDSBOROUGH 1843-

Feeling the claims of the Southland so just and important and suspending his medical studies, Goldsborough left his Talbot County home. Starting for the Confederate lines in the early fall of 1862 he fell into Federal hands at Port Royal when he and his companions, Lloyd Lownes and Sidney Winder, were confined in prison. After three months young Goldsborough luckily made his escape and this time was successful in reaching the capital. Being qualified for service in the medical department he was assigned to Hospital No. 1 in Richmond as a hospital steward. He served at this point while pursuing the study of medicine at the Medical College of Virginia. At this school he received valuable training in military medicine and surgery from which he graduated. On April 28, 1864, he accepted a commission as assistant surgeon in the Southern Navy and was assigned to Drewry's Bluff. He was then transferred to the iron-clad steamer *Fredericksburg* in the James River squadron. Assistant Surgeon Goldsborough retired from Richmond with Rear Admiral Raphael Semmes' Naval Brigade to Danville and subsequently to Greensboro where he was paroled on May 1, 1865. Returning to Talbot County he practiced medicine until relocating to Baltimore in 1868. In 1875 he removed to Washington where he continued to devote himself to his profession and was a member of the District of Columbia Confederate veterans.

DANIEL SMITH GREEN 1812-1864

Born in Culpeper County, Virginia, and graduating in medicine from the University of Pennsylvania in 1832, he came to this state to practice and soon entered the U. S. Navy serving during the Seminole Indian and Mexican Wars. Surgeon Green was with Commodore Perry's expedition to Japan. At the outbreak of the War Between the States he resigned from the Pacific squadron but his name was stricken from the rolls after leaving his ship at Panama. Reaching Baltimore for a short stay, Dr. Green ran the inter-national blockade and received an identical rank in the Southern navy on June 20, 1861. Surgeon Green was sent to Culpeper to organize and establish a hospital, then he was sent to Lynchburg in charge of a clinic that would become General Hospital No. 2. Requesting active sea service he was relieved on September 5, 1862, and assigned to service aboard the C.S.S. *Patrick Henry*. This steamer was in the James River Squadron, which was commanded by French Forrest, another conspicuous Marylander of the old navy who had come to the assistance of the Southland. In the fall of 1863 when the Confederate Naval Academy was established under Captain William H. Parker, another "Free Stater" from the old navy, Surgeon Green was relieved. The steamship *Patrick Henry* was chosen as schoolship for the midshipmen. Taking his place as medical officer on board and as a member of the school's academic staff was Assistant Surgeon W. J. Addison whose biography has already appeared. Surgeon Green was assigned to station duty and contracted an insidious disease that, through his occupation he had fought for thirty some years, took his life on March 5, 1864, at Lynchburg. Actuated only by high sense of honor and duty to the cause he loved and the principles he advocated, his life was offered up, "devotatus civibus suis in meridie," devoted to his fellow man and the South.

WILLIAM GREEN

William was a son of Surgeon Daniel Smith Green. He completed courses at the University of Virginia and the Jefferson School finishing in 1858. Dr. Green was working in the city hospital at Brooklyn, New York, when he obeyed his heart's impulse to answer the South's call to arms. He enlisted as a private in the Lanier Guards; this unit of Marylanders was mustered into the 13th Virginia Infantry as Company G. The nucleus of this group was composed of Baltimoreans. George Lanier, of Lanier Brothers who were dry goods merchants, equipped them in Baltimore. During these exciting times this scheme was adopted to get out of the city without being arrested. A funeral procession was planned; loading a coffin with guns, a hearse, followed by a solemn procession of overloaded carriages of mourners, proceeded to Loudon Park Cemetery. When a safe distance from the city the casket was opened and quickly each armed man said good-bye to those remaining at home. The empty hearse and sparsely populated carriages returned to the city as the Lanier Guard tramped to Harper's Ferry where they were mustered in. Private Green was detailed to the medical department just after the Battle of Manassas. As an assistant surgeon he was ordered to his father's hospital at Culpeper. In the spring of 1862, the institution was moved to Lynchburg where he was promoted to surgeon. In the fall of 1863, Surgeon Green was reassigned to the artillery of the Second Corps under General J. Daniel. During the long investment of Petersburg he was appointed Chief Surgeon of Artillery and served in this capacity until, dragging his weary body to Appomattox, he wept. Dr. Green remained in Virginia until 1867 when he returned to Baltimore. In 1871, he accepted a professorship of materia medica and therapeutics at Washington Medical University.

PHILIP D. GROVE

He wished the doctrine of secession had never been heard of and that our country could have remained as our fathers left it — prosperous, happy and united. The issues had been long ago made between the two sections and Old Maryland would no doubt eventually link her fortunes to those of the South. But on May 24, 1861, Federal troops crossed the Potomac taking possession of Arlington Heights. The promise that government soldiers were only to be used to protect the capital was broken by the Washington authorities. Maryland was bound hand and foot to the Union by the overwhelming force of the army of occupation. Dr. Grove was one of the true sons of this state who stepped bravely to the front when the rights of citizenship ceased by coming to the support of the Southland. On September 17, 1862, he was appointed acting assistant surgeon while working in the General Hospital in Danville. Being passed to an assistant surgeon he was ordered to the 2nd Maryland Cavalry which was organized May and June of 1863. Harry Gilmor of Mason's Maryland cavalry company obtained permission to organize a cavalry troop for the 7th Virginia Regiment. This was also a complete unit of men from the "land of pleasant living," but instead of being affiliated with their state kinsmen of Company G they were sent to the 12th Virginia Cavalry where they became Company F. The 2nd Maryland Cavalry was an independent battalion of partisan rangers composed of courageous riders who were born under the black and gold flag. Gilmor's Battalion consisted of five new companies and his former Company F, but by August this company was recalled to the 12th Virginia due to the protest of Colonel A. W. Harman who felt that although they were Marylanders they had been mustered into his regiment and he needed them. Assistant Surgeon Grove was captured on October 15, 1863, at Sharpsburg and incarcerated in Fort McHenry. On November 21, he was sent to City Point to be exchanged and he returned to the battalion to receive the accolades of their daring exploits.

CHARLES L. GWYNN

Enrolled in the scholastic program of medicine at the University of Maryland where his brother had graduated three years prior to him in 1860, he was working under his brother when Chief Justice Roger Brooke Taney of the United States Supreme Court issued the writ of habeas corpus to the commander of Fort McHenry. This required him to produce John Merryman, the first lieutenant of the Baltimore County Horse Guard who was arrested, before the district court on May 27. An aide of General G. Cadwallader appeared without the defendant and said Merryman had been arrested for open and avowed hostility to the U.S. and that the President had authorized the suspension of the writ. The chief justice ordered an attachment to issue against General Cadwallader and sent a marshal to arrest him. The marshal and deputies proceeded to Fort McHenry but could not gain entrance. Chief Justice Taney ordered the court records to show the General in contempt. He subsequently ruled that the President of the United States can have no authority at anytime, under any circumstances, to suspend the writ of habeas corpus. But in these hectic days the cruel despotism of the Federal military ruthless ruled without cause or legal process. Cherishing the guaranteed principles of America, Gwynn departed for the Confederacy and in early 1862 enlisted as a private in the 26th Virginia Infantry Company B. On July 22 he was acting assistant surgeon assigned to the 46th Virginia Infantry. He returned to his regiment on September 12 again as a private and after an illness requested back pay as a contract surgeon. On August 11, 1863, Dr. Gwynn was detailed from the ranks to Wise Brigade Hospital, then he was working in Chaffin's Bluff Hospital as an acting assistant surgeon. By the next year he can be found as a contract physician employed by the government.

ALEXANDER L. HAMMOND

Alexander bore a very common last name associated with Anne Arundel County medicine in the 1850's. In 1860 Annapolis had a population of 4,658 inhabitants with 1,056 free negroes and only 475 slaves, yet this was the slave trade center of the state. The greatest portion of the white citizenry were of Southern convictions but the politicians who held power were strong Union proclivities. The *Annapolis Gazette* was violent in its denunciation of secessionists and the diabolical crusade. During the spring of 1861 it maintained such a staunch Union stand, becoming so notorious, that by August sales had declined to a point that they were forced to cease publication. Northern troops occupied the capital for three weeks prior to the garrisoning of the state. The army was encamped at the Naval Academy and by this time the cadets from the Southern states had resigned and returned to their respective homes which left the student body strongly of Union feeling. Of the seventeen Maryland middies, seven would resign; their principles were so deeply entrenched in the Constitution under Southern interpretation they joined the Confederacy. One would become a seaman in the U.S. Navy while another had feelings so diversified he didn't return after that semester. Eight completed their studies, graduated and were commissioned. West Point had six Marylanders in the corps of cadets, four were so influenced with such strength of their convictions they felt justified in reversing their allegiance and joined the Confederacy. Dr. Hammond was accepted as acting assistant surgeon on May 28, 1864, and prior to this he had been a contract physician. Practicing in Howard Grove Hospital in Richmond until relieved on July 7, Hammond was then ordered to the Confederate States Hospital at Petersburg.

GEORGE B. HAMMOND 1832-1898

George received his M. D. at the University of Maryland in 1854 and then worked in the therapeutic trade at Millersville. Anne Arundel County had seven prewar militia units and all were in support of the American Confederacy. The elite honor guard of the governor was composed principally of the gentry of Annapolis. Their captain was a staunch Unionist who disassociated himself with the militia company in the spring of 1861. He organized a second outfit and saw that the men were well screened to contain only the purest and unadulterated anti-secessionists. The earlier remained in tact and performed its official duties but the *Annapolis Gazette* expressed "it a great outrage to permit them to keep up their organization as they would join the Confederates if the opportunity presents itself." As events unfolded under the control of the Federal army, the matured squires of the county found it wise to be discreet. But a group of teenagers, who were too young to be arrested, boldly dressed in red, shouldered wooden guns and paraded the streets of Annapolis. After several outings, to the joy of the snickering prejudiced population, pressure from Federal authorities was brought to bear upon the parents and the bold young secessionists of the ancient city ceased to parade. During the early summer of 1861, boats owned by Unionists had groups of secessionists come aboard and tear the national flags from the masts, trampling them under foot with lusty cheers for Jeff Davis. Dr. Hammond left the oppressive and tyrannical power of the military at home and went to the aid of Dixie. On August 24, 1862, as an assistant surgeon, he was assigned to the 11th Georgia Infantry. In the spring of 1863, he was transferred to the 18th Virginia Battalion of heavy artillery. Assistant Surgeon Hammond was consecutively administering to soldiers at General Hospital No. 8 in Raleigh, Way Hospital in Wilmington and Wilson North Carolina Hospital. On February 13, 1865, he was advanced to the rank of surgeon and became a part of the Richmond defenses. After being paroled, he returned to the county of his birth and practiced at Chesterfield, and in later years near Crownsville.

HARRY HAMMOND

Harry, also of Anne Arundel County, went to the assistance of the bonny blue flag that bears a single star. On October 1, 1861, documents show him as acting commissary of subsistence in the Army of the Potomac. On March 24, 1862, Dr. Hammond resigned as a captain in the commissary department. He was appointed to the staff of General Maxcy Gregg as aide-de-camp. It does not appear that he used his medical knowledge in an official capacity; however, at Fredericksburg when the left was driven back General Gregg was rallying the second line when he fell mortally wounded. Dr. Hammond rushed to his aid but was unable to save him. Before the end of 1862, he was promoted to major as quartermaster of General S. McGowan's Brigade. He served in the field until January 12, 1865, when he became inspector of field transportation of Robert E. Lee's army. After the surrender of Appomattox Dr. Hammond returned to his home and resumed the profession from which he had been diverted by miraculous principles. By the mid-1870's he had relocated in Baltimore. The author has been unable to establish the relationship of the three Hammonds other than they all came from the same county. Another famous practitioner, wearing the blue of the foe, of which no correlation can be documented, was William A. Hammond of Annapolis. After nine years in the medical corps of the army he resigned in 1859 to accept a teaching position at the University of Maryland. When hostilities broke he reenlisted but received no credit for his prior military service and entered at the bottom of the list of assistant surgeons with a rank lower than he previously held. On April 25, 1862, William A. Hammond was unanimously confirmed as surgeon general of the U.S.A.; he jumped from the rank of captain to brigadier general which created a furor in the Medical Bureau. On January 17, 1864, he was arrested and court-martialed with only two days to prepare a defense. He was found guilty on three charges of illegal authority in purchasing medical supplies and was dismissed from the service. Going to New York he mounted a campaign to restore his name in 1878 and a year later the court-martial was annulled.

JEROME HUMPHREY HARDCASTLE 1840-

Born at Dayton, Ohio, of an old Eastern Shore family, he was a collegian when the war caused most academic schools to close for there were not enough students to defray the expenses. Military medicine men received so much activity that their operating techniques vastly improved. But young Hardcastle was one of the very few who received a degree in a seceded state during the revolution. Only the Medical College of Virginia located in the capital of the Confederacy was able to withstand the impact of war. Orienting itself to wartime conditions, the Medical College of Virginia shortened its sessions and graduated two classes each year. The faculty of eight included Dr. James Brown McCaw, head of Chimboraza Hospital, an institution that trained approximately four hundred students. The valuable training in military medicine and surgery could be observed in the twenty hospitals in the city where practically every kind of wound and disease was visible. In addition, the school had a small infirmary where disabled soldiers were treated. There was a distinct relationship and area of cooperation between the medical department and the college. The Surgeon General, in an address delivered after the conflict, stated that in trying to meet the needs of the services for medical officers "a certain number of young gentlemen were annually appointed hospital stewards with the privilege of attending the lectures of the Richmond Medical College, and on graduation, letters of invitation were issued them for examination for appointment in the corps." Dr. Hardcastle used this college as a training school to obtain a commission in the medical department as an assistant surgeon in early 1865.

HIRAM W. HARDING

Harding espoused the medical course at the University of Maryland completing his scholastic training in 1860. To the South went thousands of independent Marylanders; there are no reliable statistics to show the exact number. Crossing the Potomac from its upper waters to the bay, singly or in squads under danger and difficulties, they went into service where accident or inclination led them and fought under the banners of every state in the Confederacy. Not liable to conscription, they were the very epitome of volunteers. Dr. Harding enlisted on April 1, 1863, at Camp Fisher as a private in the 9th Virginia, Cavalry Company D. By November of 1864 he was addressed as Acting Assistant Surgeon Harding in Breckinridge Infirmary at Marion, Virginia. There were many that stayed in Maryland but assisted the Confederacy as non-combatants. Adalbert Johann Volck was one of these, a chemist who taught at the Baltimore College of Dental Surgery and also completed the dental course in 1852. As a dentist in Baltimore he was a Confederate agent, carrying dispatches, assisting volunteers, smuggling medicines and other contraband. He also expressed himself through his artistic abilities working under the assumed name of V. Blada which was an abbreviation of his first name in reverse. There were three series of his vitriolic sketches that carried a false London imprint. He not only worked in silver, bronze and brass but also ivory carving, oil painting and sculpturing. Even when the war ended he continued harsh sketchings and etchings of General Benjamin F. Butler, former garrison commander of Maryland. These likenesses of Butler were used by Volck and the opposition during Butler's political career.

JAMES HOWARD HARRIS 1834-1910

Born in Albemarle County, Virginia, he studied dentistry by the apprenticeship method from Dr. William Chapam at Staunton. After receiving his M.D. degree he came to Baltimore, then attended the Baltimore College of Dental Surgery which was founded by Chapin A. Harris in 1839 and was the first of its kind not only in the country but the world. After graduating in 1861 he entered the Confederate army in the 4th Virginia Cavalry Company I. A letter from W. A. Covington to Surgeon Davis on November 3, 1864, states "Private J. H. Harris is assigned as dentist to Harrisonburg General Hospital. He will examine each soldier and officer attended and in conference with the senior medical officer will perform all dental operations required." It became apparent during the war that soldiers stood greatly in need of dental services. A plan to contract with dentists engaging in private practice was discussed by the Confederate medical authorities but this proposition was not adopted. Instead dentists were conscripted and they held the rank of hospital steward which was that of a second lieutenant. Their insignia were chevrons on the sleeve and a black stripe down the trousers like that of the medical officers. Dentists were assigned to infirmaries throughout the Confederacy, their rooms were to be well lighted, with an operating chair constructed by the hospital carpenter, and a tin basin serving as a spittoon and a servant or soldier to assist. The author has been able to find a few dentists of our state who later would serve in such a capacity. James Baxter Bean was manufacturing dental materials; John Bland, a rider in the 1st Maryland Cavalry, Samuel John Cockerville and John Hamilton Dickson were members of Mosby's Rangers. Since some were compelled to travel to other infirmaries and take their equipment and instruments, an ambulance was at their disposal; this was not available to physicians and caused frequent discussions. Dentists not only assisted surgeons in cases of fractures of superior and inferior maxillary bones but soon in many facial operations. The C.S.A. attitude toward the dental profession, at a time when its members were struggling to obtain a respected professional status, meant much to dental practitioners of the future by the official recognition of dentistry's importance. It was not until 35 years after this that the United States Dental Corps was established. After the war Dr. Harris returned to Baltimore and in 1872 he became a professor of operative and clinical dentistry at his alma mater in the University of Maryland. Three of his brothers came to this school and were graduated as dentists.

THOMAS A. HEALEY 1892-

Completing his training at the University of Maryland Medical College in 1835, then practicing in Cumberland, he was a member of the state Medical and Chirurgical Faculty. Dr. Healy would become one of the noble twenty some thousand Marylanders who wore the gray. This state in the next four years would be credited with 33 commands of troops furnished to the Union army comprising 50,316 white soldiers and 8,718 colored soldiers. This includes the 100 days men, the 9 months enlistments, the emergency troops, and the galvanized Confederate prisoners who had taken the oath. Desertions were high; in the 3rd Regiment Maryland U. S. Cavalry 398 troops deserted, 4 dishonorably discharged and 1 shot to death after being court martialed. Although many of the old state families were divided in allegiance, there were 77,536 foreign born persons living in Maryland in 1860. These emigrants naturally had but minor understanding and consideration for the struggle of Southern independence and were inclined toward the North. The German Quakers of Western Maryland had come from Pennsylvania in the post Revolutionary days; they had been in the state for several generations and became acclimated as well as Americanized. The Baltimore Germans, however, were an entirely different breed. Their residence in Maryland had been limited, most remained unnaturalized, they spoke in their native tongue and were a definite ethnic group. Our state would furnish 17 generals or flag rank men to the Confederacy and 12 to the Federal service, of the 12 only 5 were born in Maryland. Dr. Healey was commissioned a surgeon on October 28, 1861, and sent to the General Hospital at McPhersonville. On December 27, he was to proceed to Cooshawhatchie, South Carolina, to General R. E. Lee's command. On November 27, 1863, special orders had him relieved to report to Marietta's Academy Hospital. Surgeon Healey ended the war seeing field service with South Carolina troops and returned to Cumberland.

HORACE M. HEATH

Leaving the University of Maryland to help sway the fate of the South he forsook his scholarly endeavors in medicine. On July 18, 1861, McDowell moved the Northern army out of Alexandria as General P. G. T. Beauregard retired his forces behind Bull Run. By daylight of the twenty-first the first major conflict of the war began and by midday the Confederates were in retreat, their line broken and their position forced. Kirby Smith's Fourth Brigade arrived at Manassas Junction by train; disembarking they heard their first hostile fire. They struck out in a trot; after a run of a few miles the column was halted to breathe and load. The Fourth Brigade kept steadily on as General Smith was knocked over the neck of his horse by a volley and Arnold Elzey, leader of the 1st Maryland Infantry, assumed command. About four o'clock they had pressed on to the left and charged a battle line that stood on a ridge. Colonel Elzey pressed on behind McDowell's right, he never stopped to draw a breath as the entire Union line crumpled before them and First Manassas was won. As the Maryland colonel rode proudly down the line of his baptized men Beauregard dashed up filled with enthusiasm — "Hail Elzey, Butcher of the day!" and in a moment President Davis came up with General Johnston. "General Elzey, I congratulate you," said the man who made generals. Horace M. Heath had been administering to the sick and wounded at Chimborazo Hospital No. 5 in Richmond as an acting assistant surgeon. On June 1, 1864, he was promoted to assistant surgeon and assigned to Young's Virginia Battery of the Reserve Artillery Battalion. He was wounded in November and taken to Stuart Hospital in the capital city. As he recuperated he practiced in this hospital where he was assigned until April 1, 1865, when he was relieved and fled the enemy.

JOHN WISE HEBB 1840-

Hebb was born at Tower Hill Homestead and reared in St. Mary's County, graduating from Charlotte Hall College. Then with courage and fortitude he departed from the campus of the University of Maryland Medical College to devote his abilities to the southern interpretation of the laws. On June 15, 1861, he was appointed assistant surgeon and was administering to the wounded amid the hail of lethal hot steel at the great victory at Manassas. It became apparent that this war would not be a summer episode, determined in a few days or months. Before the two governments, in all its hideousness, was the spectre of a prolonged bitter and bloody struggle. The Federal Army lost 2,896 men of which 460 were killed, 1,124 wounded and 1,312 captured or missing. The Confederate loss was 1,982 men of which 387 were killed, 1,582 wounded and 13 captured or missing. The South captured 26 Pieces of artillery, 34 caissons and sets of harness, horses, wagons, ambulances, several thousand stands of small arms, as well as large quantities of all types of military supplies. The Confederate medical corps had procured a large amount of medical and surgical stores at the military depots and installations that were seized by the various states when they seceded. This victory yielded such a vast number of cases of fine surgical instruments and enormous stock of medicines that the medical staffs would be adequately prepared for another major engagement. In August Dr. Hebb was delegated to the 7th Louisiana Infantry of the 8th Brigade. On November 21, he resigned, receiving a position under his uncle, James A. Wise, who was commissary-general of Louisiana. His two brothers also followed him into the Southern army. Thomas A., older and a sucessful druggist, was killed at Front Royal. Herbert J., two years younger, served in the 1st Maryland Infantry and after the war continued to follow the subject of this sketch in the medical profession, working at Randallstown. Dr. Hebb returned to this state and practiced in Howard County and entered the Maryland Line Confederate Soldiers Home at Pikesville on January 7, 1908.

WASHINGTON M. HILLIARY 1862-

Being one of those many Marylanders who left a shining future to go to the assistance of Dixie, he went not for the prestige, not for riches, not for fame, not for advancement, not for acclaim, but to uphold the ideals of Southern chivalry. He enlisted as a private in the 1st Maryland Artillery on November 28, 1861, at Evansport for the war. Dr. Hilliary was a member of Company B section that saw service in Hampton Legion South Carolina Artillery. As soon as the heavy smoke of their guns cleared this tired cannoneer would grab his brass bound, walnut medical kit to alleviate their combat inflictions. At Mechanicsville the Flying Artillery Battery was hotly engaged and lost heavily in men and horses. Dr. Hilliary was killed in action on June 26, 1862, in the destructive artillery duel. He was a private soldier who filled a nameless grave. Fame did not herald his name and deeds to posterity. He fought without reward and died without distinction. It was enough for him to hear the voice of obligation, then to follow it and it led by a rugged path to a bloody grave. He was not a soldier of fortune but a soldier of duty, who dared all that men can dare, endured all that men can endure and gave all that men can give in obedience to what he believed the sacred call of his country. He loved his home, he loved his state, but he also loved something larger than himself, those who stood in need. He was no politician and probably knew little of the theories of constitutional interpretation. But he knew that armed legions were marching and it was his duty to hurl them back at any cost. It is for this we need to honor and revere the nameless memories of our forefathers. If ever Maryland men lived of whom it could be truly said that their hearts echoed their sentiment, "dulce et decorum est pro patria mori," these were the men.

WILLIAM RINGGOLD HODGES 1825-1887

Liberty Hall estate in Kent County was his birthplace. In the 1850's he was working with his older brother, James, in the trade firm of Hodges Brothers in Baltimore. At the ripe age of thirty-five he enrolled in a two-year medical program and then departed from the University of Maryland Medical College facilities with a heart deeply sympathetic to the principles of States Rights. The medical corps was very busy with the early epidemics and now the extensive casualties at Manassas caused a query. It became evident that many more doctors were needed. The insufficiency was helped as physicians serving in the ranks were detailed to assist. Twelve Richmond hospitals were hastily established but only a fractional part of the wounded and sick were hospitalized. Surgeon Edward Warren wrote that the disabled were "scattered through hotels, private houses, public halls, and wherever it was possible to spread a blanket. . . . from what I could gather, the whole country, from Manassas Junction to Richmond in one direction, and to Lynchburg in another, was one vast hospital, filled to repletion with the sick and wounded of Beauregard's victorious army." This early period of confusion was characterized by the lack of proper hospital facilities. President Davis was authorized to appoint additional medical officers from civil life on a temporary basis and it was in this way Dr. Hodges was employed.

Cardboard patriotic envelope
Erick Davis collection

He was ordered to proceed to General A. S. Johnston's command in the winter of 1862. Successfully passing the rigid professional requirements this candidate had the qualifications for appointment to the medical corps. Assistant Surgeon Hodges was assigned to the General Hospital at Grenada, Mississippi. As a prisoner of war he was paroled on May 19, 1865, and can be found practicing in Ellicott City in 1874.

ROBERT RANDOLPH HOLDEN

Holden completed his study of medicine at the University of Maryland in 1861. Southern legend dominated the faculty of the University of Maryland. Professor Nathan Ryno Smith was accused of helping Federal deserters escape into the Confederacy. The medical faculty delighted in flaunting their sympathy one step short of treason. Each year the college ostentatiously refused to fly the National flag at commencement. Graduates known to be Southern sympathizers received great applause and bouquets while the Unionists were roundly hissed. Rumor spread that Unionists seemed to fail their final examinations but the faculty announced proudly that the 1862 class included two known Union sympathizers. So blatant was faculty disloyalty that one newspaper demanded the officers of the institution to take an oath of allegiance and they were accused of keeping open vacancies in the staff to be filled after the war by Southern doctors. From the faculty Edward Warren would become Surgeon General of North Carolina in the C.S.A. and William A. Hammond Surgeon General of the U.S.A. From the dental school two professors would fight for the Confederacy, from the pharmacy school two would fight for the Union. One from the undergraduate school would go in the service of the South while the agricultural school had three professors leave to wear the gray and one that wore the blue. This young physician enlisted as a private in the 37th Alabama Infantry Company F. On March 19, 1863, he was admitted to the First Mississippi Hospital at Jackson, Mississippi with chronic diarrhea. Dr. Holden had applied for a transfer to be with his fellow free staters and was consigned to the 2nd Maryland Infantry Company F. He joined the regiment just prior to Gettysburg and on Culp's Hill three hundred Marylanders and eighteen North Carolinians were ordered to charge a position defended by three brigades. Flesh and blood could not withstand such fire and the survivors fell back towards Rock Creek. The 2nd Maryland lost one hundred and ninety-six devoted men in killed, wounded and captured. Among this number was Private Holden who was listed as severely wounded. Upon recovering he became an applicant for appointment before the army medical board. On February 2, 1864, he was favorably received as an assistant surgeon and ordered to Jackson Hospital, located about two miles above Richmond.

EDWARD LLOYD HOWARD 1837-1881

Edward Lloyd was a grandson of Francis Scott Key and John Eager Howard. He was an intern of Dr. Charles Frick in Baltimore and attended medical class at the University of Maryland until the spring of 1861. Joining the C.S.A. as a private in the Weston Guard, Company A of Weston's Battalion on May 17 at Richmond, he was detailed to the hospital at Manassas. The medical picture of the aftermath for the South found overworked doctors and newly formed hospitals. While among the Federal wounded the living squirmed among the dead. Their regimental surgeons refused to treat the soldiers of any command save their own, as the poor creatures cried and begged for someone to hack off a mangled arm or leg. The civilian ambulance drivers hired for the occasion had fled back to Washington after the sound of the first shots. U.S. hospitals were old and filthy, they were soon filled to the rafters and for days wounded soldiers wandered the streets pounding on doors. The image of the North's medical corps was a catastrophic disaster. On November 2, the Courtney Artillery obtained an assistant surgeon named Howard. In September of 1862, during the advance of the Southern army into his state, two Federal enrolling officers came to the Howard home and asked Mrs. Howard, "Have you a husband or sons capable of bearing arms? She said yes, a husband and six sons. Your husband, what is his name and where is he? Charles Howard, he is a prisoner in Fort Warren. And your eldest son? Frank Key Howard, he is also in prison with his father. And your next son? John Eager Howard, he is a captain in the Confederate Army. And the next? Charles Howard, he is a major in the Confederate Army. And the next? Edward Lloyd Howard, he is a surgeon in the Confederate Army. During this the men had become more and more flustered and faltered out. And your youngest son? McHenry Howard, he is in the Southern Army with Stonewall Jackson and I expect he will be here soon and she shut the door in their faces." Assistant Surgeon Howard's only other post was in General Hospital No. 4 in Richmond. Returning to the city of his birth after the war to practice, he became a member of the staff at the Baltimore Dental College as professor of anatomy in 1868. In 1870 he became editor of the *Baltimore Medical Journal*. Then he was affiliated with the Physicians Marine Hospital from 1876 until his death. He served as secretary of the State Board of Health 1874-76, then as president for the next five years. In 1879 Dr. Howard was Commissioner on yellow fever in the South.

ALFRED HUGHES 1824-

Born at Wheeling, now West Virginia, he received his collegiate education at the Homeopathic Medical College in Philadelphia. In 1851 he began the practice of homeopathy at Wheeling and encountered considerable opposition. Frequent unsuccessful attempts had been made to establish this new system in that city of those who essayed the task and failed; two practitioners were from Philadelphia and one from Baltimore. Homeopathy was a system of medical practice based on a theory of Dr. Samuel Hahnemann of Leipzig and was brought about in the early 1800's. This theory was that a drug which will produce certain disease symptoms in a healthy person will cure a sick person who has the same symptoms. Popular prejudice and the bitter opposition of the allopathy of the old school were hard on the new societies that sprang up. Dr. Hughes, however, after a hard fight and many newspaper controversies, succeeded in vindicating the advantages of homeopathic medicine. When the cholera made its appearance in 1854 he labored day and night meeting with unprecedented success in the treatment of the fearful scourge then in epidemic form. After becoming firmly established in practice he turned to the arena of political controversies as a correspondent for the Baltimore Exchange newspapers. As was the case of most of this state's editors he was arrested and held in prison at Camp Chase, Ohio, for nearly eight months until exchanged for a Union political prisoner held at Salisbury. After a short stay in Baltimore Dr. Hughes and his family were sent by boat to City Point and exchanged. He was very busy in Richmond; not only did he start a private practice, where Mrs. Robert E. Lee was one of his patients, but he contracted with the government and was elected to the Virginia Legislature. By the end of the confrontation he was back in Baltimore practicing and trying to sell his homeopathic ideals.

JAMES FRITZ HUGHES

This physician was never taught about the nightmare of torturous sickness and wholesale death that he would experience after leaving the University of Maryland Medical College. Obviously the Confederate Medical Department was faced with a stupendous and frightful task. During the Mexican Wars, records show that ten men died of disease for every man killed in battle. The competence of the doctors not only improved in surgical areas but their fight with morbidity progressed even without clinical thermometers or stethoscopes. The medicos in blue and gray faced a bloody picture from start to finish, an impossible job with inconceivable means. Many of the young boys of rural America who volunteered were rugged individualists. Hair, beards and feet entered and left the army camps uncombed, matted and dirty, respectively. The boys, as in all pre-antiseptic wars, really let themselves go; as the feet got dirtier their habits in general became worse. Those company officers who were sticklers for sanitation were far better to their troops than the complaining soldiers realized. Dr. Hughes was a free lancer known as a contract surgeon and received the pay of a first lieutenant. In 1863 he was working at Rogersville, Tennessee, with General J. Longstreet's command and then at Atlanta under Medical Director S. H. Stout. He was commissioned an assistant surgeon on June 1, 1864, and was stationed at General Hospital No. 24 in Richmond. Later he also practiced in Scottsville Hospital and Ocmulgee Hospital at Macon, under the command of a stately Cecil Countian who wore the wreath of a brigadier general, William Whann Mackall.

FREDERICK HUNTER

Dr. Hunter enlisted in the 1st Maryland Flying Artillery C.S.A. for the war in Richmond on August 7, 1861, and was the fourth medical physician to join this company as a private. Serving with distinction in this battery he was on leave in the capital during the first two months of 1862 when he passed the medical examining board. On April 17 Assistant Surgeon Hunter was assigned to General J. J. Pettigrew's command, which included his former commander, Richard Snowden Andrews' Artillery Battalion. While serving in this capacity he treated his companions of the Flying Artillery and the 4th Maryland Battery known as the Chesapeake Artillery. The usual divisional organization of the Southern Medical Corps of field medicine went something like this: The surgeon-in-chief of a division selected a regimental surgeon to head the field infirmary and two assistants to carry out his orders. One assistant supervised the pitching of tents, providing of straw, fuel, water, etc., and had direct charge of the hospital stewards and nurses. It was the other assistant's job to record the patient's name, rank, company, regiment, nature of wound and decide which needed emergency treatment. From the entire division three surgeons were selected to do the major operations or at least be responsible for them, with as many supporting doctors as available. The remaining medical officers of the division except one, were required to act as dressers of wounds. That one physician who stayed with the regiment as it went into action was the first to give aid. This paper strategy was very seldom realistic, the medical department of a division rarely was close to maximum strength, the shortage of ambulances and horses were major stumbling blocks. At Cedar Run on August 6, General Charles S. Winder, the accomplished, meritorious Maryland leader of the Stonewall Brigade, died in the arms of Major Andrews. Then he, too, was struck by a piece of shell, in the inguinal section of his trunk. This cut the peritoneum, spilling out his viscera into his hands as he fell from his horse and lay along the dusty road for several hours before being moved to a farm house where he and General T. J. Jackson had spent the previous night. Finally, obtaining medical assistance, his abdomen was sutured and under the care of Dr. Hunter and an orderly he recovered from this dreadful wound.

OSBORN S. INGLEHART

Completing his academic medical education at the University of Maryland in 1857, he received an appointment in the United States Navy as an assistant surgeon that same year. Resigning his commission to the war department he tendered his abilities to the C.S.A. where he was granted the same rank as he previously held. Assistant Surgeon Inglehart saw hospital duty at naval stations at Selma and Mobile until being assigned to the C. S. S. *Gaines* in the Mobile Squadron. After an engagement in which extensive casualties were experienced the medical staff was frequently overwhelmed with patients. Naval operations were done on board ship but preferably hospitals were established on land. The operating surgeons were surrounded by those awaiting surgery. Night often fell before they finished their work; torches or candles were then lighted to provide illumination although operations were known to have been performed with no light other than that provided by the moon. On January 7, 1864, he was promoted to passed assistant surgeon. Under Admiral Franklin Buchanan he participated in the Battle of Mobile Bay. On August 5 the *Gaines* was hit by an eleven-inch shell, she was leaking badly and had to be abandoned. As they were sinking Passed Assistant Surgeon Inglehart directed that the wounded and dead be removed in the boat first. The entire crew of a hundred plus a detachment of marines were evacuated. For the remainder of the war he was on duty with the Battery Buchanan, named in honor of the gallant Maryland admiral. He surrendered on May 4, 1865, and was paroled six days later at Nanna Bubba, Alabama.

MARTIN L. JARRETT

Martin learned the medical trade at the University of Maryland and in the office of his older brother, Dr. James H. Jarrett, in Jarrettsville. Harford County was strongly Southern in its sympathies and opposed the invasion by the Northern troops upon its soil. Every member of the Jarrett family, parents, five sons and one daughter, were advocates of the Confederacy except James. When he announced that he was in favor of the Union and intended to enter the U. S. Army his course was bitterly opposed by the family and caused a sensation in the community but he joined the Purnell Legion as assistant surgeon. Young Martin Jarrett departed from Harford County upon hearing that the Army of Northern Virginia was near the Potomac. He became acting asssistant surgeon of the 1st Maryland Cavalry Battalion C.S.A. when they crossed into their native state in early July of 1864 at Poolesville. He was captured on October 4 at Halltown near Martinsburg, while ill. Being sent to Old Capitol Prison at Washington he was then conveyed to Fort Delaware after 14 days. He had been in declining health since joining the Confederates, suffering from the greatest enervating ailment of the Southern fighting men, intestinal disorders of diarrhea and dysentery. Inadequate rations, poor cooking, impure water, fatigue and exposure were the prime causes of the chronic diarrhea. He declined to be exchanged; taking the oath of allegiance on December 21, he was released but could not go south of the city of Philadelphia. By 1867 Dr. Jarrett's professional practice was in the Monumental City until 1874 when he returned to Jarrettsville, where he was school commissioner of Harford County. In 1909, he was commander of the James R. Herbert Camp No. 657 United Confederate Veterans and was a member of the committee in charge of the Admiral Raphael Semmes Centennial Celebration.

Large Confederate field medical tin canteen, 8 1/2" x 10 1/2" in height with a 1 1/4" spout having a 3/4" opening.

G. Craig Caba collection

JAMES THOMAS JOHNSON, JR. 1826-1869

He was born and raised in Charles County. Following his deceased father's footsteps and wanting to become a practitioner, he was sent to Dr. J. R. W. Dunbar for training. He was also schooled in medicine at the University of Maryland in 1848 prior to joining Dr. Eldred W. Moberley at New Market where they served the area. In 1845 he was elected to the House of Delegates for one term. At the convention which met in Frederick on January 16, 1861, he expressed his sympathy with the Southern cause and was a delegate from Frederick County to the state convention which met in Baltimore in February and March. Dr. Johnson, anxiously awaiting the peaceful separation, saw the cherished hope grow fainter as the violent coercion of the republican politicians became more apparent. He was one of three brothers who followed the stars and bars: Otis and J. Newman rode in Company A of the 1st Maryland Cavalry. J. Newman was killed on July 4, 1864, at Shepherdstown as they prepared to return to their cherished state in the Baltimore and Washington Raid. Dr. Johnson was commissioned an assistant surgeon on September 9, 1861, at Manassas Hospital and then Farmville Hospital. In the spring of 1862, Ephraim Howard Poole, also of Frederick County, after recovering from a battle field injury, began to assist his healer. Poole obtained a transfer to the medical department and in 1863 accompanied Dr. Johnson to Salisbury, North Carolina, where he not only helped him but was also compelled to belong to an infantry company that guarded medical supplies. Assistant Surgeon Johnson was then transferred from Way Hospital No. 3 to Charlotte where he was Medical Purveyor, continuing at this diligent post until the Confederate cause had fallen. Before the end of June, 1865, he had reported to the provost marshal at Frederick, but being unable to use his chosen profession he practiced in Virginia. After a year, Dr. Johnson returned to the county in the Urbana area for several years, then going to Huntsville, Alabama, he served as health officer of that city.

RICHARD POTTS JOHNSON

He was born and reared in Frederick County and was probably the namesake of Dr. Richard Potts. For several years the author felt they were one and the same man but this is not true. Dr. Johnson enlisted in Richmond on May 17, 1861, as a private in Company A Weston's Infantry Battalion. This company was transferred to the 1st Maryland Infantry where they became Company C. On September 13 he was appointed surgeon of this Maryland regiment until they were mustered out because their enlistment had expired on August 17, 1862. In the fall of this year, recruited in Richmond and organized at Winchester, the 2nd Maryland Infantry was mustered in and Surgeon Johnson became medical officer. General George Hume Steuart, Jr. was ordered by T. J. Jackson to proceed to organize Marylanders into the Maryland Line but with the coming of the spring campaign of 1862, he was given command of a brigade and the recruiting was postponed. In the summer of 1863, Major General Isaac Ridgeway Trimble was to form all the Maryland troops into brigades but the army was in enemy country in Pennsylvania. In the winter of 1863, under the third general from our state, Bradley Tyler Johnson, a cousin of Dr. Johnson, the Maryland Line became a reality. It was composed of the elite of this state, young men charged with devotion to duty, honor, country, liberty, justice and right. Their gallantry in battle became an ideal of the Army of Northern Virginia all through their service. The Maryland Line consisted of an infantry regiment, a cavalry battalion and three batteries of 16 artillery pieces, with Surgeon Johnson as medical director. He was privileged to administer to men from the "land of pleasant living" until June 25, 1864, when he was wounded during the seige of Petersburg. He was sent to the General Hospital at Lynchburg after recovering and on January 11, 1865, was acting surgeon-in-chief of the institution.

WILLIAM HILLEARY JOHNSON 1827-1901

Graduating with a medical degree from the University of Maryland in 1849 he practiced at Petersville in Frederick County. He was elected a 2nd lieutenant along with Captain Robert H. E. Boteler and 1st Lieutenant Jacob G. Thomas who were also medical physicians and officers in the secession company known as the Adamstown Minute Men. Going into the medical bureau of the Confederate army he was commissioned an assistant surgeon and ordered to the Missouri State Guard. These men were formed for the service in defense of that state and on September 15, 1862, they were turned over to the Confederate authorities. Assistant Surgeon Johnson saw service with the Missouri State Guard from the fall of 1862 until the following summer. He continued his doctoring in field duty in the Trans-Mississippi army. The majority of Southern practitioners who became medical officers had little prior experiences or training in military surgery. Although there had been an increased use of the lancet and scalpel by physicians and no doubt the medical school dwelt on this, there were few doctors who treated many gunshot wounds. It was believed that all needful operations must be performed within twenty-four hours, so the scenes in and around the field hospitals, where most of the amputations were performed, became increasingly grim as the wounded were brought in for surgical attention. The fatality rate for amputations was as follows: fingers, 3%, toes 6%, forearms 14%, upper arms 24%, legs at the thigh 54%, at the knee joint 58%, at the ankle joint 74%, and at the hip joint 83%. After tranquility had been reestablished Dr. Johnson returned home and worked in the profession at Adamstown.

HENRY M. JONES

Upon obtaining the knowledge of a physician in 1860 from the University of Maryland Medical College, he migrated to Harrison, Texas. Dr. Jones, with an unrestrainable spirit, joined Lane's Company 1st Texas Rangers as a private when the war clouds broke. He was employed as a medical officer by contract at Tyler until September 26, 1862, when he received an appointment as assistant surgeon. Outrageous statements of the ghastly butchery practiced by field and hospital surgeons found credulous listeners who in turn became narrators. Circumstances at times necessitated an unusual number of amputations. Many of the Shiloh wounded lost limbs as a result of the heavy casualty list of this bloody engagement and the consequent inability of the medical officers to attend the wounded more promptly. In many cases there was little choice, almost certain death without surgery and probable death with it. There were some who were too rapid with the knife and saw; these were usually young practitioners who were more interested in acquiring or displaying surgical skill than in preserving life and limb. Compound fractures were usually amputated, in rejecting amputations more lives were lost than limbs saved. As the war continued the Southern surgeons became more conservative with the knife. The general rule was those medical men who had read much and seen little were too conservative while those who had read little and seen much were the reverse. Assistant Surgeon Jones was with the Trans-Mississippi Department and was paroled on June 24, 1865, with the army of General E. K. Smith. After a year he returned to this state, then settled in the District of Columbia where he practiced.

LEVIN SMITH JOYNES 1819-1881

Joynes was born in Accomac County, Virginia. Receiving his A.B. at Washington College in 1835, A.M. at the University of Virginia in 1837, and M.D. at the University of Virginia in 1839, then studying in Philadelphia, Paris and Dublin, he settled in Baltimore in 1843 to practice. In 1846 he was appointed professor of physicology and legal medicine at Franklin Medical College in Philadelphia. Two years later Dr. Joynes was back in Baltimore until 1855 when he began to teach at the Medical College of Virginia until the war came. He was appointed assistant surgeon and was with the Virginia forces from April until June of 1861. He was dean and professor of institutes of medicine and medical jurisprudence at the medical school in Richmond. Only this school located in the capital of the Confederacy was able to withstand the impact of war, all the other medical schools in the seceded states were forced to close their doors. There was a distinct relationship and area of co-operation between the C.S. Medical Department and the medical college. When the Association of Medical Officers of the Army and Navy of the Confederacy was organized it was unanimously voted to grant honorary membership to all members of the college faculty who were not already attached to the army or navy. Dr. Joynes remained in that city where he became president of the Richmond Academy of Medicine in 1866. In 1872 he was secretary of the first Virginia State Board of Health.

JOHN THOMAS KEATS -1905-

A native of Queen Anne County, Keats had a listening ear toward the South to hear about the many sons of Maryland who were clad in gray and butternut. Eighteen young men who had served one year in Company K 1st Virginia Cavalry proceeded to Richmond and began to organize a complete Maryland regiment in May, 1862. Other cavalry companies of Marylanders had been immediately absorbed by Virginia regiments. As the recruiting for this unit went on briskly, it was stipulated that it would be one around which future companies of "black and gold" cavaliers could rally. This first company was needed in the spring campaign and was attached to the 2nd Virginia Cavalry but by November 25 this battalion of dashing horsemen was officially organized. A more chivalrous crowd of riders would never flash a blade or answer a bugle call. They would bear the reputation of a gallant troop, faithful in the execution of orders and brave in the face of danger on many bloody fields of war where many comrades would perish. Dr. Keats enlisted on April 1, 1863, in Richmond in Company B 1st Maryland Cavalry with the rank of a private. By that fall, he was delegated to medical officer Wilbur Richard McKnew as acting assistant surgeon. After several months, he was nominated as assistant surgeon and received the two bars of a captain on his collar. He was taken prisoner on May 8, 1864, in Talbot County while returning from his home on furlough. Foremost on the minds of Maryland Confederates were their loved ones at home and few could resist paying those a quick visit when on leave, so a huge number of rebels were captured within the province. Assistant Surgeon Keats was incarcerated in Fort McHenry until May 9, 1865, when released. He settled in Ibinville Parish, Louisiana, for a decade before returning to the Eastern Shore. Dr. Keats was a member of the Society of the Army and Navy of the Confederate States in the State of Maryland. On April 5, 1892, he became a resident of the Maryland Line Confederate Soldiers Home and is buried on Confederate Hill in Loudon Park Cemetery in Baltimore.

JOSEPH KENT, JR.

Graduating from the University of Maryland Medical College in 1830 he attended the ill at Davidsonville. With a common consecration to a precious and honorable cause he departed from Anne Arundel County to the Confederacy. He was appointed a surgeon and assigned to the 1st Arkansas Infantry. Due to the epidemics of casualties the rigors of obligation were more than his years could bear and he was compelled to resign after a short term of duty. Going into private practice he became an embalming surgeon. Embalming prior to this time was used primarily for the preservation of anatomical specimens by physicians. With the presence of thousands of troops in an area, diseases went wild, and combat caused many deaths. Physicians saw an opportunity to make a profit by embalming. Many families, upon receiving news that a son or husband was ill or wounded, would make arrangements to go to their aid. Upon arriving the family would help nurse him back to health. If by chance he had lost his life the family would arrange for a funeral. When the families learned that embalming made it possible to transport the remains home for burial, those who could afford to have their loved ones embalmed agreed to it gladly. Thus the practice of embalming gained acceptance; families thought little of spending a hundred dollars for the embalming if they were able to return the remains home for burial. The embalming surgeons did arterial embalming by the extensive use of the vascular system, injecting a combination of zinc chloride and arsenic for preservation. Although cavity embalming was not done, restoration work was extensive. The army had no organized way to deal with the dead, many times the identification of these fallen heroes was made impossible by the pursuit or retreat of the enemy. The embalming surgeons realized the inadequacy of this system and with the hope of increasing their business would try to identify the deceased. This became a common sight to the soldiers and he knew the embalmer's earnestness and resourcefulness. If he was killed he wanted his remains brought home for positive identification and buried in the family plot, not left in a nameless common grave on a distant field. The preservation of remains introduced into the culture during the war has been accepted by the populous and continues to serve the same function today.

JOHN KER

Dr. Ker, from 1855 to the war period, was a member of the Vaccine Society of Baltimore working with the board of health. He was an ardent and impulsive sympathizer with those who allied themselves with the cause of the sister states to the south. The only record of his service in the army of the Confederacy shows him as an acting surgeon in Richmond's Chimborazo. Dr. Ker is probably being referred to as a contract surgeon. Gunshot wounds of the abdomen and chest constituted about nineteen per cent of the war wounds. Those penetrating the viscus were regarded as almost certainly fatal. Protruding viscera was seldom returned; it was considered inevitable death. Wounds of the chest were regarded as hardly less serious. Hemorrhage and infection were the chief causes of death. Wounds of the face, head and neck constituted about twelve per cent of the total. Gunshot wounds of the extremities constituted about sixty-five per cent of all. From the stand point of capacity and overall arrangement the most impressive hospitals in the South were located in Richmond. The Southern capital early became the chief medical center of the Confederacy. There were twenty infirmaries in the city after the medical situation was brought under control and in early 1864 there were forty-three surgeons, sixty-five assistant surgeons and eighteen acting assistant surgeons on duty. There were twenty-nine hospitals not in the city limits, located on the periphery where there were fifty-six surgeons, fifty-seven assistant surgeons and eight acting assistant surgeons. This did not include contract surgeons such as Dr. Ker.

HENRY J. KEY 1840-

Fitting himself for the practice of medicine when the conflict became imminent, the Baltimorean Key, through self-denial, devoted his aptitude and professional acquirements to those who resisted the advance of an invading army. On July 21, 1862, he was appointed to the C.S.A. medical corps by the Secretary of War and officially commissioned an assistant surgeon on September 6. He was ordered to the artillery in the Army of Tennessee with Courtney's Battery. Chloroform was the anesthetic choice in the Southern army, while ether was favored in the North. Although there were thirty-seven deaths from chloroform and three from ether reported for the period of the war on the Union side, Southern surgeons claimed that there was no danger in anesthesia if properly given. On January 5, 1863, at Murfreesboro he was captured and sent to his native city in the dungeons of Fort McHenry. After being exchanged Assistant Surgeon Key was transferred to Garrities Battery. The many casualties of the Army of Tennessee in the battles of Chickamauga and Missionary Ridge were so great that they were compelled to obtain additional hospital accomodations—many times utilizing churches, courthouses, former colleges, all types of public buildings and unoccupied private structures. As a consequence of the frequent necessary movement of the hospitals behind this army and the many bloody battles it became a serious problem to obtain establishments for infirmaries. By the summer of 1864, the inability of the government to provide proper accommodations for the treatment of the Army of Tennessee's sick and wounded was very serious. Failure of the quartermaster department to supply hospital tents caused the impressment of large privately owned buildings for hospital purposes. There was opposition manifested by the businesses that were impressed and they were inferior and inappropriate as hospitals, causing the ingenuity and resources of the medical officers to be taxed for want of supplying many necessities. Assistant Surgeon Key again became a prisoner of war at Meridian, Mississippi, being paroled on May 10, 1865, and he then proceeded to a parish in Louisiana to practice.

WILLIAM C. KIRKLAND

Enlisting in the 6th Alabama Infantry Company G on June 2, 1861, with a number of his kinsmen, he served in the ranks as a private for twelve months when he was discharged. Dr. Kirkland entered the C.S. Navy as an assistant surgeon. Social life in Baltimore was almost obliterated; spies, male and female of all social ranks, permeated everything. You could not tell whether the servant behind your chair at dinner or the lady by your side whom you had taken to the table were not in the employ of the Federal provost-marshal. But force never compels ideas and hearts are beyond the power of bayonets. During this time nurses were arrested because the babies in their arms wore red and white socks, young ladies were marched to the guard house because they crossed the street rather than pass under the suspended Union flag. Communication with Richmond was incessant and reliable, word would be passed by a nod on the street, by a motion of the hand, time and place given in a breath. In the parlors of the aristocratic houses, in every luxury that wealth and culture could buy, scores of beautiful women would meet to see the messenger and hear the news from Dixie. Every exploit of a friend and achievement of a Marylander were recited and repeated until human nature could stand no more, then "In Dixie's land I'll take my stand and live or die for Dixie" would burst from the throng. The address and destination on Assistant Surgeon Kirkland's parole was 804 North Avenue, Baltimore, Maryland.

KARL H. A. KLEINSCHMIDT

As a resident of Georgetown he received his A.B. degree at the Catholic University at the beginning of the war and continued his pursuit of a medical degree. The medical college of Georgetown University was established in 1849. Upon receiving his diploma with the class of 1863 he forsook worldly materialism and personal aspirations to follow the courage within his soul. On March 3 at Fredericksburg he was commissioned an assistant surgeon in the Southern army and attached to the 3rd Arkansas Infantry. Going into battle the assistant surgeon on the field would equip himself with a pocket case of instruments, ligatures, needles, pins, chloroform, morphine, alcoholic stimulants, tourniquets, bandages, lint and splints. He was in charge of the infirmary corps comprised of detailed men from each regiment who were the least effective under arms. The infirmary corps was no place for cowards because they advanced with the first line troops. They were armed with bandages, sponges, tourniquets, splints, and a canteen. Litters were used to transport the wounded to ambulances. The assistant surgeon on the field applied bandages, administered stimulants and superintended the wounded to field hospitals. No elaborate surgical procedures were undertaken by him unless there was an urgent necessity. Assistant Surgeon Kleinschmidt served with the "razor back" boys until their muskets were stacked at Appomattox on April 9, 1865. Upon being paroled the next day he started walking to Georgetown. He worked as a general practitioner in Washington holding membership in the District of Columbia Medical Association and the Medical Society. In 1876 he returned to his former university as professor of physiology in the medical school.

WILLIAM C. KLOMAN 1835-1907

Born in Germany Kloman came to Somerset County in 1837. Going to Baltimore he was educated in medicine and was graduated from the University of Maryland in 1855. Dr. Kloman remained in this city to practice and was an active member of the Baltimore Medical and Surgical Society and the Baltimore Pathological Society until August of 1862, when he passed the C.S.A. medical examining board and was assigned to the 6th Virginia Infantry on December 4. After Chancellorsville Assistant Surgeon Kloman was transferred to Chimborazo Hospital in the fourth division. To each hospital was assigned a surgeon-in-chief, to each division therein a surgeon in charge, and to each ward of the division an assistant surgeon. The surgeons in charge usually made an inspection each day of the wards after the assistant surgeons had attended those of their wards twice a day and made prescriptions. In cases of danger the assistant surgeon called in a surgeon, to consult or advise. The surgeons in charge made a daily report to the surgeon in chief. Each ward had a corps of stewards who supervised the nurses, the steward's clerks, the apothecaries, the quartermasters, the baggage-masters, the forage-masters, the wagon-masters, the ambulance drivers, the cooks, the bakers, the carpenters, the shoemakers, the ward-inspectors and the forgotten hanger-oners whom the soldiers called hospital rats. In the spring of 1864, Assistant Surgeon Kloman was detailed to Hick's Ford. After the fall of Petersburg he was promoted to surgeon and was paroled at Greensboro. In December, 1865, he returned to Baltimore to continue his profession and was a member of the Society of the Army and Navy Of The Confederate States In The State of Maryland. In 1875 he was appointed professor of anatomy in Washington Medical University.

Apothecary medicine chest 9 3/4" x 11 7/8" x 7 3/4" of cocoabolo wood. Twelve side compartments contain six 49 milliliter glass bottles with glass stoppers, center compartment contains large 137 milliliter bottles. Top drawer accomodates a hand-held balance scale, weights, spoon and two small 9 gram glass vials. Bottom drawer holds a mortar, two 15 gram bottles with silver plated tip tops, and 3 pewter 30 gram jars. In the back is a hidden compartment for four large bottles.
Dr. Gilcin F. Meadors, Jr. Collection

THOMAS SARGENT LATIMER 1839-

He was born in Georgia and at fourteen moved to Shrewsberry, Pennsylvania, with his mother and in 1857 they were residing in Baltimore. His education in the art of medicine at the University of Maryland was interrupted by the North's hostile invasion of this state. Espousing the cause of the Southland with all his nature he mustered into the C.S.A. Army as an enlisted man on May 17, 1861, at Richmond in the Weston Guard in Weston's Battalion. This Maryland battalion was broken up and Company A was ordered to join the 1st Maryland Infantry Regiment where they became Company C. He served as a private until October 8 when his abilities were put in requisition in the line of his schooling when he was detailed to the General Hospital at Mt. Jackson. Upon being commissioned on November 16, Assistant Surgeon Latimer was returned to the Maryland Regiment. On February 2, 1862, he was appointed medical purveyor in the field with the Army of Northern Virginia until late 1864 when he became surgeon-in-charge of Robinson Hospital in the capital city. The nurses unfortunately were not practiced or experts in their duties. They, a short time earlier, had been the sick or wounded men who were convalescing and placed in this job until strong enough for field duty. This arrangement bore very hard upon all involved and even harder upon the patients. It entailed constant supervision and endless teaching but the demand for men in the field was too imperative to allow those who were fit for their duties there to be detained for nursing purposes, however skillful they may have become. Surgeon Latimer surrendered at Charlotte after the hostilities ended and like many Confederates, if they could afford it, left the States and went to the Spanish West Indies. After a short time he was back in Richmond practicing medicine and then returned to this state's largest city. From 1866 to 1868 he was resident physician at the Baltimore Infirmary before entering private practice. Dr. Latimer was active in the Society Of The Army And Navy Of The Confederacy In The State Of Maryland.

GEORGE WASHINGTON LAWRENCE 1823-1890

Born at Plymouth in Montgomery County, Pennsylvania, he attended Concord Seminary and Germantown Academy, then came to Baltimore and the office of Dr. J. H. Miller who was his preceptor. In 1843 he entered the U. S. Navy as an acting assistant surgeon for two years. Attending the medical courses at the University of Pennsylvania and graduating in 1846 he began to practice in the Monumental City. In 1850 he went to California, then returned to this state at Catonsville. Going to Arkansas in 1859 Dr. Lawrence was resident physician at Hot Springs Hospital. Going into the service of the South as an assistant surgeon he was soon advanced to surgeon. In early 1862 he was hospital inspector for the Central Army of Kentucky and then medical director of the 3rd Corps of the Army of Mississippi. Medical Director Lawrence then became president of the army board along with his previous duties. The common soldier had a horror of a hospital for probably he had never been that sick or swallowed such starch, flavorless, compounds that young assistant surgeons were so fond of prescribing. Whiskey was the main stimulant to relieve the suffering in medicinal practice and it was drawn at the dispensary under the guardianship of the apothecary and his clerks. There was a tremendous demand for spirits. Many times the diseased and wounded were the ones who did not get their issue. A hospital bill passed by Congress provided that liquors, in common with other luxuries, belonged to the matrons department to stop the pilfering. On May 8, 1862, Surgeon Lawrence was induced to resign for language alleged to be disrespectful but General W. H. Arnold requested that his resignation not be accepted and that he be ordered to report to him. Surgeon Lawrence then became inspector of mines until October 15, 1864, when he was assigned as chief surgeon of the bureau of conscription, Trans-Mississippi Department. After receiving his parole at Shreveport, Louisiana, in June of 1865, he returned to Hot Springs Hospital.

WILLIAM M. LEEMAN

Leeman is listed as a medical physician in the Confederate Record Book - Marylanders Who Were In The Confederate Services Outside Of Maryland Commands, located in the Maryland Historical Society manuscript collection.

G. T. LEWIS

He is in the records of Harry Wright Newman as a Confederate surgeon from this state. The author has been unable to locate evidence of his military service. Through the documents in the National Archives two assistant surgeons are found, George W. Lewis and Greenville R. Lewis, but it cannot be established if there is any correlation to the first named Lewis.

ALEXANDER LINDSAY 1831-

A Baltimorean by birth, he was of Southern conviction and enlisted as a private on May 14, 1861, in the 154th Senior Tennessee Regiment Company A. This unit became the 1st Tennessee Infantry and on May 3 he was advanced to corporal. After his twelve-month enlistment he was discharged. The next reference to Dr. Lindsay was as an acting assistant surgeon in General Hospital No. 4 at Wilmington, North Carolina. Although the hospital contained an almost endless horde of personnel a problem arose with the so-called hospital rats. These were invalids who resisted being cured from a disinclination to combat. Many were poor, destitute cripples who were physically unfit for the field and were simply trying to survive. On July 26, 1864, Acting Assistant Surgeon Lindsay was ordered to Greensboro's Way Hospital. He was paroled at Greensboro on April 26, 1865.

LEONARD E. LOCKE 1833-

Locke was surgeon of the 53rd Alabama Partisan Rangers. They were organized as rangers but were never mounted and served a dismounted cavalry. Back in Maryland the populous had to bear under a vulgar and reckless military despotism of brute force, upheld and approved by those who abused administration of justice, blotted out by blood and violence. On May 25, 1862, Judge Richard Bennett Carmichael, while sitting in his court in Easton, was dragged from the bench bleeding by Union troops and imprisoned. On June 28, Judge Bartol of the Court of Appeals was also arrested and confined. The rights of property and the safety of citizens were brutally trampled on by Northern ruffians aided and approved by pro-Unionists within the state. Only through constant watchfulness and arrests, with the unflagging presence of a large number of Federal troops, could the inhabitants be forced into subjugation. On August 1, 1862, Surgeon Locke was elected first lieutenant of Company F and on November 5 he was promoted to captain. While serving as a line officer he still signed several discharges as surgeon to soldiers of the regiment for disabilities. On May 28, 1863, he was captured near Florence. By June 12, he was sent to City Point for exchange but then to military prison at Alton, Illinois, and then Johnson's Island. Perhaps it became known to Federal authorities that Dr. Locke was a line officer and not eligible for quick exchange as those of the medical corps. He was finally exchanged on February 24, 1865. After the restoration of peace he came to Baltimore.

THOMAS F. MANEY

As surgeon of the 1st Virginia Infantry he is embraced under the title Marylanders In The Confederate Service in the book of W. W. Goldsborough 1900 edition of The Maryland Line in the Confederate Army 1861-1865.

THOMAS CLAY MADDOX 1836-1881

Receiving his formal education at the Alexandria Academy in 1851 and then the Winchester Medical College, he came to Washington County and practiced in Hagerstown. At the dawn of the conflict he went to Montgomery and from April 1 to June 23 he was with the Southern forces at Fort Sumter as a surgeon. In the fall of 1864 Surgeon Maddox was stationed at Barnesville, Georgia Hospital. Matrons were blessed women who undertook the nursing of soldiers during the war and were the only bright spot in the hospitals. They were entering a domain that was reserved for males and encountered considerable opposition on all sides. The matrons were allowed by the law of September 27, 1862, and were to exercise a superintendence over the entire domestic economy of the infirmary. Each hospital had a chief matron; if they were fortunate they had a matron per ward plus two assistant matrons whose duties encompassed nursing, cooking, laundering and any and all necessary responsibilities that were left undone. The feminine touch of these good samaritans revolutionized the care of the sick and maimed as they proved to be strong morale builders and were recognized by the patients to be a cardinal element in recovery. Most physicians did not readily appreciate the angels of mercy, they often resented the intrusion into their domain especially when the wretched females saw fit to try mother's pet home remedies. The doctors had been used to the Catholic sisters who, in their devotion, were as Florence Nightingale's dictum of silent obedience. Although never silent these hallowed matrons clearly demonstrated they were not the weaker sex. After peace was restored Dr. Maddox practiced in Richmond until 1872 when he came to Baltimore and in the following year was a vaccine physician. Dr. Maddox was killed in the election fracus at Odenton in Anne Arundel County in 1881.

AUGUSTINE SMITH MASON 1834-

Born in Stafford County, Virginia, Augustine was graduated from the Medical College of Virginia in 1855 and came to Washington County. He was commissioned an assistant surgeon on July 1, 1861, and opened the first hospital in Fredericksburg which became known as the general hospital. In March, 1862, he was transferred to Richmond to establish another hospital at Manchester. On September 5, the "Free Staters" in the ranks of the Army of Northern Virginia went wild with joy as they forded the Potomac at several points near White's Ferry, Cheeks Ferry and Noland's Ferry. Proceeding to Frederick General Lee appointed Colonel Bradley T. Johnson, a native of the city, as provost marshal. Five days later Lee sent half his army to Martinsburg and then the others moved west to Hagerstown where they held Crampton's Gap, Fox's Gap, and Turner's Gap. Surgeon Mason hurriedly left the infirmary to join the army near his former residence. Early on the morning of September 14 Union forces attacked the three passes through South Mountain. After heavy fighting the out flanked Confederates withdrew and by midnight a general retreat began westward. Of the 28,500 Union soldiers who took part in the Battle of South Mountain about 1,800 were killed, wounded or missing. The 17,600 Confederates lost 2,700 in casualties. On September 24 Surgeon Mason was assigned to General G. W. Smith's command as assistant medical director. By December 17 he was announced as chief surgeon of General Arnold Elzey's command. In the spring of 1863 Medical Director Mason was chief surgeon in the Department of Richmond, a position he held for the remainder of the war. After two years he returned to Hagerstown which became his permanent abode. Dr. Mason was a member of the Society Of The Army and Navy Of The Confederate States In The State Of Maryland.

FRANK J. MASON

Frank J. organized the first complete Maryland unit of cavalry in the spring of 1861 under Turner Ashby in Loudoun County. Many Maryland lads were superb horsemen; they had no trouble recruiting a valiant troop of cavaliers. They elected Dr. Mason as their captain and were mustered into the 7th Virginia Cavalry as Company G. This company was the heart from which the future Maryland cavalry units would draw their leaders. Three celebrated lieutenant colonels would also emerge from Company G and form heroic battalions of Maryland cavaliers: Harry W. Gilmor—2nd Maryland Cavalry, Elijah V. White—35th Virginia Cavalry and T. Sturgis Davis—Davis's Maryland Cavalry Battalion. In the spring of 1862 the company was reorganized and Dr. Mason was not reelected. On September 16 General Jackson returned from the capture of Harper's Ferry to strengthen Lee's line between Antietam Creek and the Potomac River near the town of Sharpsburg as the clash started. At dawn the next day the bloodiest single day battle of the war occurred. The Federals launched several atttacks first on the Confederate left, then at the center and finally at the right. Bitter and bloody combat continued all day with first one side and then the other winning brief gains. The fighting was especially desperate around the

Dunkard Church, on the Confederate left, near the stone bridge across Antietam Creek on the right and along the sunken road at the center called "bloody lane" where the blood literally flowed. Of the 75,300 Union troops 12,400 were killed, wounded or missing, and of the 40,000 Confederates nearly 10,700 were casualties. Thus, in one day, over 23,000 men were lost in the two armies and for weeks after the engagement the surrounding countryside for miles and miles was a huge hospital. Dr. Mason served as an aide-de-camp on the staff of Brigadier General Lloyd Tilghman of Talbot County. On the retreat from Holly Springs on May 15, 1863, while handling the rear guard at Champion's Hill, Mississippi, General Tilghman dismounted to give directions for sighting a piece of artillery and was wounded by fragments of an exploded shell from which he soon died.

JOHN THOMPSON O. MASON 1817-1891

John, of Baltimore, was an assistant surgeon in the navy during the Mexican War. He was with Commodore M. C. Perry aboard the *Vandalia* for the 1852 expedition to Japan. It was Assistant Surgeon Mason's good fortune to then serve under Captain Franklin Buchanan. He had entered the United States Navy at the age of fifteen and rose to prominence. Assisting in founding the Naval Academy at Annapolis, he became the first superintendent. On April 22, 1861, he resigned his commission and retired to his family home in Talbot County. On August 31 he appeared before a Justice of the Peace in Easton to legally acknowledge bills of sale of all his personal and real property to his family. By September 5 he was in the Southern navy and soon he was addressed as Admiral Buchanan. Dr. Mason also resigned and offering his services to the Confederacy, on June 10, 1861, he was appointed assistant surgeon. At the battle of Hampton Roads under Franklin Buchanan during the famous duel of the *Monitor* and the *Merrimac* Assistant Surgeon Mason was on the *Patrick Henry*. He was transferred from his ten-gun sidewheel steamer of one hundred and fifty officers and men to hospital duty. In June of 1863 he was medical officer on board the ram *Baltic* of the Mobile naval forces. Scorbutic symptoms were the most hindering illnesses affecting the Confederate seamen. The prevention and treatment of scurvy was a well-rounded diet of fresh meat, vegetables and fruit. On board ship if there was a scarcity of salted meat and dried fruit the sailors could hardly have a nutritious meal. His next tour of duty was on the C. S. *Huntsville*. Dr. Mason was not paroled but took the amnesty oath at Macon on September 8, 1864, and applied for a pardon that he might return to Maryland.

Cardboard patriotic envelope
Erick Davis collection

CHARLES MACGILL 1806-1881

Educated at Baltimore College class of 1823, Medical University class of 1828, he entered the office of Dr. Charles G. Worthington to read medicine. In 1829 he started his doctoring at Hagerstown becoming one of Washington County's prominent physicians and politicians. He was a candidate for presidential elector on the Van Buren ticket and in 1836 he was one of the "glorious nineteen" electors of the state senate who brought about the constitution reform. He was also active in the state militia, rising from a 2nd lieutenant to colonel of the 24th Regiment, then on July 30, 1857, major general of Western Maryland. Dr. Macgill had gotten into trouble early with the government because he was a leading spirit among the Southern sympathizers. He openly assisted his son-in-law Robert Swan, a veteran of the Mexican War, to leave Hagerstown and join the C.S.A. Swan was on the staff of Brigadier General James J. Archer and became major of the 1st Virginia Cavalry. General Archer of Harford County rose to prominence in the famous light division. After being confined in the Northern bastilles for a year and exchanged he volunteered for field duty too soon after his rigorous confinement and died from the effects of a wound just as he was about to be promoted to major general. Dr. Macgill was arrested and imprisoned in Fort McHenry, Fort Hamilton and Fort Lafayette as a political prisoner. In November, 1862, he was unconditionally released and returned to his home resuming his practice. When Lee's army crossed over the state in the summer of 1863, Dr. Macgill established a hospital in Hagerstown for broken down Confederate soldiers. On the return of the army from Gettysburg on July 7 his hospital was used for wounded Southerners. Upon the evacuation of Hagerstown five days later he cast his fortunes with the Confederacy. Leaving his family he received a commission and an expression of gratitude from Jefferson Davis. As a surgeon he worked in Lynchburg Hospital until made a prisoner on April 15, 1865. He was paroled three days later and going to Richmond he continued to reside and practice there.

Surgeon Charles Macgill
courtesy of
Miss Virginia Carmichael

CHARLES G. W. MACGILL 1833-

Charles G. W. completed his higher education at St. James College and the medical school of the University of Maryland in 1856. Returning to his home in Hagerstown, his preceptor was his father, Dr. Charles Macgill. The elder Macgill had eleven children, four of whom were old enough to carry a sword for Southern rights. David, James and William D. were troopers in the 1st Maryland Cavalry Company C. The oldest son was Dr. Charles G. W. Macgill who continued the family medical practice while his father was illegally held by the administration in Northern dungeons for over twelve months. On June 15, 1863, when Confederate forces entered Hagerstown, he assisted his father in establishing a hospital. When the Army of Northern Virginia crossed the Mason-Dixon Line into Yankee land young Dr. Macgill was with them as a volunteer surgeon. On the retreat he stopped for a short time at his father's hospital and then was appointed assistant surgeon of the 2nd Virginia Infantry. After a year's service, he was advanced to surgeon and became regimental surgeon of the Stonewall Brigade until May 4, 1865, when he was paroled at Danville. In December he returned to his native state and established himself in practice at Catonsville, where he was also surgeon at the Maryland Military Institute in 1866 along with another professor, Lieutenant Colonel Leewellyn G. Hoxton, who also served in the Confederacy. He was a member of Franklin Buchanan United Confederate Veterans Camp No. 747 and the Maryland Society Of The Army And Navy. In medical circles he was vice-president of the state Medical and Chirurgical Faculty in 1889-90. Dr. Macgill was a commissioner on the Baltimore County school board and president of the first national bank of Catonsville.

RICHARD B. MAURY

On March 22, 1862, Maury of Georgetown was appointed surgeon and ordered to the 28th Mississippi Cavalry. On June 9, 1863, he was transferred to hospital service. In October of 1864, he signed papers as surgeon-in-charge of the Greenville, Alabama Hospital. In routine hospital life meals were served by the ward-masters three times a day. Breakfast was at seven in the morning in summer and eight in the winter. Tea, milk, bread, butter and molasses and whatever meat that could be saved from the previous day were served. After breakfast the assistant surgeons visited their respective wards, making out their diet lists as light, half or full and the quantity of whiskey desired for each. Dinner at two might be poultry, beef, ham, fish and vegetables. Supper at six according to the doctor's instructions was chicken soup, beef tea or tea and toast depending upon prescribed rations. As the war progressed this luxurious diet could not be maintained and the starchy compounds of wheat, corn and arrowroot prevailed. In January of 1865, Surgeon Maury was working in the Brodie General Hospital. Records show him at Way Hospital at Meridian, Mississippi, on March 29, 1865. He surrendered at Citronelle and was paroled at Jackson on May 15.

The silver Maryland cross was worn by Surgeon Charles Macgill during the war and the United Daughters of the Confederacy cross of honor was presented to Surgeon Charles G. W. Macgill after the war.

Daniel C. Toomey Collection

THOMAS J. McGILL 1812-1886

He pursued his brother Charles B. McGill to the course of lectures at the University of Maryland medical school in 1834, then joined him in practice at their native community of Jefferson. In 1856 he moved to Frederick where two of his sons, Samuel and Wardlaw, followed his footsteps in medicine. Dr. Thomas McGill, like the majority of Marylanders, favored the Southern understanding of the Constitution and issues of the day but was unwilling to make the ultimate sacrifice and sever the ties of home. There were many who wanted to go South but for one reason or another couldn't or didn't. Drs. William Smith McPherson and Lewis H. Smith of Frederick County both sympathized strongly with the Confederacy and were commissioned in the medical corps by Stonewall Jackson during the Antietam campaign but did not accept owing to impoverished health. Dr. Thomas McGill, after being arrested a second time, was sent within Southern lines on August 1, 1864, with about twenty other Frederick Countians among whom was Reverend Joseph H. Jones and Dr. William Turner Wooton. He went to Richmond where he was appointed acting assistant surgeon and was paroled April 20, 1865, then returned to Frederick.

WILBERFORCE RICHARD McKNEW 1839-

Born in Prince George's County he attended Hobart College in New York, then was admitted to the University of Maryland. While preparing himself for the profession of medicine the conflict became imminent and he was a medical officer of the Baltimore volunteer militia for three weeks. After order was restored the despot's heel was indeed on thy shore as military control was established. He returned to his course of study and saw the University of Maryland Hospital taken over by Federal ailing soldiers. Graduating with the class of 1861, he bore his breast bravely to the foeman's steel by joining the 1st Maryland Cavalry on November 12, 1862. Assistant Surgeon Wilber McKnew was officially appointed by the Confederate government on November 12, 1862. He was captured at Greenland Gap in April of 1863 and held for one month at Fort Norfolk before being exchanged. He was ordained medical officer of this sublime command which was conspicuous for devotion, efficiency and reliability. One of the most annoying and prevalent diseases to the fighting men was camp itch as it was commonly designated. It was not a disease in which the animalbule of scabies, the acarus, was ever seen, it was not even a vesicular disease. Sulphur, arsenic or alkaline baths were considered routine treatment, or washing with a strong decoction of poke root for mild forms. Twice Medical Officer McKnew was admitted to the hospital during the war, both times suffering from chronic diarrhea. On January 24, 1865, he was assigned to Robertson Hospital in Richmond. When peace was restored he returned to Prince George's County until 1869 when he made Baltimore his home. When the state militia was reorganized it contained an enormous amount of former Confederate officers. Dr. McKnew was surgeon of the Maryland National Guard on the staff of General James R. Herbert, previously commander of the 2nd Maryland Infantry C.S.A. He was also a member of the Society Of The Army And Navy Of The Confederate States In The State Of Maryland and Isaac R. Trimble Camp No. 1025 of Confederate Veterans.

JAMES W. McSHERRY 1833

McSherry was born in Martinsburg, now West Virginia, and sent to college at Baltimore. In 1850 he received his degree from St. Mary's College, which became a theological seminary, then entering upon the study of medicine he was graduated from the University of Maryland in 1855. After practicing this profession for a year in the Monumental City he returned to Boone County to administer to the sick until the beginning of hostilities in 1861. Dr. McSherry had been serving as a surgeon in the state militia for several years and at the outbreak of war, he enlisted in the Virginia service as captain of the Boone County Rangers. They were formerly Company D of the 2nd Kanawha Regiment but on July 1 they became Company B 36th Infantry. After reorganization he was on medical duty as a contract doctor. Another Baltimorean who received much notoriety was Brigadier General Lewis Henry Little of the Army of the West. On September 19, 1862, at Iuka, Mississippi, while commanding the left wing, Generals Price and Little were conferring on horseback when a minnie ball struck Little above the left eye. Falling into the arms of a comrade he died without speaking a word and buried in a little garden behind the headquarters at midnight by torchlight. After the war his remains were exhumed and reinterred in Greenmount Cemetery, Baltimore, which received the bodies of six other C.S.A. generals. Later on staff duty with General Floyd's command McSherry went to Kentucky and Tennessee and was wounded in the side at Carnifex Ferry and in the leg at Fort Donelson. Captain McSherry received a staff appointment under his former commander, General John McCausland, and on November 19, 1864, he was captured in Kanawha County. He was subsequently held in confinement at Fort Delaware until after the close of hostilities when officers of his rank were released. Dr. McSherry returned to Baltimore to practice medicine for a short period, then resided back in Martinsburg. He was a valued and influential citizen and rendered substantial service to the community during a career of seven years on the city council and two terms as mayor.

ALEXIUS L. MIDDLETON 1833-1906

Receiving his medical doctor's diploma from the University of Maryland in 1860, he followed the banner of liberty during the tragic Civil War as acting assistant surgeon in the 2nd Texas Infantry. Statistics on alumni of the 1860 classes of the four schools composing the University of Maryland who were participating in the war indicated that thirty per-cent fought for the Confederacy and almost ten per-cent for the Union. From the medical class of 52 graduates 17 saw Confederate service and 5 Federal service. The dentistry class of 35 diplomas had 11 in the army of the Confederate service and 3 in the United States Army. From the undergraduate class of 4 graduates 2 entered the Southern forces and one the Union forces. It was not easy to make the decision to fight against one's friends and classmates after having experienced two gay, harmonious years together. The Agricultural College was only in its second year when the long sectional conflict erupted; of the 78 students and 6 professors only 17 students and 3 professors remained until commencement in July of 1861, while 20 joined the Confederate troops and 9 the Union troops. Dr. Middleton was soon made assistant surgeon and in February of 1864 the 2nd Texas was mustered out at Galveston. He continued to serve in the Trans-Mississippi Department until the tattered battle flag was furled forever. Returning to his home he established a practice at Upper Marlboro.

FRANCIS TURGUAND MILES 1827-1903

Dr. Miles received his A.B. at Charleston College and his M.D. at the Medical College of South Carolina. In 1856 he obtained a teaching appointment at the Medical College of South Carolina and a year later was named assistant demonstrator. He then went to Cambridge, Massachusetts, to study comparative anatomy and from hence to Paris before returning to his alma mater. He was a volunteer surgeon on James Island at the taking of Fort Sumter, then he enlisted as a private in the Phoenix Rifles. Dr. Miles was elected lieutenant of the Calhoun Guards and when they mustered into the C.S.A. on March 24, 1862, he was captain. This Company E 1st Charleston Battalion of Infantry was stationed at Fort Sumter. At the battle of Secessionsville on June 16 he was shot through the thigh but continued in active service. By the consolidation of commands about September 30 this battalion became a part of the 27th South Carolina Infantry and Miles Company became Company A. On August 17, 1863, at Morris Island he was slightly wounded. During a critical period of the siege of Fort Sumter in 1864 Captain Miles commanded the fort for several days. Having been recommended for an appointment in the medical bureau he resigned on April 3, 1864. The following day he was a surgeon in the Provisional Army and ordered to report to the surgeon general. He joined a medical department that was faced with a stupendous and frightful task. The competence of the doctors who wore blue or gray were about the same but for the South in this period in the struggle, the dearth of clothing, food and medical supplies was a significant hindrance to health and recovery. Some Confederates marched in bare feet while the Federals had mighty mills and factories and supplies of all kinds increased even to the point of such a luxury as a dehydrated carrot. In 1865 he resumed his chair but soon removed to Baltimore. Dr. Miles became professor of anatomy, histology and pathology in 1868, at Washington Medical University. In 1880 he became a lecturer of physiology in the University of Maryland Medical College. He was also founder of the Clinic Society of Maryland and served two terms as president of the American Neurological Association. Dr. Miles was author of *Pepper's System of Medicine* and *Keating's Encyclopaedia of Children*.

JOHN N. K. MONMONIER 1896-

John N. K. was one of two sons of Dr. John Francis Monmonier who became doctors. The Monmonier of this sketch was graduated from the University of Maryland as an M.D. in 1858 and worked with his father in Baltimore. He had the sincerity of his belief in the sacredness of the cause of the Southland by going to Richmond. There he enlisted as a private in the Maryland Guard of Company D Weston's Battalion. On June 13, 1861, the secretary of war began to shift companies into regiments as troops were needed. Each soldier of Weston's Battalion signed an individual petition which was sent to President Davis requesting that the battalion not be separated. The Marylanders were broken up and the Maryland Guard became Company H 1st Maryland Infantry. On November 16 he received an appointment from the medical department and prepared to leave his regiment. By December 10, he was at Camp Florida in Virginia. He then spent his time and talents to further the comfort and well being of his patients at Camp Bragg near Swift Run and was listed as a senior assistant surgeon of the 3rd Division Department of Northern Virginia. On March 24, 1863, he was promoted to surgeon. Confederate medical regulations published early in the war listed a total of 130 diseases for prevalence and treatment. The great enervating ailments of the brave boys in gray were the intestinal disorders, diarrhea and dysentery. Some idea of the high incidence of the intestinal disorders may be gained from figures: 226,828 of the 848,555 cases of disease reported east of the Mississippi during the first two years were diarrhea and dysentery. Of the 50,350 soldiers admitted to Chimborazo Hospital suffering from some specific illness 10,503 were diagnosed with one or the other intestinal disorders. In the spring of 1864 Surgeon Monmonier was working for the inspector of hospitals office and was stationed near Raccoon Ford. On January 6, 1865, he was admitted to Jackson Hospital and soon returned to duty until the new republic sank to rise no more. By 1867 Dr. Monmonier was an assistant professor of anatomy at the Washington Medical University in Baltimore and the following year became a full instructor. In his many writings he drew from his experience in the war and reflected gun-shot injuries and their treatment.

CHARLES McL. MORFIT 1838-

Charles McL. was a son of Henry Mason Morfit who was a member of the state general assembly in 1861 and while moving for the question of secession he was taken into custody by union troops. No charges were brought, no trials were granted and he was thrown into prison while his three sons joined the C.S.A. Clarence was captain, Mason a major and Charles was commissioned an assistant surgeon in the navy on June 10, 1861. After receiving his A.B. degree he studied under Doctors N. R. Smith and W. A. Hammond in Baltimore. In 1859 he received his A.M. degree at Loyola College and was named attending physician at the Eastern Dispensary in Baltimore. After receiving his M.D. degree from the University of Maryland in 1861 he joined the U.S. Navy but resigned after only several months. Assistant Surgeon Morfit's first sea service was aboard the C.S.S. *United States*. He was then ordered to the C.S.S. *Ivy* before going to the New Orleans Naval Station. After a short stay Dr. Morfit was working at his profession on the steamer *Arkansas* then at Jackson Naval Station. After Christmas of 1862, he was assigned to the C.S.S. *Oconee* and was captured on August 20, 1863, while trying to escape from his seized ship just off Tyler Island, Georgia. He was sent to Old Capital Prison in Washington, then to Fort McHenry before being exchanged on November 21. His next duty was aboard the ironclad *Raleigh*. While serving at the Wilmington Naval Station he was promoted to passed assistant surgeon on July 28, 1864. His next assignment was on the steamer *Albemarle* and in the next seven months he was twice moved by the war department, first aboard the *Richmond* then the *Chickaneuga*. Passed Assistant Surgeon Morfit was paroled on May 19, 1865, at Augusta, returned to the city of his birth where he practiced and was active in Confederate veteran affairs. In 1867 he was made lecturer of practicing medicine at the Washington Medical University. From 1869 until 1880 he is listed as a vaccine physician working with vaccination against small-pox. In 1880 Dr. Morfit was appointed coroner for the east district of Baltimore.

WILLIAM T. MONTGOMERY 1831-1881

William T. was a son of Dr. James Montgomery, an old defender during the War of 1812. Completing the medical course at the University of Maryland in 1851 he established his occupation with his father at their home in Clairmont Mills in Harford County. Dr. Montgomery had wrapped around his heart the Southern cross; making his way to Richmond he mustered into Company A Weston's Battalion as a private on June 2, 1861, when it appeared the Weston Guard was going into action against the blue bellies. The Weston Guard were transferred to the 1st Maryland Infantry where they became Company C. By November he was on detached service with the hospital of the Maryland Regiment. Dr. Montgomery applied for an appointment with this regiment from his state but he was assigned to the 48th North Carolina Infantry as acting assistant surgeon. Measles caused by a filter-passing virus was recognized as another great scourge. This infectious sickness regarded as a disease of children created havoc in the first year. Bad hygienic conditions no doubt contributed heavily in early epidemics. Medical officers learned that drugs were of little value in limiting the duration of the disease and most recommended abundant ventilation. A solution of ammonium acetate given in doses of 40 to 50 drops three times a day in a cup of warm tea seemed to possess a particular eliminating action. On October 14, 1862, he was made assistant surgeon and on April 13, 1863, he was passed to the position of surgeon and ordered to the 10th Alabama Infantry Battalion. In the late summer of 1863 Surgeon Montgomery was court martialed under general order No. 88 Department of Northern Virginia. By September 10, he was serving in the Commissary Department in the Department of Alabama, Mississippi and East Louisiana. After all the armies were defeated and the banner went down in blood he returned to Harford County to resume his medical knowledge, for those in need.

Apothecary scale made of brass and black and white marble, flanked by two blue glass bottles that contained a powdered disinfectant of santonim and hydrargyrl chloridum corrosivum.
Maryland Pharmaceutical Association collection

RUSSELL MURDOCK 1829-1905

Educated at the University of Edinburgh in 1856-58 and the University of Virginia 1859-61, Dr. Murdock of Baltimore was resident physician at the Alms House and the General Dispensary there until his heartstrings drew him into the Southern services. In the fall of 1861 he was appointed acting assistant surgeon and summoned to Libby Prison Hospital. Most prison hospitals in the Confederacy, like the prisons themselves, were established in warehouses and factories. Libby Prison Hospital was located in a large four-story warehouse on the James River. It was described as being admirably arranged and clean and neat to the last degree. The entire establishment was in every way a model; deaths were never attributed to lack of proper attention and it was sometimes charged that the care of enemy prisoners was receiving too much consideration. The Confederacy cared for its disabled prisoners about as well as it did for its own sick and wounded. Both were victims of severe privations in the latter part of the conflict. The three Richmond area prison hospitals had accommodations for about five hundred patients; by March of 1864 they contained over eleven hundred and the mortality rate rose sharply. In December 1862, Acting Assistant Surgeon Murdock was ordered to Winder Hospital in Richmond. On June 2, 1863, he was advanced to assistant surgeon and assigned to the 1st Regiment Engineer Corps. By November 4, 1864, he was promoted to surgeon and continued to aid those wasted by disease and torn by combat. After the crusade he returned to his home and taught surgery at the Baltimore Dental College while being very active in various circles with his colleagues. Dr. Murdock patented an improved apparatus allowing locomotion of patients without displacement of fractures; it was used with great success during the Franco-Prussian War. He received much notoriety as inventor of an eye speculum that holds the lid open and an eye forceps that combines five instruments that are required for a cataract operation. In 1882 the Baltimore Eye, Ear and Throat Charity Hospital was established with Dr. Murdock as attending physician.

SAMUEL W. MURPHY

Dr. Murphy was one of those devoted sons of Dixie who were willing to lay down their lives, their fortunes and their sacred honor in loyal obedience to the call of duty as they understood it. In 1862 he was commissioned assistant surgeon of Page's Tennessee Artillery. Rheumatism was a disease that incapacitated numerous soldiers. The Army of Tennessee from June, 1862, to May, 1863, recorded an aggregate of 9,927 rheumatic ailments while 59,772 cases were reported on field and hospital registers of the forces operating east of the Mississippi during the first two years of the war. Treatment for rheumatism or what was diagnosed as rheumatism seldom brought much relief. Colchicum and iodide of potassium appear to have been standby remedies for those who received medicinal preparations. By June 14, 1864, Assistant Surgeon Murphy was practicing in the General Hospital at Richmond and in December he was transferred to Chimborazo Infirmary. On January 2, 1872, he opened Rugby Academy for boys at Wilmington, Delaware, and conducted the school for fifteen years before selling it. By the turn of the century he became a resident of the Maryland Line Confederate Soldiers Home at Pikesville and then chose to return to his own home.

WILLIAM H. MURRAY

Born in Anne Arundel County and coming to our state's largest city to practice in the early 1850's, Dr. Murray embraced the cause of the South, a priceless heirloom to be handed down. He became an acting assistant surgeon in October of 1862 at a brigade hospital on Taylor's farm. He was then a contract surgeon until regularly appointed assistant surgeon on November 3, 1864, serving with his many fellow Marylanders in Stuart's Horse Artillery under the profound Dr. James Breathed. Numerous respiratory ailments attacked the Confederate soldier, the most deadly of which was pneumonia, although the problem of diagnosis was a difficult one. Pneumonia diminished as the temperature became more elevated and the vicissitudes of the season eased. Prior to the war practitioners had relied heavily on antimony and the lancet but now it met with little success, while the mortality rate was alarmingly high. The infection was asthenic and demanded a sustaining rather than a depleting treatment. The tartar emetic, other preparations of antimony and bleeding in civil practice were dispensed with in favor of a carefully regulated diet, brandy, opium and quinine. Indigenous remedies were prescribed consisting of local applications of mustard seed, stramonium leaves and hickory leaves along with butterflyroot and sanguinaria. Dr. Murray was paroled on May 20, 1865 in Richmond. Settling in the Norfolk, Virginia, area he was a member of the Norfolk County Medical Society in 1870.

WILLIAM HENRY NEWELL 1830-1913

As a son of Reverend D. Newell, he was born in New York but resided after his father's death on East Second Street in Frederick. He completed his studies at the University of Pennsylvania as a physician in 1859. He felt that the banner of the Southern cross was studded with the stars of God's heaven, like those originally on Old Glory before it was tainted. Crossing the frontier into the Confederacy he was appointed acting assistant surgeon and participated in the Battle of South Mountain. After Antietam he was in the hands of the enemy. His mother, Analanah Ritchie Newell, went to Hagerstown to visit her son who was ill. She was accompanied by several young ladies from Frederick but they were arrested. After being roughly treated and all the little comforts they had brought for the wounded Southern were taken from them along with their personal belongings, they were finally escorted back to Frederick. By October 24 Acting Assistant Surgeon Newell was back with the Confederate army. In the spring of 1863 he was practicing in the General Hospital in Richmond and on June 13 he was promoted to assistant surgeon. On July 2, he was transferred to Charlottesville General Infirmary. Smallpox was the most dreaded of the sicknesses that harassed the Confederate soldier. Medical authorities had not been unaware of the danger of a smallpox epidemic and medical authorities ordered vaccination of all troops. Vaccine crusts from patients and the civilian population, particularly children, were sent to the medical bureau to produce the vaccine virus. Smallpox victims were isolated, sores were often covered with ointment made from linseed oil and limewater; flax opaca, a plant, was used as a diaphoretic. Saline purgatives, cooling drinks and enemata were used, operates prescribed once or twice a day to moderate the delirium. The eyes were carefully washed with water and vinegar, the pustules of the eyelids touched with lunar caustic to prevent dangerous ophthalnia. Mercurial ointment was also smeared on the face. On January 23, 1864, he was dropped from the rolls but by March 1st he was on the register of the medical director's office in Richmond.

CHARLES E. V. NICKERSON

In 1856 he was graduated from the University of Maryland Medical College and administered to clients in Baltimore. After the stirring scenes of April 19, 1861, volunteer civilian companies were organized and called to arms to repeal the Northern invasion that now cried for vengeance to burn the rebellious city. Dr. Nickerson volunteered as a member of the civilian volunteer militia surgical staff. Every sentiment of his nature and aspirations of his soul were with the Southland so he departed for the Confederacy becoming a contract physician and entered into the following: "This contract entered into this 8th day of December 1862, at Richmohd State of Virginia between Surgeon General Moore of the C.S. Army and Dr. C. E. V. Nickerson of Baltimore in the state of Maryland witnesseth, that for the Consideration hereafter mentioned, the Said Dr. Nickerson promises and agrees to perform the duties of a Medical Officer agreeably to the Army Regulations, at Hospital Duty, Knoxville, Tennessee. And the Said Surgeon General Moore promises and agrees, on behalf of the Confederate States, to pay or cause to be paid to the Said Dr. Nickerson the Sum of Eighty dollars for each and every month he shall continue to perform the services above stated, which shall be his full compensation, and in lieu of all allowances and involvements whatsoever. This contract to continue till determined by the Said doctor, or the Commanding Officer for the Time being, or the Surgeon General." In the fall of 1864 Dr. Nickerson was working in Walker Hospital at Columbia, Georgia, then Reed Infirmary at West Point. On March 30, 1865, he is listed as in charge of the Wayside Hospital when the end came.

HENRY REGINALD NOEL 1836-1878

Noel was born in Essex County, Virginia, schooled at Fleetwood Academy and the University of Virginia. Coming to Baltimore in 1859 he began his medical treatment in the Alms House. He was a member of the American Medical Association and the Baltimore Medical and Surgical Society. With the South he held with great unanimity to the doctrine of state sovereignty, believing that sovereignty was inviolable by the general government. After the occupation he went to Virginia to burst the tyrant's chain and was commissioned an assistant surgeon at White Sulphur Springs at the headquarters of Wise's Brigade in the summer of 1861. On September 13 he was assigned to the 16th Virginia Infantry. Receiving the star of a major on his collar on November 16 Surgeon Noel was sent to duty at Pocataligo. By March 31, 1862, he was transferred to the 60th Virginia Infantry. The so-called continued fevers appeared at field registers with considerable frequency. This term usually encompassed typhoid fever, typhus fever and fevers that could not be identified clearly were assigned to this category. These cases were isolated in a well ventilated area and treated with saline purgative followed by stimulants. Oil of turpentine produced dramatic results but was accompanied by much tympanitis, dryness, a fuliginous condition of the tongue, fauces, gurgle and pain in the right fossa iliac and moderate diarrhea. Externally much reliance was placed upon cold cloths and sponge baths. Typhoid and typhus progressively diminished during the progress of the war. In April of 1864, Surgeon Noel was stationed at Narrows in Giles County. With breaking hearts they laid that tattered battle flag down and he returned to his residence. In 1867 Dr. Noel was teaching physiology and pathology at the Baltimore College of Dental Surgery. By 1873 he was also instructing physiology and hygiene at the College of Physicians and Surgeons.

WILLIAM AUGUSTUS BLOUNT NORCOM 1836-1881

William A. B. of Edenton, North Carolina, was the son of Dr. James Norcom. After graduating as a physician from the University of Pennsylvania in 1857 he practiced in his native city. On July 19, 1862, he was nominated assistant surgeon in the C.S.A. By that fall he was working at the No. 2 North Carolina Hospital at Petersburg. Malaria was a disease which had long been both indemic and epidemic in the deeper Southern states due to the anopheles mosquito and an infected population. It was generally believed that malaria was caused by miasms emanating from areas covered by stagnant water and certain practices, such as the burning of tar in the vicinity of hospitals, were followed to prevent the malady. Quinine was a favorite remedy and was more effective than crude cinchona; however, the ever tightening blockade gradually diminished the supply and led to antiperiodics among the native plants. Tinctures of Georgia bark and dogwood mixed with whiskey became adequate substitutes. Turpentine applied externally was also a valuable remedial agent but the prophylactic power of indigenous barks saturated in whiskey was highly approved by the patient and the medical officer was carefully reminded of the hours appointed for receiving the favorite medicine. Assistant Surgeon Norcom continued his practice at Petersburg until early 1865 when he was sent to Way Hospital No. 3 at Salisbury. In 1866, he came to Baltimore to practice which became his permanent abode.

LUCIUS BELLINGER NORTHROP 1811-1894

Born at Charleston he was graduated from the Military Academy at West Point in 1829 in the class with Jefferson Davis. They served together in the West against the Indians. During the Seminole War in Florida he was severely wounded and retired on half pay. Studying medicine in Philadelphia he came to Baltimore County for a short time. Returning to Charleston Dr. Northrop practiced only occasionally for charity. When South Carolina seceded he was appointed lieutenant colonel on March 27, 1861 in the subsistence department. On June 21 he was made a colonel in the commissary department and on November 26 he was promoted to brigadier general and became Commissary General of South Carolina. A few months before the fall of Richmond General Northrop was relieved and went to Egypt, North Carolina. On June 30, 1865, he was arrested by Federal authorities at Raleigh and confined in Castle Thunder prison in Richmond. General Northrop was not released until November 2 when he was granted an additional parole and came to Baltimore. He was deported and then told not to leave the state of Virginia without notifying the government. He was a member of John Bowie Strange Camp United Confederate Veterans. Returning to Baltimore County he was a member of the Society Of The Army And Navy Of The Confederate States In The State Of Maryland. On April 18, 1893, General Northrop resided at Pikesville in the Maryland Line Confederate Soldiers Home.

JOSIAH CLARK NOTT 1804-1873

Dr. Nott was born in Columbia, South Carolina, receiving the degree of A.B. from the South Carolina College in 1824. He studied medicine in the office of Dr. James Davis and attended a course of lectures at the College of Physicians and Surgeons in New York. He graduated as an M.D. in 1827 from the University of Pennsylvania. He was a resident student of the Philadelphia Alms House for one year, then demonstrator of anatomy at the University of Pennsylvania. In 1829 he returned to Columbia. In 1833 he came to Baltimore; in 1835 he traveled among the European Centers and in 1836 he moved permanently to Mobile, Alabama. He made numerous contributions to the medical literature; most of his notable contributions were on public health. He held the chair of anatomy at the University of Louisiana but resigned to help form the Medical School in Mobile. He lectured on surgery until the war caused the school to close. He was commissioned a surgeon on October 18, 1861, and was assistant medical director to General J. M. Withers, then soon became medical director. In January of 1863, he was inspector of camps and hospitals in the District of the Gulf until resigning on March 3 at Mobile, after which he served on the medical staff of General B. Bragg as medical director. Pulmonary tuberculosis, catarrh and bronchitis harassed the Southern fighting men. The Army of the Potomac reported 19,455 cases of consumption from July, 1861, to March 1862. Standard treatment for tubercular patients included nourishing food, tonics and stimulants. For the early stages of phthisis a decoction made from the black snakeroot and iodine was administered. The most well-known remedies for coughs and colds were juice of horehound that was sweetened, lobelia, the leaves of the bene, the bark of the holly root and button snakeroot. After the war, Dr. Nott returned to Baltimore and later went to New York where his main field was gynecology.

THOMAS ZADAC OFFUTT 1829-1908

Hailing from Montgomery County, at the age of seventeen he went to Georgetown and secured a clerkship in a store. After one year he returned home and entered the Rockville Academy where he carried on his studies for three years. Prepared for the medical profession he spent one session in the University of Michigan, after which he entered the medical department of the University of Pennsylvania graduating in 1865. Going to Baltimore County he opened an office in the second district until the opening of the War Between The States when this ardent volunteer went to the assistance of the South. On October 2, 1862, he was appointed an acting assistant surgeon in Winder Hospital at Richmond. Venereal disease may have been more prevalent than has been generally supposed in the C.S.A. Army. The treatment of syphilis and gonorrhea included poke root or berries, elder, wild sarsaparilla, sassafras, jessamine, and prickly ash. They discovered silk weed root put in whiskey, given at the same time as pills of rosin from a pine tree with very small pieces of blue vitrol, would cure stubborn cases of gonorrhea. On July 13, 1863, he was advanced to assistant surgeon and assigned to Hood's division. Assistant Surgeon Offutt on November 24 was ordered to the 45th Virginia Infantry and at Keaneysville on August 25, 1864, he was left in charge of the Confederate wounded in the enemy's lines. He was with the casualties until

Anti-rheumatic oil or Indian balm, hand blown glass syringe with pewter top, 100 pills of valerianate of quinine, and a long hollow swab with a sponge.
G. Craig Caba collection

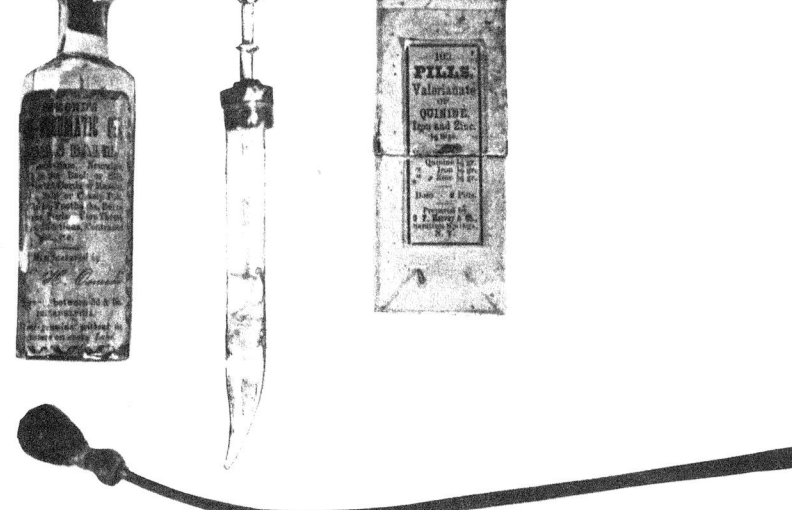

they reached Harper's Ferry when he was conveyed to Richmond by a flag of truce. In the early months of 1865, he was promoted to surgeon, sent to the 4th Virginia Infantry and was paroled on April 24 at Charleston. He returned home for a short time then went to Harrisonburg, Virginia, where he engaged in the mercantile business. In 1869 he disposed of this endeavor and again resided in Baltimore County where he enjoyed a profitable practice. In 1879 Dr. Offutt moved to Towson and again terminated his medical practice to study law in the office of David G. McIntosh, a former colleague in the Confederacy who was a lieutenant colonel and a renowned artillery commander of Hill's Corps. He passed the bar in January of 1881 and spent the ensuing three years as an attorney until being elected to the Maryland Legislature. After one term he was appointed to the staff of Governor McLane with the rank of colonel in the state militia and returned to Towson where he was engaged in business pursuits.

THOMAS OPIE 1842-

Opie was born in Berkeley County, Virginia, and graduated in medicine at the University of Pennsylvania on March 24, 1861. Instead of practicing his profession he shouldered a flintlock musket as an enlisted man and marched to war with the Augusta Lee Riflemen. Swapping his flintlock for a yankee minie musket he continued his infantry service until the Battle of Rich Mountain at which time the young physician became assistant surgeon of the 25th Virginia Regiment. In October, 1862, he was transferred to Staunton General Hospital of the Fourth Division. Dietary deficiency in the Confederate army and navy was not long in producing scurvy. Medical officers continually warned that unless vegetable rations were increased there would be a tendency to scorbutus throughout the whole army. With the commencement of the 1863 spring General Lee ordered a daily detail from each regiment to gather sassafras buds, wild onions, garlic, lamb's quarter and poke sprouts to supplement the deficiency of rations. Little medication seems to have been used in relieving scurvy besides citric acid and a decoction from pine tops or clorate of potash. Learning of the surrender of Lee's command Assistant Surgeon Opie mounted his horse and started toward General Johnson's army but before reaching his destination that corps also had surrendered. He headed his steed in the opposite direction toward Harper's Ferry thence to Baltimore. In 1872 he inaugurated the College of Physicians and Surgeons of that city and was elected dean for twenty-four successive terms. In 1873 Dr. Opie was a vaccine physician. His main field was obstetrics and he became attending physician at the Baltimore Maternite Hospital which he founded the following year. He was a member of the Society Of The Army And Navy Of The Confederate States In The State Of Maryland and the Franklin Buchanan Veteran's Camp. In 1886-87 he was vice-president of the state Medical and Chirurgical Faculty.

CHARLES ORDEMAN 1862-

He was born and raised in Frederick County at Park Mills. Both Charles and his brother John H. were members of the Manor Mounted Guard at Carrollton Manor. This cavalry militia was organized in 1859 and was very Southern in their feelings. A number of members of this company joined the Confederacy and none were known to don the uniform of blue. Dr. Ordeman was in the "volunteer State" when the calamity began and enlisted as a private in the 21st Tennessee Regiment Company G on April 26, 1861, as a private. He was detailed to the infirmary as a hospital steward. Soon he passed the army medical board and was granted a commission as assistant surgeon with the Army of the West. The medical departments were furnished with a moderate number of narcotics and sedatives and an abundant supply of tonics, astringents, aromatics and demulcents. While the list of anodynes, emetics and cathartics remained in a comparative degree incomplete, the Confederacy made every effort to develop its internal resources by the appropriation of its indigenous medicinal substances of their own soil. The most widely dispensed medication was whiskey. Liquor was eagerly sought by the military thus delerium tremens of alcoholism was prevalent. Assistant Surgeon Ordeman was killed and is buried in Tennessee. There are two references to his death but no particulars. Fate prevented him from a lucrative practice and worldly goods to leave behind. High and chivalrous principles will always stir the hearts of those who truly appreciate honest devotion to a superb cause by his "fortitudo indomitabile et devotione exemplaria" indomitable courage, and unwaivering devotion.

ISHAM RANDOLPH PAGE 1834-

Isham was born in Richmond and entered the University of Virginia. Pursuing the medical course at the University of New York, he completed it in 1859. In the early spring of 1861, Dr. Page left his practice at Bellevue and Charite Hospitals in the Empire City and returned South. His first medical work was with the Virginia Military Institute cadets until the 18th Virginia Regiment was formed and he was appointed to them on May 4. Assistant Surgeon Page was officially commissioned on July 1 and was then sent to Yorktown Hospital. On February 5, 1862, he became a surgeon and was reassigned to field service in General W. N. Pendleton Artillery. At Fredericksburg he was wounded, but after recovering, was made chief surgeon. Psychosomatic medicine was unknown at this time but some medical officers were aware of the acute mental depression of many soldiers. All the men were naturally subject to homesickness at times. The adversities of combat, the afflictions of the wounded and the aches of the sick caused mental depression and anxiety. The medical officer placed emphasis upon proper food as the principal agent to assist in the cure of the physical system of the sick and wounded. The promise of a furlough to return home was found to be superior to the entire pharmacopoeia and would literally rescue a nostalgic soldier from the jaws of death. This psychological maneuver would not work on Marylanders; they were excommunicated from those whom they loved the most and their only hope was to fight that their state might be liberated. In November of 1864 he became assistant medical purveyor working in the capital city. Ordered to Danville upon the evacuation of Richmond he established and took charge of an infirmary until June of 1865. After being paroled he settled in Baltimore by 1871. Dr. Page was a vaccine physician from 1873-80 while teaching turgery at the Washington Medical University.

JOHN RANDOLPH PAGE 1830-1901

John was born in Gloucester County, Virginia, and received his M.D. at the University of Virginia in 1850, then attended medical and surgical clinics in Paris and London for two years. Returning to the county of his birth to practice until 1856 Dr. Page then came to Carroll County and was a member of the Maryland Medical and Chirurgical Faculty. Determined at once which cause to take up arms to defend he realized that the huge hostile army held our state in subjection so he removed to the seat of war and became assistant surgeon of the 10th Virginia Infantry on July 19, 1861. He was elevated to surgeon on February 5, 1862, and ordered to Yorktown where he organized and was in charge of the new general hospital. Here he was especially successful as a diagnostician and was advanced and sought in his views on sanitation and hygiene. By mid-April of that spring Surgeon Page was assigned to the Reserve Artillery Corps of General Pendleton's command. He continued through the summer in General Pendleton's staff as head surgeon of medical staff until August 17 when he was granted a leave of absence for thirty days for the benefit of his health. By mid-winter he was surgeon-in-chief of Burkeville Infirmary. On April 24, 1863, Surgeon Page was ordered to the medical director at Knoxville in the Department of East Tennessee, but this edict was revoked on May 6. Being sent to General Hospital No. 2 at Lynchburg he signed as surgeon-in-charge on June 15. Within the next year he became surgeon-in-chief and was one of the first physicians to use bichloride of mercury in

Surgeon John Randolph Page
Daniel D. Hartzler collection

the treatment of infected gunshot wounds. He also used tar water—antiseptic property being creosote and crude carbolic acid at a time when antiseptic treatment was not recognized. He was cognizant of the infection and fatal nature of glander in horses, so he condemned and destroyed all horses and stables infected with glanders within the spheres of his limits. On March 24, 1865, Surgeon Page was called to report to Richmond but the war ended before he could get to the medical director. His practice was established in the fallen capital city where he was a member of the Richmond Academy of Medicine. Going to Louisiana State Seminary at Alexandria he taught until 1869 when he accepted a teaching position at the Washington Medical University in Baltimore.

JOHN WILLIAMSON PALMER 1825-

Completing his courses at the University of Maryland Medical College in 1846, he left Baltimore, the city of his birth, three years later for San Francisco where he continued his learned occupation. During the Burmese War, Dr. Palmer was surgeon on the steamer *Phlegethon* and was employed by the East India Company from 1852 to 1857. When it was evident that the Union was not faithful to the laws of the land, Dr. Palmer sought to protect his heritage by seeking the hospitality of the South as an aide-de-camp on the staff of another Baltimorean, General Robert Charles Tyler. Tyler entered the army as a private and won distinctions to the rank of a brigadier. At Missionary Ridge he was dangerously wounded and his leg was amputated. While sojourning near West Point, Georgia, he organized convalescents and state militia against a Federal cavalry raid. Defending an earthwork fort called Fort Tyler on April 16, 1865, the little garrison was overrun and the gallant general on crutches was instanly killed by a sharpshooter's ball that struck his head. Dr. Palmer is best remembered for his literary contributions as author of "Golden Dragon", "Queen's Heart", "The Old and The New", and of the popular song "Stonewall Jackson's Way". He also translated Michelet's, Hugo's and other French works. His wife, Henriette Lee Palmer, was also a native Baltimorean and a well-known authoress.

JOHN THOMAS PARKER 1839-1917

Parker was born at Arcadia in Worcester County and graduated from Washington College at Chestertown in 1856. He studied at the University of New York then completed his medical courses at Philadelphia, Pennsylvania. He opened his office at Snow Hill, but saw his friends armed with truth and right in their hearts go South and become martyrs. As the thunder clouds in Maryland grew blacker the wail of the South wind whistled vengeance of the soul to a beleaguered land and Dr. Parker answered the battle cry of the Confederacy. He was commissioned an assistant surgeon on October 14, 1862, and was placed in Polk Hospital in Atlanta. Ailments as neuralgia, meningitis, headache, chorea, cerebrities, apoplexy, paralysis and mania were classified as diseases of the brain and nervous system. It was not until the conflict entered its final year that the number of soldiers suffering from mania or temporary insanity caused much concern. The patient was taken before a justice of the peace and in accordance with his decision might be sent to an asylum. Finally, Louisiana Hospital in Richmond was used for the treatment of all troops of unsound minds. Assistant Surgeon Parker resigned on January 11, 1864, and became a citizen physician. In October he filled a military post at Montgomery, Alabama, and then he was assigned to field duty with the 19th Virginia Battalion. Assistant Surgeon Parker was captured by the enemy in early February, 1865, and imprisoned at Johnson's Island until June 20 when he was released upon taking the oath of allegiance. On June 24 he reported to the provost marshal at Salisbury and two days later at the Union camp at Snow Hill. He hung out his shingle at Girdletree in Worcester County, then settled in Stockton where he met with success in his chosen occupation. In 1872 Dr. Parker was elected to the state legislature representing his county in the House of Delegates.

FRANCIS W. PATTERSON 1835-

Born in Saulsbury, Connecticut, and moving to Ohio at the age of two, he attended Ohio Wesleyan University, then was a pupil in medicine of his uncle, Dr. R. J. Patterson. He later attended Starling Medical College for two years and took a third course at the Medical College of Ohio. In 1859 he began practice at Elyria but that same year moved to Jackson, Mississippi, to work at the State Lunatic Asylum. He enlisted after the state withdrew but his military career as a private didn't last long. By September of 1861 he was an assistant surgeon at Camp Pickens near Manassas. On July 3, 1862, Assistant Surgeon Patterson was to report to General Lee's army for duty with the 25th Georgia Volunteers. Six days later he was promoted to surgeon. Many times Surgeon Patterson was surrounded by casualties as he operated. They were lying upon the ground awaiting their turn with patience, some dead and some dying but the majority with painful wounds of the extremities. The operating table was a tail gate of a wagon, the communion table of a church, or a door laid upon barrels or boxes. These makeshift operating tables were slimy with blood and as fast as one patient was removed another took his place to be anesthetized by the merciful chloroform and undergo the necessary surgical treatment. The soldiers all appeared to bear their wounds cheerfully and it was only now and then when the knife cut deep that a smothered groan revealed the sharp pang of pain. When the lamented end finally came Surgeon Patterson surrendered at Appomattox Court House. In 1865 he settled in Catonsville where he practiced for several years; gradually withdrawing he devoted himself to farming and raising stock. In 1886 he became United States inspector of contagious disease in animals doing extensive investigation of bovine tuberculosis.

HENRY McEWEN PETTIT, JR. 1836-1913

He was born in Cumberland and raised in Frederick. Graduating from Frederick College he went to Philadelphia to study medicine in a drug store and after two years he went to Pittsburgh working as a pharmacist. When peace was shattered he returned to Frederick then enlisted into Zarvona's Maryland Zouaves and when their celebrated commander, Colonel Richard Thomas, was captured the first company was ordered to the 47th Virginia Infantry and became Company H. After their twelve months term was concluded in July 1862 they were sent to the Arkansas Battalion where private Pettit was made a prisoner. On November 18, he was exchanged from Fort McHenry and on December 19 was appointed a hospital steward at Petersburg. Hospital Steward Pettit, after duty at Howard Grove Infirmary, was then sent to General Hospital No. 8 at Raleigh. On March 15, 1864, he was transferred to Atlanta where he received a favorable recommendation from the medical board. Assistant Surgeon Pettit was involved in hospital construction until reassigned to Pettigrew Infirmary. The medical officers, in spite of their deficiencies as we see them today, labored courageously with all their knowledge, experience and skill to administer to the Confederate soldiers who were relentlessly stalked by the enemy and disease. They were up against almost overwhelming problems created by lack of supplies and military situations but the sublime conduct of the wounded excited their most profound admiration. A sentiment of genuine heroism pervaded the Southern boys; each regarded himself as a martyr to a holy cause and seemed proud of the blood which he had shed for it, and even of the death which he was called upon to die in its behalf. Under the spell of this patriotic enthusiasm there was no murmuring because of the want of comforts and conveniences or over the fate which condemned them to suffering and to mutilation or at the decree which banished them from home and friends. With brave hearts and smiling countenances they met their doom, sustained by the reflection that they had done their duty as men and soldiers, for they bled for the land which they loved. After the close of the war, Assistant Surgeon Pettit remained at Raleigh to care for the sick and wounded who were not well enough to go home where he contracted typhoid fever. He returned to Frederick near the end of June, 1865, going to Baltimore for several years then to Carrollton, Missouri. The practice of medicine became repugnant and he farmed for a short while, then went into the drug business.

Maple field surgeon's pocket kit 7 1/2" x 3" stamped "Gemrig Phila." on the aneurism hook, forceps, director, bone spreader and three scalpels.

G. Craig Caba collection

AARON SNOWDEN PIGGOT 1822-1869

Aaron was born in Philadelphia, attended Yale College finishing in the class of 1841, the University of Maryland Medical College class of 1844. Settling in the Monumental City he was a professor of anatomy and physiology in the Washington Medical University in 1848. Dr. Piggot was a member of a number of medical societies and literature societies while producing a number of literary works. He went to the assistance of the stars and bars as a military medicine man. On July 19, 1862, he was assigned to duty at the C.S. laboratory of the medical purveying department in Richmond. Being advanced to the rank of surgeon on September 26, 1862, he was superintendent of all the apothecaries and chemists. This pharmaceutical laboratory was established to manufacture and prepare various medicines. There was no lack of materials for the construction of apparatus such as drug grinding mills, steam distillation apparatus, and contrivances for the production of high-grade alcohol from corn whiskey. Medical supplies such as opium, morphine and quinine that were smuggled into Richmond through the blockade were examined and diluted in this laboratory. Indigenous and other products manufactured at the depot were also examined closely, hence the laboratory served for both pharmaceutical manufacturing and as analytical control station. On November 10, 1863, Surgeon Piggot was relieved and assigned to duty in charge of the new pharmaceutical laboratory to be erected near Lincolnton, North Carolina. Not only did he establish and oversee this new facility but also attended patients at the Lincolnton Hospital. This laboratory manufactured and produced many substitutes made from native roots and herbs. Surgeon Piggot was paroled at Lincolnton on July 19, 1865, and returned to his home where he became professor of chemistry at the Baltimore College of Dental Surgery at the University of Maryland in 1865. He was known as a thorough scientist in his specialty of chemistry and was equally at home in any and every part of the field of literature with a brilliant pen.

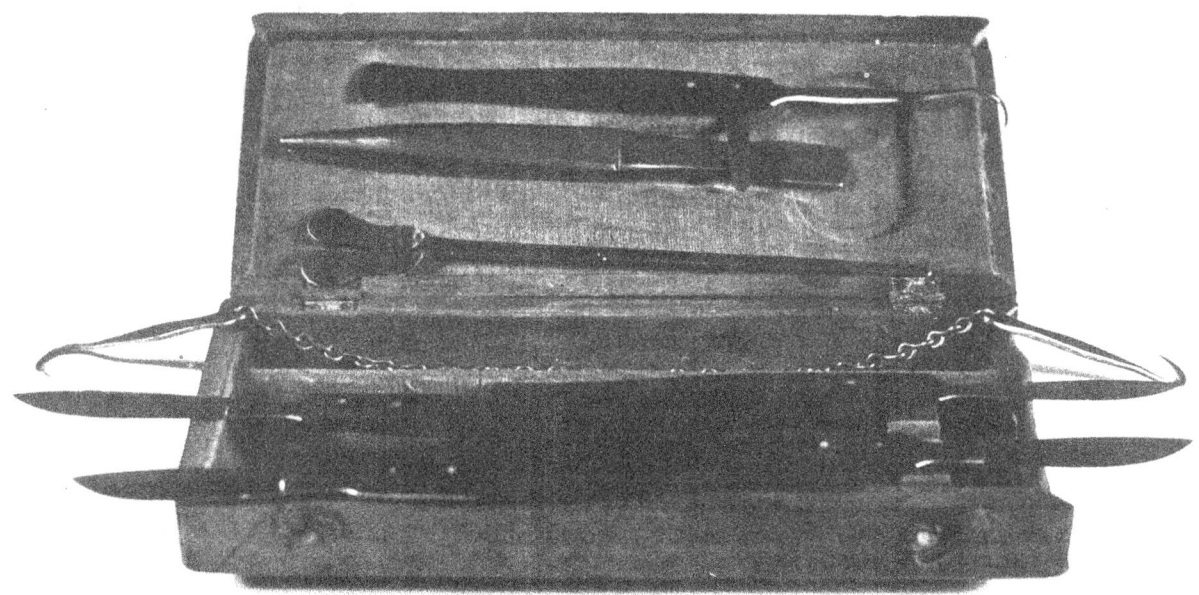

JOHN WILLIAM PITTS 1842-1910

Born in Berlin, son of Dr. Hillary R. Pitts, he was a graduate of Buckingham Academy and the University of Virginia as he studied medicine at the elbow of his father until the fiery hatred was upon the land. He enlisted on May 25, 1862, with his brother Marylanders in Company K 1st Virginia Cavalry. On the 27th of June, 1863, General J. E. B. Stuart, with three brigades of horsemen, crossed into this state at Rector's Crossroads and the next day near Rockville they captured one hundred and twenty-five supply wagons. In the late afternoon of June 29 the Southern Cavalry skirmished with Federal forces at Westminster in route to Gettysburg. The following day Private Pitts was taken captive near the town and sent to Fort McHenry and then Fort Delaware and exchanged at City Point on July 31. He returned to his unit and after General Stuart's death at Yellow Tavern Company K was transferred to the 1st Maryland Cavalry of the Maryland Line. In August of 1864 he went before the physicians composing the examining board and was a successful candidate. Assistant Surgeon Pitts was in hospital service in Richmond for the next eight months. He returned to his home in Worcester County but couldn't practice medicine so he enrolled in the medical school of the University of Pennsylvania, periodically returning to keep abreast of medical advances by doing postgraduate work. Dr. Pitts was not only a valued citizen in a professional way but also as a public servant. He was a member of the county school board, mayor of Berlin when the town was incorporated in 1896, Captain of the Bond Light Horse Cavalry, president of the Wicomico and Pocomoke Railroad, vice-president of the Calvin B. Taylor Banking Company and served in the state Legislature.

RICHARD POTTS 1828-1866

Potts was born at Fountain Rock estate near Frederick. He received his medical doctor's degree from the University of Pennsylvania in 1851 and was in the therapeutic work at Frederick for two years. On September 16, 1853, he became an assistant surgeon in the U. S. Army serving in the western territories, and devoted his spare time to ornithology. Assistant Surgeon Potts followed the majority of the officers from our state in the old army by resigning on May 7, 1861, and seventeen days later received the same rank in the C.S.A. On May 27 he was to report to General Beauregard at Corinth, Mississippi, and on July 9 he was assigned to General Polk at Memphis. Although just an assistant surgeon, twenty-three days later he was made medical director of Department No. 2. On November 13 Medical Director Potts was befittingly promoted and ordered to Bragg's command. By July, 1862, he was appointed medical purveyor by the Medical Department at Jackson, Mississippi, to obtain and distribute medical supplies. He required $300,000 for the quarter ending September 30. Congress had forbade the exportation of cotton to the North but cotton was eagerly sought by the Union and the Confederates were in need of many items. Surgeon General Moore sent Medical Purveyor Potts to Montgomery about Christmas 1862 in charge of all trade with the enemy on the Mississippi. Not only did he encounter competition from other purveyors anxious to share in the trade but he was hampered by a general lack of co-ordination among the Richmond authorities. Medical Purveyor Potts' internal trade and smuggling was centered around Memphis during the Federal occupation from 1862-1865. "Memphis", declared one Union General in May 1864, "has been of more value to the Southern Confederacy since it fell into Federal hands than Nassau." Evidence to support this astonishing remark is not lacking for two months later it was estimated by the Union Congressional Committee on the Conduct of the War "that between $20,000,000 and $30,000,000 worth of supplies had passed through this city into the hands of the Confederacy." Surgeon Potts was heavily engaged in contraband until the end came. He then went up river to practice in Memphis until he was overtaken by typhoid fever and was returned to Frederick for burial.

ALFRED H. POWELL 1831-

Born in Leesburg, Virginia, he was a student of Dr. A. R. Mott, attended the University of Virginia 1850-1851 and Jefferson Medical College in 1852. Starting his doctoring in Leesburg he became coroner and health officer. Dr. Powell became assistant surgeon on July 1, 1861, of the 16th Virginia Infantry when they were transferred from state service as the 26th Regiment into the C.S.A. On February 17, 1862, he was appointed surgeon and upon reorganization of the army in that spring he was reassigned to the 19th Virginia Infantry. While the assistant surgeon was giving first aid on the field of battle the regimental surgeon was in some protected place behind a hill or in a gully where the major surgery was performed. Later at the hospitals wounds were more carefully examined, foreign bodies probed and removed, splints readjusted, dressing reapplied but the majority of amputations were done in the field. The armies were constantly on the move, advancing, retreating, traverse and flank movements and many times it was a laborious and difficult task for the medical officers to stay with the combat. The equipment and supply of the medical corps were many times separated from the physicians, at which time he had to use his own ingenuity. The pliant bark of a tree made a good tourniquet, the juice of the great persimmon a stypic, a knitting needle with its point sharply bent a tenaculum, a pen knife a scalpel and bistoury. A common table fork with bent prong was used as a bone depresser for fractured skulls, and a piece of soft pine in place of a porcelain tipped probe to bring out the leaden ball. In April of 1864 Surgeon Powell was again sent to the 16th Virginia Infantry. By 1866 he was working in Baltimore and later became assistant coroner. He was also demonstrator and lecturer of anatomy and clinical surgery at Washington Medical University.

WILLIAM H. PUE

Completing his studies at the University of Maryland Medical College in 1860, he enlisted at Richmond on June 19, 1861, as a private in the Weston Guard, Company A Weston's Maryland Battalion which was soon transferred to the 1st Maryland Infantry as Company C. At Manassas he was on detached service assisting the medical men of this command and he stayed in this position until the regiment was mustered out. On July 1, 1862, he was appointed an acting assistant surgeon and in December was working in Chimborazo Hospital. On June 1, 1864, he was promoted and continued to treat his fellow soldiers at this, the most famous of the Confederate infirmaries which was erected on the Chimborazo Heights overlooking the James River. The Richmond institution was opened on October 11, 1861, and grew to a capacity of over eight thousand patients being the largest military hospital in the history of this continent. It contained five separate divisions, each division comprised thirty wards, each ward accommodated from forty to sixty patients. Altogether it comprised one hundred and fifty buildings, each one story, one hundred feet by thirty feet and a number of tents, pitched on the surrounding slopes. There were five soup houses, five icehouses, Russian bathhouses, a bakery capable of making ten thousand loaves of bread daily and a brewery in which four hundred kegs of beer were brewed at a time. The large farm known as "Tree Hill" pastured the two hundred cows and about four hundred goats and there were hospital vessels going to Lynchburg and Lexington to obtain the food that they couldn't grow. Chimborazo was an independent army post and was by far the most successful hospital either side had of restoring patients to health. The key reason for the great recovery rate was that this hospital center was constructed with ventilation given top priority and convalescing patients were assigned to tents in the open air. In April of 1864, Assistant Surgeon Pue was assigned to the 50th Georgia Infantry in field duty.

THOMAS CLOMAN PUGH 1837-1911

Dr. Pugh of Hamilton, North Carolina, completed his studies in 1857 at the medical school of the University of Pennsylvania. Going into Confederate service as an acting assistant surgeon he was ordered to report to General Lee's army on June 5, 1862. On August 16 he was appointed an assistant surgeon and in November he was sent to the General Hospital at Warrenton. When amputation was deemed unnecessary surgical intervention not infrequently consisted of resection, that is, the removal of joints with preservation of the extremities. Resection was found to be more successful when applied to the arms than when it concerned the legs. There was some feeling that resection, except for small joints, was questionable if not reprehensible surgery. It was pointed out that in addition to the often unfavorable physical conditions that surrounded the patients, many who recovered from the operation had little use of the extremity saved. Another argument against resection was that it kept the patient in the infirmary for a greater length of time than amputation and thereby exposed him for a longer period to tetanus, erysepelas, gangrene and pyaemia. After going into field service with the 17th North Carolina Infantry Assistant Surgeon Pugh was transferred to the 21st North Carolina Regiment in Kirkland's Brigade of Hoke's Division. With the dolefulness of the dejection of defeat he came to Baltimore to practice.

Large 10 1/2" x 18 1/2" x 10" maple medical chest of Assistant Surgeon William H. Pue which has a Samuel Sutherland label. Samuel Sutherland was a gunsmith for forty-seven years, first in Baltimore then in Richmond; during the war he served in the Local Defense at Libby Prison and Belle Isle. He had two sons associated with medicine who also returned to Baltimore, Joel B. Sutherland, a dentist who was a sergeant in the 25th Virginia Infantry, Company G and R. D. Camerson Sutherland, a general practitioner who was too young during the war.

William A. Albaugh III collection

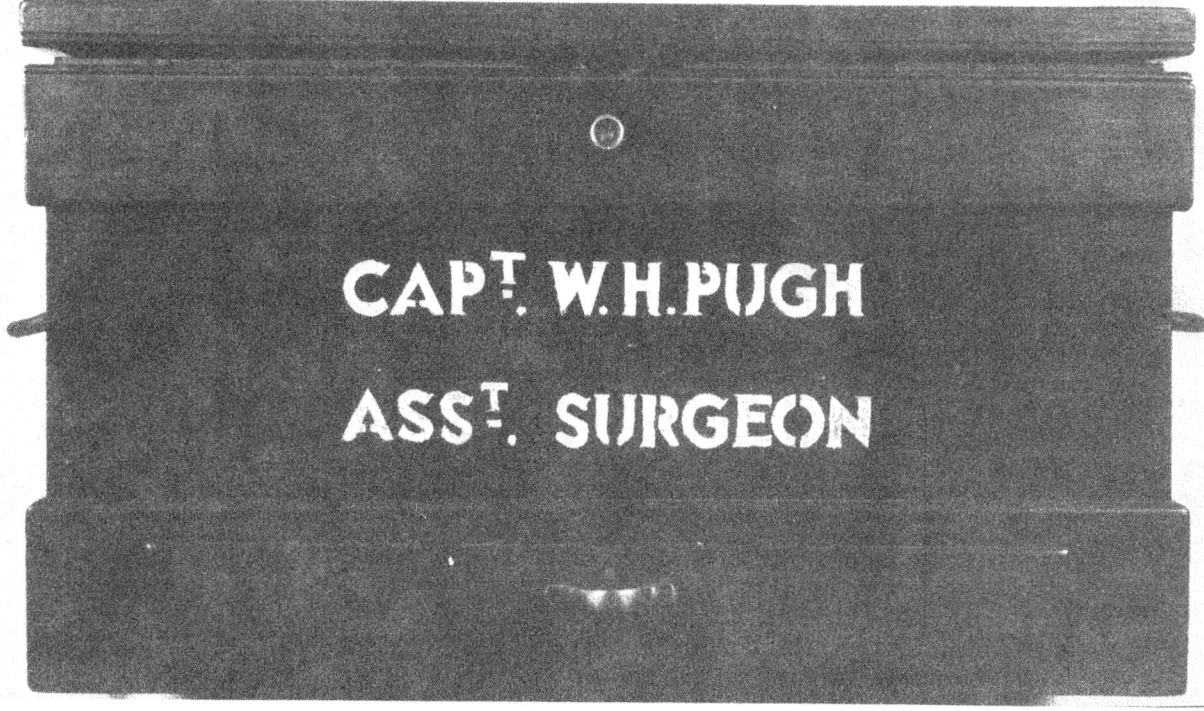

SAMUEL A. RABORG

A Baltimorean by birth, he was graduated from Georgetown University and the medical school of the University of Maryland in 1860. During the militia build-up in the third week of April, 1861, he was one of the thirty-six Baltimore practitioners who volunteered to serve the valiant citizens who resisted the Northern invasion. Their only treatment was for accidental and self-inflicted gunshot wounds that happened by chance. Crossing the Potomac he was appointed assistant surgeon on July 3, 1861, in the 1st Maryland Infantry. This regiment had fourteen medical doctors in its ranks and an abundance of military practitioners, so on August 27 he was ordered to the Culpeper General Hospital. On March 13, 1862, he was ordered to report to Coosawhatchie, South Carolina, for hospital duty at Atlanta. Assistant Surgeon Raborg was next sent to General Hospital No. 2 at Lynchburg. The enrollment of the University of Maryland Medical College fell from about 150 in 1860 to 100 in 1863; the country needed doctors and this school of medicine was one of the few colleges in the state that not only remained open but prospered. The faculty created a new up-to-date course in military surgery. The college hospital made a handsome profit from the war, the government used whatever facilities needed for United States wounded soldiers. They paid $5.00 per soldier per week, private patients could use what beds were available and were charged only $3.00. The medical professors were required to attend army patients. The College of Pharmacy maintained its antibellum enrollment of 20 to 30 students annually. The College of Dental Surgery saw enrollment fall from over 100 to less than 30. The Undergradute College barely struggled through the war; it produced 4 graduates in 1860, 3 in 1861, 1 in 1863, and 1 in 1866. The Agriculture College awarded 2 degrees in 1862, 2 in 1863, and 4 in 1864. Reconstruction was harder on the agricultural college than the war for there was only 1 graduate in the next eight years.

N. M. READ

Enlisting in defense of the Southern way of life, he was commissioned an assistant surgeon on July 1, 1861, in the C.S. Army. He was sent from the Richmond area hospitals to Culpeper Court House. On October 15, 1862, he resigned from the army and left Lynchburg Hospital where he was practicing. On November 26 he was appointed assistant surgeon in the C. S. Navy from Maryland and assigned to the Mississippi River defenses. After seeing service aboard the C.S.S. *Pontchartrain* as medical officer he was ordered to the naval batteries at Fort Hindman, Arkansas, where Dr. Read was captured on January 12, 1863, and sent to Sandusky prison. He was sent to Fort Monroe on May 1 to be exchanged but then he was confined in Fort McHenry until being reciprocated on November 21 at City Point. In matters of "pure medicine" not much appears at the first glance but a respectable number of developments, revelations and the like come into focus upon close inspection. Certainly great experience was gained in handling the knife and the saw. Many surgeons were becoming less squeamish in entering the chest, abdomen and even the cranial vault. Anesthesia had come into its own and its safe usefulness assured a better ratio of successful operations. The connection between disease and microbes was beginning to be appreciated by the growing ranks of avante garde as was the significance of antisepsis and asepsis. Orthopedics received quite a boost in the appearance of more practical splints and workable artificial limbs and the widespread use of plaster of paris. Interest was also beginning to show in methods of rehabilitation. Assistant Surgeon Read was sent to the Mobile Squadron and surrendered on May 4, 1865.

Top View

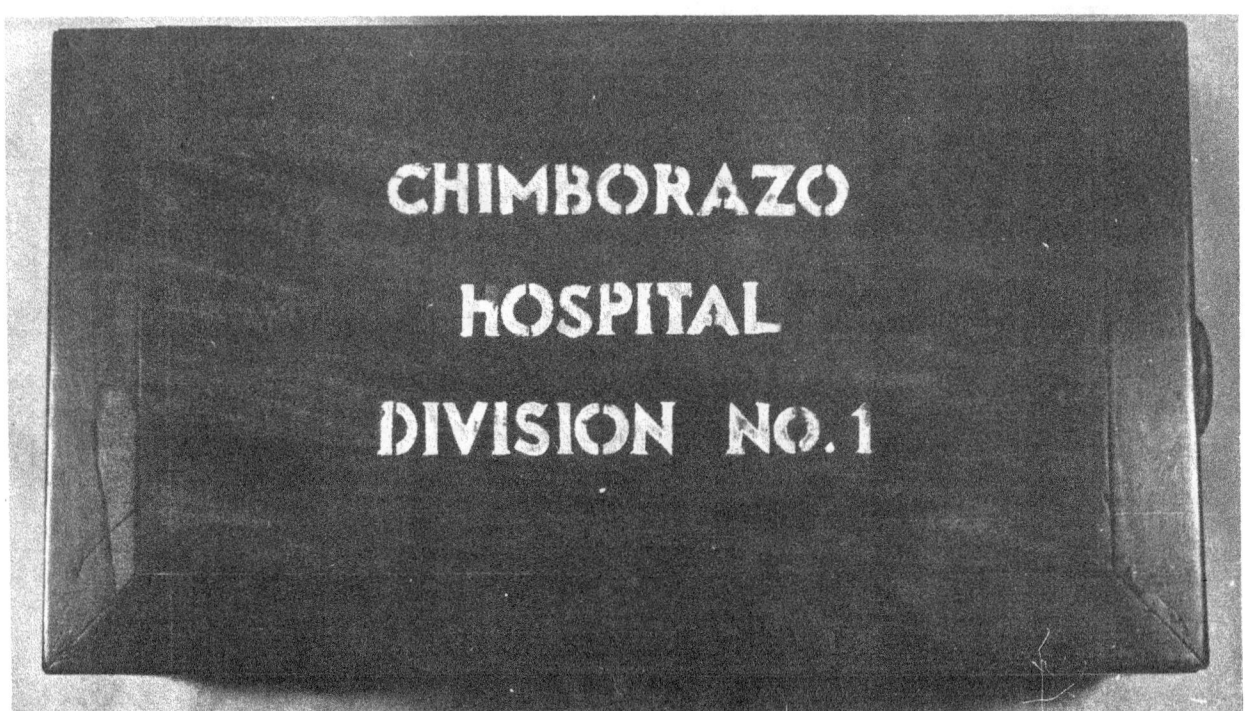

JOHN SUMMERFIELD RICHARDSON 1845-1862

Richardson was born at West River in Anne Arundel County. He was studying under Dr. Frank Rogers in the preceptor method when this vivacious youth saw humanity and compassion of the populous change to hostility and hatred. Those loyal to the star spangled banner, as the true sons of Maryland had seen it, had to whisper with voices without noise of those who were across the Potomac but it made their pulses throb. Young medical student Richardson left home for the army amidst gorgeous cheers and a mother's benediction to the wondrous lulling of a hero's dream. He enlisted as a private in Company H 51st Virginia Infantry on July 20, 1862, for the war and after a month's tour of duty he went before the medical officers comprising the army board and was accepted as an acting assistant surgeon, returning to his unit in the 23rd battalion in the Army of Western Virginia. As the Southern army approached Fayetteville near Gauley Bridge on September 10 young Dr. Richardson was killed as the enemy was driven from their works by sharp fighting. His blood had watered the same soil as had his forefathers who marched with General Washington, "Sanguis per libertate ne effundetur in vanitatae" no blood given for freedom was ever spent in vain.

JOSEPH HENRY RIDDICK -1865

Born in Hertford, North Carolina, of Maryland parentage, he was graduated from the medical school of Pennsylvania in the class of 1859. On July 1, 1861, he mustered in the 27th North Carolina Infantry Company F as a private for one year. Twenty-four days later he was detailed to hospital service as a steward with extra pay of 25 cents per day. After the conclusion of his enlistment Dr. Riddick furnished a substitute on August 1, 1862, and pursued his medical career apparently as a civilian. After the trumpets of war ceased their charging blare he came to Baltimore to practice.

R. SAMUEL RINGGOLD 1825-

The 1850 Baltimore census shows him as being born in our state and working as a male attendant at the Maryland Hospital. Making his way into the Confederacy he was appointed an assistant surgeon and on January 24, 1863, he was ordered to report to General S. Price's command in the Trans-Mississippi army. On December 7 he was rejected by the medical board and his name was dropped from the rolls. This day he was ordered to cease to be an officer along with five other physicians who were disclaimed. He apparently was successful with the military examining cabinet because in the spring of 1864 he was assistant surgeon of Charpenteer's Alabama Battery. After some large battles medical officer Ringgold spent several days and nights in constant operations and vigils. A distinguishing feature of all such field hospitals at such times was that ineffable smell of gore which no man who has passed through the experiences of four years of a bloody war can fail to recognize. By December of 1864 Assistant Surgeon Ringgold was in Temple's Battalion of Light Artillery in the Department of the Gulf. He appears on the rolls of prisoners of war on May 19, 1865, at Grenada, Mississippi.

WILLIAM H. ROBBINS 1839-1863

Robbins obtained his medical certificate from the University of Maryland in 1860 and started his apprenticeship in Baltimore. He was one of the early Southerners to retaliate for the blush upon the cheek, leaving soon after the Pratt Street massacre, from hill to hill, from creek to creek, Potomac calls to Chesapeake. Dr. Robbins enlisted on April 25, 1861, as a private in the Lancaster Greys which became Company H 40th Virginia Infantry. At the end of a year's enlistment he mustered out as a corporal and soon reenlisted but was appointed acting assistant surgeon. At 5 in the afternoon of May 2, 1863, a magnificent rainbow sprang its prismatic arch across the western sky near Chancellorsville. Jackson ordered an advance. Hooker's right was cooking supper and unconscious of the Confederates as they routed the panic stricken Federals. As the opposition was speedily brushed away the pursuit was hot; as the twilight closed the troops were entangled in the forest and Acting Assistant Surgeon Robbins was killed. Noblest of martyrs fell in a glorious fight, and by night had died to save the cause of truth and right. The dreams of loved ones, of home, of triumph and of prospective accomplishments that came in subconcious at night were no more, for his great eternal reward where all former events are understood but to mortals he was "semper paratus, semper fidelis," always ready, always faithful.

FENWICK ROBERTSON 1911-

Completing his medical profession training in 1854 at the University of Maryland, he started his practice at Kingston in Somerset County. With a vitalness of esteem to counteract that forceful encroachment of private liberties he relinquished his livelihood. He came into the Confederacy in the spring of 1863 and on May 17 was appointed acting assistant surgeon in General Hospital No. 13 in Richmond. His next tour of duty placed him in Jackson Infirmary. Armies have always had their malingerers and that of the Confederacy was no exception. Medical officers referred frequently to in correspondence of those goldbricks who had no other disease than want of heart which medicine and regimen would not cure. Some men suffered so much from battlesickness and shell fever that they shot themselves in the hand or prevented their wounds from healing. Physicians were warned by regulations to be cautious in granting disability certificates to soldiers who had not been under their care for sometime. A general order dated July 8, 1863, recommended that as far as practicable able-bodied hospital employees fit for field service be relieved by soldiers unfit for such duty. All able-bodied white men between the ages of 17 and 45 could not be retained in any capacity but were to be turned over to the conscript officer. Charges continued to be made that infirmaries were filled with troops able to undergo field service and the need for manpower was so great that in early fall of 1864 the Secretary of War sent an examining commission of doctors to hospitals with authority to return all patients fit for duty. In September Dr. Robertson became an assistant surgeon, again sent to General Hospital No. 13 where there medical officers labored with a ratio of seventy or eighty patients. After the beleagued city fell he continued to administer to the war torn wounded in Richmond until November of 1865 when he returned to Kingston. Dr. Robertson was a member of the Society Of The Army And Navy Of The Confederate States In The State Of Maryland. On October 5, 1897, he entered the Maryland Line Confederate Soldiers Home in Pikesville and is buried on Confederate Hill in Loudon Park Cemetery.

THOMAS J. ROGERS

Receiving his therapy commission as an assistant surgeon on April 4, 1863, and in October, at the reorganization of the army, he was sent to the 3rd Maryland Artillery in the Army of Tennessee. This battery was elated to have Assistant Surgeon Rogers, a brother of the "Black and Gold State," assigned to them. In addition while at Decatur they received seventy-five new men, horses, equipment and cannon for a new four-gun battery. Within the next month they also had twenty-seven transfers to them which recuperated the vast losses of the past two years in Louisiana and Mississippi. On November 27, the command proceeded to Sugar Valley and went into winter quarters; here the officers built a cabin and experienced a delightful change. They were joined by fifteen volunteer recruits and drilled twice a day. On the 7th of May the 3rd Maryland Artillery was ordered to the front and to the seven fellow officers who shared the little cabin devastation would strike in the next twelve months. Assistant Surgeon Rogers would treat two who were wounded, two were captured and he buried two others. As the weary battery dragged on this medical officer performed a dual role, not only of disease and wounds of his men but maladies of the stock which was essential to the command. The horses suffered from an epidemic of cartarrh according to this physician and there were no remedies available in the army, so separation of diseased stock was employed. This disease was produced by the want of proper feed; what was being fed was considered bad. Things did not improve as men, horses, mules and guns faded away. After Mobile was evacuated on April 11, 1865, the cannoneers with their guns were conveyed to Meridian, Mississippi. On May 4 they surrendered with General R. Taylor and on May 10 Dr. Rogers was paroled.

CHARLES A. RUTLEDGE

Coming from Harford County he was not in favor of breaking up the Union by secession but when sides had to be taken, his enthusiasm led him into the Confederate medical corps. On December 2, 1862, Acting Assistant Surgeon Rutledge was ordered to report to Atlanta. 1864 found him near Baldwin, Florida, and on May 25 Assistant Surgeon Rutledge was assigned to Medical Director W. A. Carrington in the capital city. Primary operations where amputations were involved were those amputated within twenty-four hours after the wound was received before inflamation and its results had ensued. Primary amputations had a much more favorable prognosis than secondary amputations. This was due to a soldier's weakened state from loss of blood, exposure, shock and the small, unnourishing meals he received in the hospitals which usually left his system in a declining state. The mortality rate was over 60% of the secondary amputations performed by Southern physicians. Assistant Surgeon Rutledge was sent to General Hospital No. 1 at Lynchburg in June and by October he was transferred to Warrenton General Hospital. January 26, 1865, found him working in the Richmond area hospitals and upon the evacuation he went to Greensboro where he was paroled. Returning to Harford County he practiced at Taylor.

Dental surgeon's 6" x 3½" kit, red leather box with dark blue interior and unique hidden mirror in the lid. Carved ivory handles on bone chisel, utility knife and spatula, sealer, curette, sealer, and lancer.

G. Craig Caba collection

ALEXANDER IGNATIUS JENKINS SEMMES 1828-1898

Alexander was born in Maryland and was the grandson of Captain Thomas Jenkins of Revolutionary War fame. He received his A.B. in the Georgetown University, class of 1847 and his M.D. from the same institution, class of 1850. After studying in Paris he proceeded to New Orleans and was resident physician at Charity Hospital. His brother also resided there and became attorney general of Louisiana, then a delegate in the Confederate Congress. Dr. Semmes first joined the army on June 19, 1861, and on July 4 was appointed surgeon in Richmond's Jackson Hospital. He was sent to the General Hospital at Culpeper Court House and then back to the capital city in the infirmary known as Camp Winder. On Febraury 12, 1862, he was assigned to field duty with the 8th Louisiana Infantry. By November 12, Surgeon Semmes was detailed as a member of the army medical board. On February 7, 1863, he was relieved from duty with the Louisianians and temporarily became a hospital inspector. He was transferred back to Jackson Infirmary on July 20, 1863. On July 6, 1864, General Jubal Early's cavalrymen crossed in this state near Sharpsburg. The next afternoon General Bradley T. Johnson opened an engagement to capture Frederick, which was being reinforced only to have it cancelled. Not until July 9 was the battle of Monocacy fought with the Federal army losing 1,600 men while the South suffered 700 casualties. General Johnson's cavalry brigade and the Baltimore Light Artillery were dispatched to Point Lookout to free the 17,000 Confederate prisoners of war and rejoin General Early at Bladensburg while he captured Washington. Lieutenant Colonel Harry Gilmor with the 1st and 2nd Maryland Cavalries raided the Baltimore area. Due to the disastrous delay of two days before Frederick, Washington was reinforced and General Early recalled General Johnson before reaching St. Mary's County, thus the capital and prisoners were saved. In this year Surgeon Semmes worked in two other Richmond hospitals, Stuart's and Louisiana. In 1865 all records show him as senior member of the medical examining board at Jackson Hospital and a member of the Richmond board of survey. After the withdrawal he remained in the city and was captured at Jackson Infirmary, then paroled on April 16. He practiced medicine back in New Orleans, then Savannah where he taught physiology at the Savannah Medical College. In 1878 Dr. Semmes was ordained a priest in the Roman Catholic Church and gave up medicine. By 1886 Father Semmes was president of Pio Nono College in Macon. After five years, because of poor health, he relinquished his post and was chaplain to the Sisters of St. Joseph in Sharon, Georgia.

HENRY C. SCOTT

Scott won his M.D. degree in 1857 from the University of Maryland and the city directories show him as a general practitioner in Baltimore. He was one of the early martyrs to cast his fate with the Southland, enlisting as a private on May 17, 1861, in Company A Weston's Battalion. Dr. Scott was one of six Maryland physicians in the ranks of the Weston Guard and there were eight doctors included in this study that marched with Weston's Battalion. This first company of Weston Guard was transferred to the 1st Maryland Infantry as Company C. Dr. Scott was appointed corporal on September 1 and marched with Springfield musket on his shoulder until mustered out when his enlistment of one year expired. He then became a contract surgeon working for the government until May 3, 1863, when he was appointed an acting assistant surgeon. He was soon promoted, while continuing his skill in Jackson Hospital. No words can do justice to the uncomplaining nature of the Southern wounded. The unfortunate victims bore the infliction as they had borne everything else painful—with calm patience and indifference to suffering. Whether lying in the infirmary wasted by disease or burning up with fever, torn with wounds or sinking from debility a sonorous groan was seldom heard. Jackson Hospital, located about two miles above Richmond, was opened in the summer of 1863 and was the third largest institution behind Chimborazo and Winder Its wooden barracks were able to accommodate twenty-five hundred patients and had water closets, two large icehouses, a large bakery, gardens and sixty cows. An official of the United States Sanitary Commission at the close of the war made the following report: "Jackson Hospital, as established and conducted by the rebels was excellent; in some respects few military hospitals of our own surpass it. It was excellent in its general plan of organization; in its location and its arrangement of buildings; in its administration; in its thorough policing; in the exceeding cleanliness of its bedding and in the very liberal provision made by the Rebel Government for the Hospital Fund." Assistant Surgeon Scott was captured on April 3, 1865, in Richmond.

EDWARD B. SIMPSON 1839-1898

Born and raised at Libertytown in Frederick County he pursued the medical profession. His tender college times at the University of Maryland were stained by the tyrant's chain and those sent to Fort McHenry's dungeons. Surrendering his books and shining future he departed for Harper's Ferry where on May 23, 1861, he joined the C.S.A. and enlisted as a private in Company G of the 1st Maryland Infantry. Jennie and Hettie Cary, two sisters of devoted Southern sympathizers of Baltimore and their cousin, Constance, had experimented with several melodies to the heroic poem of James Ryder Randall entitled 'My Maryland." They came to Fairfax Court House and on a July evening at the headquarters of General P. Beauregard, near a flickering campfire, they introduced this new heart throbbing song. They were surrounded in the darkness by thousands; observers record that the cheers at the end of this great anthem were deafening and there was nothing but misty eyes in the 1st Maryland. In the fall of 1862, Dr. Simpson reenlisted again as a private in Company B 35th Virginia Cavalry. This dashing troop was composed of men from along the Potomac River area and led by Lije White, a distinguished lieutenant colonel from Montgomery County. There were many from the "Old Line State" in this troop of "comanches", as they were surnamed, but Company B had been organized in Montgomery County and was composed entirely of Marylanders. On July 15, 1864, the 35th Virginia Cavalry was camped near Blackwater when they learned that "old Jubal Early" was thundering at the gates of Washington and "handsome Harry Gilmor" was riding around Baltimore. Every man immediately became possessed with an almost insane desire to go to him; during the night, without leave or license, Company B did go and left scarcely a Marylander to tell the tale of what had become of his companions. With Maryland opened and their homes inside Confederate lines they intended to get to them. When they returned their sympathizing commander did not punish them, but trooper Simpson was not with them for he had accepted a position at Jackson Hospital in Richmond as acting assistant surgeon. His brother George R. Simpson had also come into the army and was a corporal of Company D 1st Maryland Cavalry. After the war, Dr. Simpson returned to Libertytown to practice and in 1881 relocated at Harney in Carroll County.

WILLIAM BEVERLEY SINCLAIR 1819-1895

William was a son of Commodore Arthur Sinclair of the old navy. The character of this sketch graduated from Mt. St. Mary's College at Emmitsburg and the University of Pennsylvania Medical College in 1838. After working in Baltimore for several years he was appointed an assistant surgeon in the navy. He received an appointment as assistant surgeon on June 10, 1861, in the Provisional Navy of the Confederate States. Many times surgical operations of naval medical officers were conducted under adverse conditions. Sometimes flat boats or barges were used as hospitals. The removal of a limb was a serious procedure but the time involved was surprisingly short. The anesthesia was administered by a cone or handkerchief and after ten breaths the patient was under. A tourniquet was applied to stop the blood flow and a proportionate size scalpel used to cut through the skin and muscle; usually a triangular cut was utilized exposing the bone. A commensurable size saw was used, then the arteries were tied off, the triangular pieces of skin brought together and sutured. A bandage with plaster of paris was applied to stop the venous drainage. Not more than ten minutes had elapsed when this semi-concious amputee was removed from the table and another poor sailor placed upon it. Medical Surgeon Sinclair was under the command of Commodore George Nichols Hollins at naval stations on the coast of Louisiana, Richmond and Wilmington. Commodore Hollins was a native "Free Stater" who received many commendations in his long, prosperous naval career which started at the age of fifteen in 1814. Dr. Sinclair was paroled at Richmond on May 4, 1865; returning to Baltimore he was active in the medical profession until the mid-1880s when he curtailed his work.

ALLEN P. SMITH

While a medical student at the University of Maryland, he answered the call of Mayor Brown for volunteer physicians to serve the Baltimore militia during the military build-up just after April 19, 1861. Of the thirty-six doctors that came forward to compose the Baltimore Civilian Militia Surgical Staff ten would run the blockade and join the Southern army to serve the suffering Confederates. After receiving his diploma Dr. Smith was reunited in the Confederacy with Edward Warren, Alexander Clendenin, Richard Emory, William B. Everett, Arthur L. Foreman, Robert J. Freeman, Charles E. V. Nickerson, Samuel A. Raborg, and Ignatius Davis Thompson who had been on the Monumental City's surgical staff. Acting Assistant Surgeon Smith was apointed in the C.S.A. and sent to the Florida district where, in February of 1862, he was ordered to report to the army medical board. By September of that year, he was an assistant surgeon with the 21st Florida Cavalry. He now experienced first hand the unbelievable wholesale agony that Americans never really dreamed could happen through the four hideous years. He labored with the same tender compassion, not caring which color of uniform, friend or prisoner, but ministered to all because they were his brethren under the Hippocratic creed. As he worked with twisted flesh, shattered bones, burning fevers, rampant pus and oozing raw stumps, Assistant Surgeon Smith saw the terrible swift scalpel become less terrible and dank, dirty, dingy pesthouses of the past evolve into a pavilion of hope.

ARTHUR MONTEITH SNOWDEN 1869-

Arthur was born and raised in Prince George's County, graduating from Georgetown University and from the University of Maryland Medical College in 1855. He established his life's vocation at Laurel until the furious storm of the War Between the States led him into the fray. Not being a politician, a militarian, nor an orator to lead people, Dr. Snowden was passive to a commitment but not in sympathy. His temperament and a large lion heart continued to pulsate the audacious blood that binds Southern brethren together as he went into the Southern lines during the Antietam campaign. There were six Snowdens from Laurel and seven others from Prince George's County that volunteered in the Confederate Army. Dr. Snowden enlisted on October 1, 1862, as a private trooper in the 14th Virginia Cavalry Company D. This unit subsequently became Company K 15th Virginia Cavalry. By March of 1863 he was appointed acting assistant surgeon in the General Hospital at Staunton. Infection of wounds was the chief cause of mortality that followed upon the heels of operative surgery and the surgical fevers—tetanus, erysepilas, hospital gangrene and pyaemia were greatly feared. Wartime surgeons never determined the causes of these ailments although some did reach the conclusion that soldiers tainted with scurvy or in a run-down condition were very susceptible. Idiopathic tetanus was actually an incorrect designation, very little distinction was made on medical records between idiopathic and traumatic erysipelas. Those with infection were usually isolated where they could receive an abundance of fresh air. Sesquichloride of iron acquired a wide reputation as a specific and quinine was often prescribed as a tonic to counter the febrile condition often present. Dr. Snowden then turned to contract practice as things worsened and the beleaguered Confederacy drew to a close.

DeWILTON SNOWDEN 1838-1897

Giving his address as Laurel, he went to Georgetown University, finishing with the class of 1834. Proceeding to Baltimore and the University of Maryland he graduated in medicine in 1840. During the wearisome times of 1860 he was not using his medical training but was the special transportation clerk in the auditor's office of the national post office department in Washington. In April, 1861, Dr. Snowden resigned his position; leaving his wife and children he became affiliated to the glorious Confederate quest. Going to Richmond he applied for a clerkship or a surgeon's post in the newly formed government. Positions in the infant administration were eagerly sought by those from the states that had separated; there was a substantial number of Marylanders who held eminent berths and they were often rebuked as outsiders. An appointment did not readily come so the impatient doctor enlisted on July 9 in the 1st Maryland Artillery. This private cannoneer served in the flying battery until July 18, 1862, when he was given a medical discharge, being unfit for duty due to an indirect inguinal hernia. He could not return to his home nor could he continue as a noncombatant when man power was so critical. On October 2 he received a regimental appointment to the 2nd Maryland Infantry as assistant surgeon. Many times Assistant Surgeon Snowden inwardly wept when he saw the glared battle-stained faces of his brothers after their courageous charge on July 2 for possession of Culp's Hill. They had come to Gettysburg five hundred strong but left behind two hundred in hostile country. Their commander, General George Hume Steuart of Baltimore, was heartbroken at their disaster; wringing his hands great tears sealing down his bronzed weather-beaten cheeks he repeatedly exclaimed "my poor boys—my poor boys". Assistant Surgeon Snowden was with this regiment until the shattered ranks reached Appomattox where he surrendered on April 9, 1865. Starting for his home he was illegally arrested on June 14 upon reaching Washington. His medical profession was from Laurel but his membership in the United Confederate Veterans was in the Hyattsville camp.

Large brass mortar and pestle flanked by two large dark blue and white glass jars which contained anthelmintum ointment of unguentum zinc oxide and unguentum hydrargyri.
Maryland Pharmaceutical Association collection

SAMUEL E. SPALDING

As one of the area's wealthiest residents, this aristocrat from Leonardtown apparently did not go to medical school until later in life. He received a medical diploma from Georgetown University in 1858. During the war his loyalty was for sovereign rights and he was actively involved in smuggling and espionage. His son, Basil William Spaulding, ran away from school at the age of seventeen in 1862. He rode with McNeill's Rangers whose command toward the conclusion of the combat was under Lieutenant Colonel Harry Gilmor of the 2nd Maryland Cavalry. There were many arrests in Southern Maryland as vast amounts of contraband were smuggled across the Potomac. Living under a despotism against one's ideals and beliefs they were willing and justified in spite of the consequences. On February 17, 1863, a squad of Federals were sent to the home of Dr. Spalding to arrest him. The doctor had crossed the river the previous night with a boatload of goods and upon returning was told by compatriots of the seizure orders. Without saying goodbye to his family he immediately again ran the blockade and sought sanctuary in Southern lines. The contribution he then gave to this beloved country was that of a gladiator in the 59th Virginia Infantry where he became a 2nd lieutenant in Company F.

HARRY H. STEINER

On June 22, 1839, he was commissioned an assistant surgeon in the United States Army and his birthplace was given as Maryland. Dr. Steiner resigned on January 31, 1852, and returned to civilian life. On July 19, 1861, he received a commission as a surgeon of Georgia troops in the C.S.A. No other records can be found.

WILLIAM FREDERICK STEUART 1815-1889

Born in Anne Arundel County, he obtained his medical degree at the University of Maryland in 1839 and settled in Baltimore. Dr. Steuart was the medical practitioner for the 5th Maryland militia for a number of years. On April 15, 1861, he was advanced to lieutenant colonel of the 5th Regiment and served during the militia resistance of the next month. Departing for the South he ran where the brave dare not go, to a war that would have him bear with unbearable sorrow. As an assistant surgeon in line duty he had to work when his arms were too weary to fight for the right without question or a glorious quest for the world would be better for this. He had two sons who were also officers in the C.S.A., William F., Jr., of ordnance and Harry A. of the 3rd Maryland Artillery who was killed while attempting to escape from Old Capital Prison. Many times the wounded were unloaded from the ambulances beside of the road where the air and the soldiers were saturated with dust and dirt. The overworked operating surgeon's hands went from patient to patient with merely a wipe in between. A sponge was thrust in one incision after another after only being squeezed out. Their instruments were rinsed off in a muddy creek after the surgery for the day was completed and replaced in their velvet-lined cases to contaminate again. The bandages many times were any type of material that was available. But the physician cannot be condemned for what he didn't know or understand; he simply did the best he could with the knowledge he had at hand. On July 10, 1863, a star of major was placed on the collar of Surgeon Steuart and five days later he was ordered to Medical Director L. Guild's office. On November 24 he was sent to the board of examiners of conscripts for the Fifth Congressional District of Virginia. Dr. Steuart turned from a lost cause to an incomplete family and a broken fortune. He was resident physician at the Physicians Quarantine or Marine Hospital in Baltimore from 1874 to 1876.

Surgeon William Frederick Steuart
William A. Albaugh III collection

B. A. TARR

This Confederate physician had a written endorsement on the virtues of a periodical datelined Baltimore which appeared in the Volume I *Confederate Veterans Magazine* in June 1893. Prior to the war, there were two practitioners, Charles E. Tarr, and William H. Tarr, working in our state; however, no military references can be found on any of the three.

THOMAS PRICE TEMPLE 1830-1891

Temple was born in Hanover County, Virginia, and received his M.D. at Jefferson Medical College in 1850. He started his practice in Richmond but soon moved to Baltimore and by 1855 Dr. Temple was located in Harford County. Turning all his endeavor in the defense of the Southland he was appointed an assistant surgeon in the Richmond hospitals. On May 28, 1862, he was released from the 4th Georgia Hospital in the capital and ordered to report to General J. E. Johnston. On July 16 he was promoted to surgeon and on August 27 was assigned to the 61st Virginia Infantry. On February 17, 1863, he was dropped from the rolls and ceased all duty. The special orders of March 24 ordered him to resume his duties with the 53rd Virginia Infantry. In August Surgeon Temple was surgeon-in-charge of Howard Grove Hospital on the Mechanicsville Turnpike one mile from Richmond. On April 23, 1864, he was transferred to the medical director's office of the Army of Northern Virginia. Being paroled at Appomattox Court House on April 10, 1865, Dr. Temple returned to this state and was established at Clarksville until 1874 when he practiced at Ellicott City. He was a member of the Maryland Medical and Chirurgical Faculty. To the casual peruser of medicine the general impression seems to be that the Rebellion's greatest calamity brought forth little more than hundreds of fetid hospitals and thousands of botched amputations. Yet a serious student simply cannot come away from this fascinating segment of American history without sensing the ingredients of an incipient revolution in the medical picture of the period. For the first time medical and surgical activities were systematically reported, and analyzed and post-mortems were seriously studied. In pharmacy there was a giant step from the mortar and pestle to the elaborate coils and kettles of the pharmaceutical industry. The professions of dentistry and embalming were firmly stabilized. The virtues of cleanliness brought about the initiation of public health on a national level. In paramedical matters the modern hospital and female nurses were rapidly incorporated into civilian institutions.

I. PENBROKE THOM 1828-

Born in Culpeper County, Virginia, he was an alumnus of the University of Virginia. In 1846 he was commissioned a 2nd lieutenant in the 11th Infantry Regiment and upon his return from Mexico he studied medicine at Jefferson Medical College in Philadelphia. In 1852 he was appointed an assistant surgeon in the navy where after four years he resigned and settled in Baltimore. When the call to arms came, Dr. Thom tendered his services to the South. On May 17, 1861, he was made a captain of the Irish Battalion by the governor of Virginia. With his past military training he was a warrior first, a physician second. At Kernstown on March 23, 1862, while leading Company C 1st Battalion Virginia Infantry he was wounded in the right hand, right leg, and over the heart by a ball that penetrated through a testament in his pocket, while his sword was also hit with minnie balls and was bent double. A concussion caused him to be left on the field for dead, but afterwards was found to be alive and was cared for. On sufficiently recovering he was detailed at Richmond forwarding troops and supplies down the James River. After being ordered to Mississippi, in December he was compelled to resign because of his health. Going to Niagara by a blockade runner from Charleston in 1863 Dr. Thom was reunited with his family and went to England until returning to Baltimore in 1866. In the fall of 1877 he was elected to the city council and was a member of the Society Of The Army And Navy And The Veterans Association of Washington.

JACOB G. THOMAS 1827-1894

Jacob G. was the son of Dr. Robert L. Thomas and was licensed as a medical doctor in 1848. He was a cousin of Dr. John Hanson Thomas, a member of the 1861 state Legislature who was arrested and made a political prisoner for several months. Dr. Jacob G. Thomas graduated from the Washington Medical University, returned to his home in Frederick County and was elected 1st lieutenant in the Adamstown Minute Men. This Southern militia company was officered by two other medical practitioners, Drs. Robert H. E. Boteler and William Hilleary Johnson who would serve in the C.S.A. The character of this sketch came to the assistance of the Southern banner and in May of 1862 was serving as surgeon of the 39th Alabama Infantry. On November 2, he was relieved and transferred to the Richmond area hospitals. The army of General R. E. Lee in Virginia surrendered April 9, that of General J. E. Johnston in North Carolina April 26, that of General R. Taylor in Mississippi May 4, that of General E. K. Smith west of the Mississippi River May 26, 1865. All other organized bodies of Confederate troops, as well as individual soldiers wherever they happened to be, reported to the nearest officer in command of Union troops, surrendered and received their paroles. The surrender of the Confederate armies was universal and sincere; there was no reservation in this relinquishment, no desire or effort to continue the struggle as guerrillas or otherwise. There was complete submission to the authority of the United States government by all in official and private capacities. President Jefferson Davis, Vice-President A. H. Stephens and other distinguished citizens of various parts of the South were immediately arrested and imprisoned. Dr. Thomas went west, then practiced at Columbus, Ohio, before returning to Frederick County.

THOMAS H. THOMAS

Thomas H. of Cambridge carefully made his way through the Federal blockade to the Confederacy and was enrolled on September 15, 1862, in the 31st North Carolina Infantry. As a private in the ranks of Company C, Dr. Thomas experienced the hardships of an enlisted man and was captured on June 1, 1864, at Gaines Farm. He was held at Elmira, New York and Point Lookout before being exchanged on March 2, 1865. He proceeded to Wayside Hospital or General No. 9 at Richmond where he signed his parole as assistant surgeon. Foremost in the minds of the undernourished, ragged Maryland lads who laid down their arms when the end came was of those loved ones at home and on returning to their domiciles to rehabilitate their lives they were molested and imprisoned. These were legally paroled Confederate soldiers who had taken the oath of allegiance and complied with all the surrender terms but resolutions by the Unconditional Unionists were passed refusing to let the returning ex-Confederates join the loyal Maryland communities. Large numbers of Southern veterans were arrested; a very great many fearing criminal prosecution for service in the Confederacy did not return to Maryland. Others were clandestinely hidden in their former homes by parents or relatives until the witch-hunt subsided. Most were released after a few weeks and the general populace gladly renewed acquaintances with a friendly hand. The military authorities then allowed former residents to return within the state but ex-rebels who had not resided here were refused. Those professional veterans such as doctors, lawyers, and teachers were not allowed to practice.

IGNATIUS DAVIS THOMPSON 1836-1881

A Frederick Countian by birth, he received his M.D. degree from the University of Maryland in 1861. After being a volunteer on the Baltimore Militia surgical staff during the first invasion of the state his heartstrings pulled him to the bleeding Southland; freedom was worshipped next to Thee, so to the flaunting flags of the Southern Cross he had to go. Dr. Thompson was a successful applicant before the tenured physicians of the army medical board and on June 2, 1863, was ordained an assistant surgeon. He was ordered to Ladies Relief Hospital at Lynchburg. This is one of the few infirmaries in the Confederacy where there was anything close to an abundance of appetizing food on the hospital tables. As the finale approached, rising prices and the inability of the subsistence department to furnish adequate stores had a detrimental effect on the diet of the incapacitated. The extreme illegal wrongs of the Unconditional Unionists to the ex-Confederate soldiers in this state, as to their returning, were soon corrected. The Republican party could no longer accuse Maryland of liberalism in its franchise laws. Only 10,000 out of 40,000 in Baltimore could vote and only 35,000 out of 95,000 in the entire state were entitled, two-thirds of the voters were disenfranchised. It was not until April 2, 1866, nearly a year after Appomattox, that the state was released from the heel of Federal military control. Marylanders began once again to breathe a little more freely but even then the native Unionists were still in control. Dr. Thompson made his home in Baltimore and was a member of the Junior Physicians to Mount Hope Retreat for the Insane. Later he was surgeon of the North Central, Baltimore and Potomac, and Western Maryland Railroads.

Large 18" x 8" surgeon's amputation kit in walnut case with green velvet interior. All eighteen instruments marked "Evans" of England, tourniquet handle, tourniquet, bone saw, bougie's, three amputation knives, aneurism needle, spring-catch forceps, two ivory probes, lancet, small saw, needles, and trocar.
                          G. Craig Caba collection

MEREDITH THOMPSON

Dr. Thompson is listed as a surgeon in the Confederate Record Book - Marylanders Who Were In The Confederate Service Outside Of Maryland Commands, which is located in the manuscript collection of the Maryland Historical Society.

ALEXANDER TINSLEY 1832-

Alexander was born in York County, Virginia, receiving his college degrees from William and Mary, Medical College of Virginia, University of Virginia and the University of New York. In 1858 he was house surgeon at Brooklyn City Hospital; a year later Dr. Tinsley was on Coast Survey and by 1860 he was doctoring in Baltimore. He was one of the sincere liberty lovers who came without hesitation to sustain a true cause by applying for and receiving an appointment to the C.S.A. Medical Corps on September 13, 1861. Assistant Surgeon Tinsley was assigned to Gwathney Hospital in Richmond. In early 1862 he was sent to field duty with the 16th Virginia Infantry. Upon reorganization in May he was transferred to the 6th Virginia Regiment. His next infirmary service was at Richmond's General Hospital No. 9 and Williamsburg Hospital. The complete collapse of the Confederate government was typical of the total exhaustion and prostration of the South in the almost superhuman effort she had made to sustain herself against great odds in men and resources which the United States had brought to bear against her. The Confederacy had enlisted an army of a little over 700,000 men and had fought over 2,200 battles. The struggle was almost over every foot of the Southland. She lost the flower of her youth in the death of 325,000 men from the casualties of this awesome war, and more were disabled and ruined in health. The paroled soldiers returned to find their homes desolate; they were disheartened and humiliated. They had nothing at hand with which to begin life anew except their knowledege, experience and the brave hearts which had carried them through four years of war that ended in the defeat of a cause they knew as just and honorable. Dr. Tinsley returned to the Paris of the South to practice and was a member of the Medical and Chirurgical Faculty of Maryland. As long as Federal forces held Maryland the well known rebel influence was neutralized by military disfranchisement. In January of 1866 the humiliated majority who were disqualified organized behind Montgomery Blair to regain their franchise. This movement brought the call of an anti-registry law asking eloquently for removal of disabilities because the war was over and Maryland needed the services of her own sons.

WILLIAM MASON TURNER 1836-1877

He earned his Ph.D. in 1855 at Brown University and was graduated from the University of Pennsylvania in 1858 as an M.D. and was a member of the Maryland Medical and Chirurgical Faculty in the latter part of the 1850's. Following his unrestrainable spirit to aid in re-establishing the divine rights of justice, he crossed the Potomac and was appointed an assistant surgeon in the Confederate Army on July 19, 1861. On April 1, 1862, he was commissioned in the C.S. Navy and assigned to Norfolk as assistant medical director. After a month's service, he resigned this post and was stationed aboard the steamer *Chicora*. In June 1864, records show Assistant Surgeon Turner serving in the Naval Battalion at Drewry's Bluff. He became a prisoner of war after the evacuation of Richmond when he was captured with his patients at Jackson Hospital on April 3, 1865. The Naval Battalion, under the auspicious Marylander Rear Admiral Raphael Semmes, destroyed their James River Squadron, evacuated the position at Drewry's Bluff on April 2 and withdrew. This brigade of soldiers and marines was fighting with muskets as infantry. At Saylor's Creek, General Ewell's depleted ranks were enveloped and when the Naval Brigade was informed of their surrender they continued the fighting fifteen minutes. The naval colors were the last to come down. Then when the bravery of the sailors was observed along the Federal line and when they did surrender the enemy cheered them long and vigorously. The Navy had given the final proof of the strength of their convictions which enrolled them under the Southern colors and of their unswerving fidelity in the painful hour of irresistible disaster. Assistant Surgeon Turner was turned over to the provost marshal on April 14 and not released until June 20. He had sought every opportunity to strike a blow for the liberties he loved, he unflinchingly obeyed orders leading him into combat, and his unsmirching record proved him a loyal patriot. The Republican minority in the Maryland Legislature could see its position slipping fast. The only hope for these radicals was for Congress to enfranchise the blacks to swamp the rebel majority.

HENRY W. TURPIN 1848-

His medical course at Georgetown University was interrupted when he joined the 2nd Maryland Cavalry as they returned from their ride around Baltimore in early September of 1864. By fall he was serving as a clerk in the Richmond Medical Department. Going before the Examining Board he was accepted as an acting assistant in December and ordered to Bristol, Tennessee. Acting Assistant Surgeon Turpin was captured before reaching his destination and exchanged at Fort Monroe on January 8, 1865. Going again to the Army of the West he surrendered at Greenville on April 30 and signed an oath of allegiance in Nashville. The general statistics of this disastrous war compute that there were 2,500 engagements by name and a number of minor skirmishes. The U.S. put 2,773,304 enlisted men in their armies and the C.S. under 800,000. Upon the supposition that these numbers represented many reenlistments, deductions must be made from both sides, still leaving the disparity of about four Federal soldiers to one Confederate actually employed in the war. One million soldiers and seamen of the two armies and navies suffered death or permanent disability, not including those who died after the surrender from wounds and diseases contracted in service. There were also thousands of survivors who suffered from the effects of this hard warfare. To the expenses of the two national governments in maintaining war, add the expenditures of all the states and many municipalities. Include in the amount the actual destruction of property of which no reliable data can be obtained. Taking all data into calculation the sum total of the cost has been reasonably computed at $10,000,000,000. Dr. Turpin worked in Washington, D.C. until he joined other veterans on April 3, 1917, in the Maryland Line Confederate Soldiers Home.

WILLIAM WARD VIRDIN, JR. 1829-1897

Born, raised and educated in North Carolina, he began to work in the field of medicine in the Monumental City. He was exposed to more Unionist malice than he could bear so even though he wasn't in sympathy with secession he was forced to become its adversary. He was appointed assistant surgeon of the 63rd North Carolina Infantry but did not hold this position long. A number of medical officers were weeded out by the examining boards. Some proved unequal to the duties of their station, others were found incompetent from carelessness and neglect, while in some instances there was gross ignorance of the very elements of the profession. There can scarcely be any credit side to a civil war, not one foot of territory was added and no material advantages were gained as a result of this struggle between the sections. Yet there were some inestimable results: states secession ceased to be a remedy for redress of popular grievances, the statehood of the state put in peril first by coercion and next by reconstruction stood its trial by both adversaries and at last triumphed at a judgment bar which recognized the legal and political worth of the Constitution. The solidness of all the states under the great instrument which formed it would be demonstrated to be better than a division of sections as the years went by and the Constitution was worth fighting for against those who would subvert it. The fighting qualities of the American soldiers were sublime; the steadiness, celerity, courage and intelligent obedience to orders were made apparent to all nations. The prominence of a United States began to develop into a world power. Dr. Virdin returned to Maryland but, not being able to practice, he took medical courses at the University of Maryland and then continued his professional knowledge abilities at Lapidum in Harford County where he was a member of the Medical and Chirurgical Faculty.

EDMUND RHETT WALKER 1836-1891

Born in Beaufort, South Carolina, he completed his study at the College of Columbia in 1856 and the medical course at the University of Virginia in 1857. In 1858 Dr. Walker was employed on the staff of Bellevue Hospital until 1860 when he came to the Eastern Shore of our state. In May of 1862, he was practicing in the South Carolina Hospital at Petersburg and on August 16 he was officially appointed as an assistant surgeon in the Provincial Army of the Confederate States. On July 2, 1863, he was ordered to report to Surgeon L. Guild of the Army of Northern Virginia and was assigned to the 8th South

Red velvet, brass bound, 9 1/2" x 13 1/2" walnut dental case of ivory handled cavity filling gold foil instruments and above a piece of soft gold foil leaf. The bottom contains five extraction forceps and an elevator all marked "Daily & Arnold Balto."
Baltimore College of Dental Surgery Museum

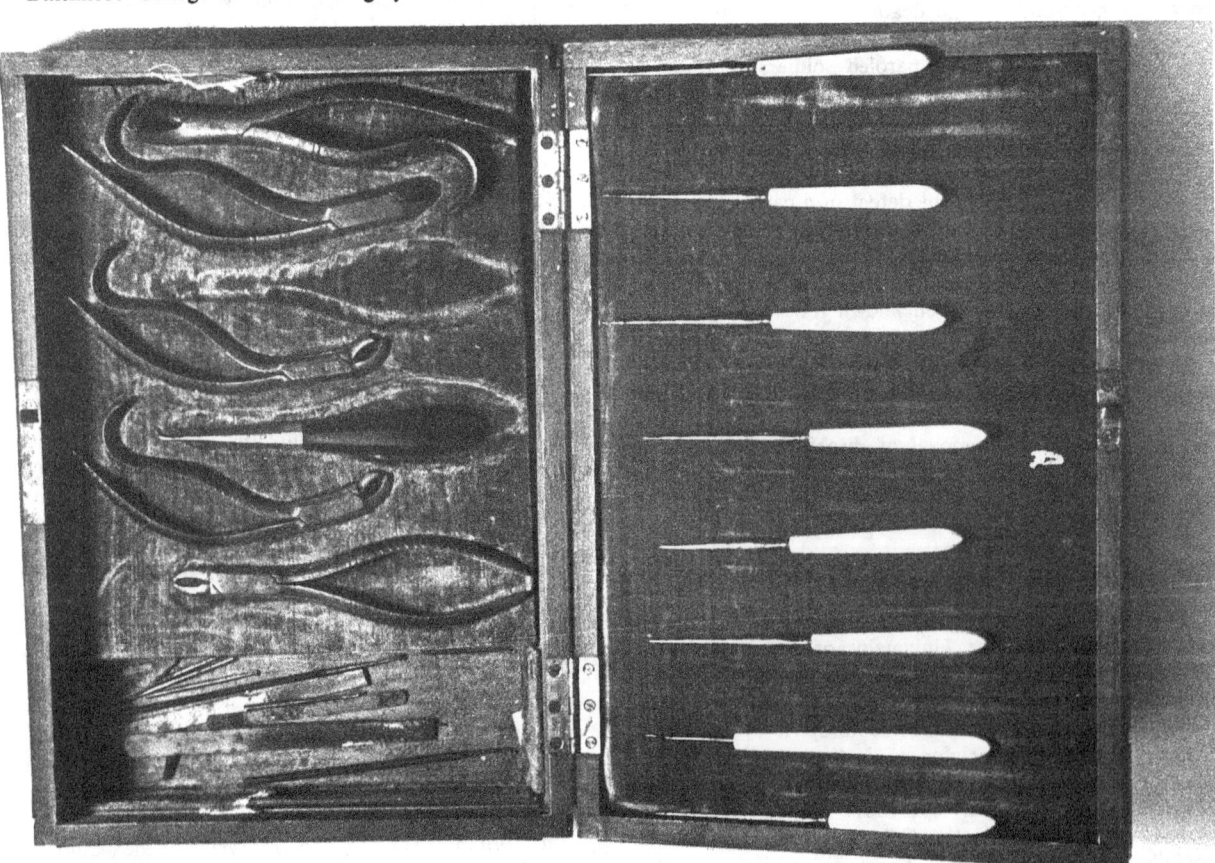

Carolina Volunteers. Assistant Surgeon Walker's next service was in the hospital at Charlottesville. After the war he settled in Baltimore where he became coroner. In 1876 Dr. Walker was professor of surgery at Washington Medical University for two years, afterward attending physician at Church Home and Infirmary. It was not until January 24, 1867, our state legislature restored to full citizenship, with the right to vote and hold office, all persons who were deprived by the provisions contained in the fourth section of the state constitution. On March 23 they also repealed the act which required an oath of allegiance. Local radical Unionists cried for universal suffrage to disqualify impoverished traitors and to continue to confine the ballot only to the loyal. They demanded to know why the Federal government which saved Maryland from treason would permit traitors to rule the state and ruin them.

HIRAM H. WALKER

Completing the two year medical course at the University of Maryland when the nation was plagued with the state of war, he went to Montgomery where he received a captain's commission in the Confederate Army. Dr. Walker was assigned to the 40th Virginia Infantry in December of 1861 as a lieutenant colonel. On April 23, 1862, this regiment was reorganized and he was not elected by the men to his former capacity so he resigned on August 26. Dr. Walker then chose to follow his medical training outside of the military. Our border state passed through the same ordeal of adjustment between war and peace and had a more revengeful and vindictive experience than some of the states which were reconstructed by Congress. The population sympathized with the defeated people of the South but the minority upheld by the army of the Union was kept in power. Their legislation was bent on one purpose to retain themselves in power which they did by disfranchising all who were suspected of sympathizing with the South. Those of the North who were radical reconstructionists felt that the treason of Maryland, by the return of Southern leadership, was a horrible example of what secessionism in defeat could accomplish. The state militias had legislated out the the loyal officers and placed ex-rebel soldiers as leading officers. Thus the seceded states continued to suffer because of the rebellious acts of the return of local government by this border state.

Dental operative set of twelve ivory-handled instruments in a 5" x 6" cardboard case.
Baltimore College of Dental Surgery Museum

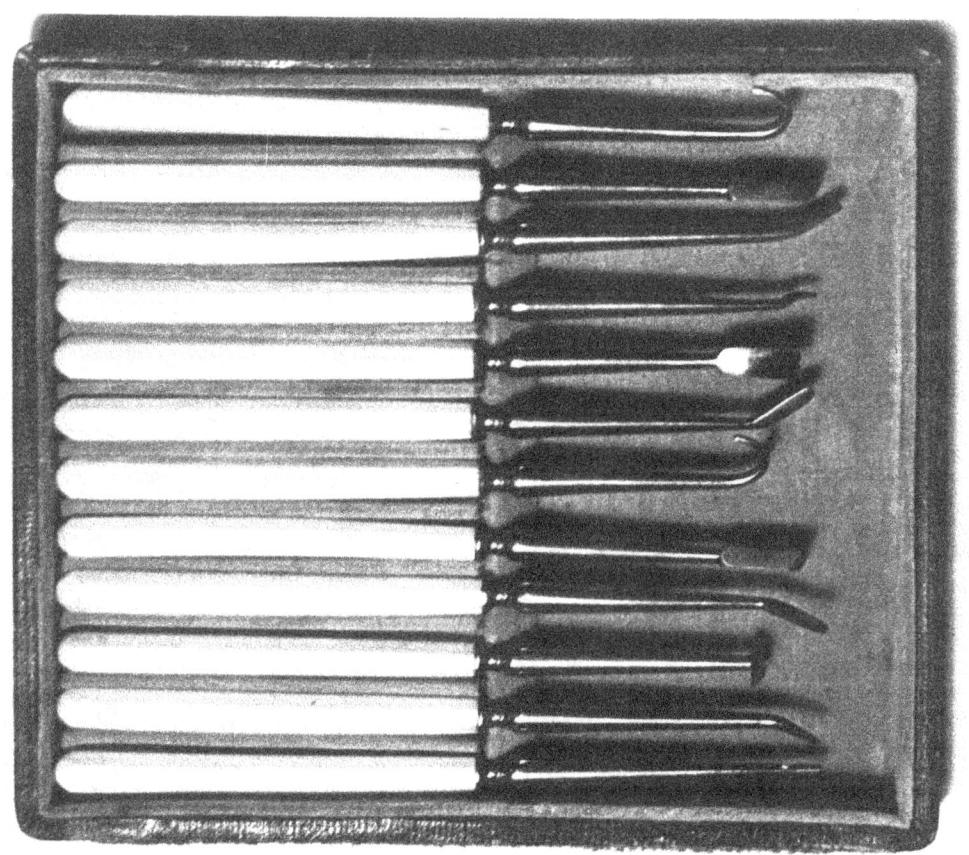

J. WILLIAM WALLS 1835-1881

Born at Harper's Ferry, he received his M.D. degree at Winchester Medical College, and came to Washington County for his chosen profession. After practicing in this state for four years, he accepted a position at his former alma mater as professor of anatomy and physiology in 1861. On November 16, he was appointed a surgeon in the Provincial Army of The Confederate States. By January 7, 1862, he signed papers as surgeon of the 10th Alabama Regiment. On June 16, he was relieved of this duty and sent to General T. J. Jackson commanding the valley district. By the end of September he was at Winchester's Senseney Hospital as surgeon-in-charge. On November 20, he was assigned to the headquarters of the First Brigade, First Division Jackson's Corps as senior surgeon. Senior Surgeon Walls was transferred in the fall of 1864 to Salisbury, North Carolina. Just after the new year of 1865, he was again with the Army of Virginia amidst the storm of shot and shell and the rattling crash of musketry with the 5th Virginia Infantry. After the remorseful end, he came to the city known as the Paris of the South and in 1867 Dr. Walls was professor of anatomy at the Washington Medical College in Baltimore. The terrible ordeal of reconstruction lasted for twelve years after the war ended. The statesmen of the Republican Party in control of the government were mad with absolute power to place those who had been slaves in charge of framing governments in the deep south. The carpet-baggers were a bird of prey, they lived only on corruption; coming from the Republican Party they sprang as naturally as maggots from putrefaction. Wherever the negroes gathered they were there like a leprous spot is seen and their cry, like the daughter of the horse leech, was always give us office. Without office they were nothing; with office they were a pest and public nuisance. Out of office, they were as beggars, but they grew rich till their eyes stuck out with fatness until the carcass was picked.

JAMES H. H. WARFIELD

Warfield was graduated from the Maryland Medical University of Baltimore in 1862 and immediately worked his way with assistance from the underground into the C.S.A. He was commissioned an acting assistant surgeon and was administering to the sick and wounded in the new General Hospital at Yorktown under Surgeon John Randolph Page. He can also be found in Poplar Lawn Hospital at Petersburg. The war had served as a catalyst for the state colleges in education by weakening classical aristocratic ideals and strengthening the force of unity, practicality and democracy. Most colleges hovered between defeat as proponents of the old and victorious renaissance as proponents of the new. The University of Maryland, Dr. Warfield's alma mater, prospered because of the professional schools in Baltimore, through their Southern loyalty and the non-functioning colleges further south attracted a large postwar enrollment. The Undergraduate College was closed and never reopened. The Agricultural College, after bankruptcy, was reestablished but for several years operated in the red as the other colleges, Medical, Dental and Pharmacy, flourished.

EDWARD WARREN 1828-1893

Born in Tyrrell County, North Carolina, he followed in his father's footsteps after he completed his studies in the medical department of the University of Pennsylvania in 1851. He had received his earlier education at the University of Virginia. After a year in the hospitals of Philadelphia he went to Paris and in 1857 became a member of the medical faculty of the University of Maryland filling the chair of Materia Medica. He was also editor of the *Baltimore Journal of Medicine*. When the dark war clouds broke upon the horizon in Baltimore on April 19, 1861, Dr. Warren tendered his abilities to city militia leaders and was appointed surgeon-in-chief of the municipal forces and organized a corps of surgeons, seizing all necessary instruments, appliances and stores. He was kept on military duty for a number of days while the entire city resounded with Southern martial music and glittered with uniforms and bayonets. During a momentary lull, anticipating subsequent trouble, he carried his family to Norfolk and returned immediately to the city for an impending emergency. The civilian militia was sufficient in men but sadly in need of arms. Dr. Warren was sent bearing letters to the governors of Virginia and North Carolina asking for one thousand stands of arms from each. His traveling companion happened to be Charles S. Winder of this state who had resigned a captaincy in the U. S. Army and was proceeding South to offer his sword to the Confederacy where he would yield his life as a brilliant general. Completing his mission, Dr. Warren was enroute to Baltimore when he learned that the Federal army had taken his city; his office was still open and he lost all of his professional possessions. Going to Raleigh he was made surgeon-in-chief of the North Carolina Navy at Portsmouth. After four months of uneventful service, he went to Richmond and obtained a position in Maryland Hospital in that city. Surgeon Warren was then ordered to report to the University of Virginia and after several months he was sent to Richmond where he was a member of the board of inspectors. On June 27, 1862, on the battlefield at Gaines Mills he was appointed medical inspector by General Lee. Surgeon Warren prepared a manual of military surgery entitled *An Epitome of Practical Surgery For Field and Hospital* of which there were several editions. In the summer of 1862, he became Surgeon General of North Carolina, a position he held until the war's end. He had hoped to return to resume his course of lectures at the University of Maryland with a triumphant army. After Gettysburg he was notified that his vacant chair would be filled because of his absence and it was evident to him after this battle that he would never return with a victorious army. Dr. Warren did return to Baltimore bereft of prosperity but he did secure the charter of a defunct school in 1867 reestablishing the Washington University Medical College in that city where he taught surgery. On April 2, 1873, he sailed for Egypt where he was chief surgeon on the staff of the Khedive. After several years, he practiced his profession in Paris until his death.

JULIUS B. WEEMS 1842-1865

Julius was able to subdue the passion of relinquishing his medical studies until his last term was completed. He was now ready to answer the strong appeal of his heart as he ran the blockade into the Confederate lines. He must have known the grave situation of the Confederacy but he had to try to right the un-rightable wrong, to dream the impossible dream, to beat the un-beatable foe. It was the glorious quest, no matter how hopeless, no matter how painful, to march into Hell for a heavenly cause with his last ounce of courage. Going before the medical examining committee he was appointed from Maryland as an acting assistant surgeon on October 5, 1864. He was to report to Surgeon F. W. Hancock in charge of Jackson Infirmary in Richmond and was assigned ward surgeon of the Fourth Division. Young Assistant Surgeon Weems had never even lanced a boil and now he was involved in life and death procedures. On December 5, he was unable to execute requirement number 52 of the surgeon general's current series due to a disability so he was relieved from Jackson Hospital. His orders were to report to Medical Director Kinlock at Charleston but while in route he was captured. Being exchanged he signed his parole in April 18, 1865, and received permission to go to his home in Baltimore where he died of consumption. The cost of war to the South was of a great magnitude but her citizens did not repine but slowly worked with a will to revoke all improper and corrupt legislation, to restore economy in public expenditures, to reduce taxation, to do away with useless offices and to rebuild the waste places. In May of 1872 Congress passed a general amnesty bill removing political disabilities from almost all citizens who had been disfranchised, still accepting those who had been officers in the judicial, military service of the Confederate States. The Supreme Court had rendered several decisions tending to recall Congress from its proneness to legislate beyond the limits of the Constitution. The negroes who could not resist being led to extremes in the hands of the masterful carpet-baggers now readily yielded to the will of the Southern Anglo-Saxons. Two-thirds of the wealth of the Southern people had been swept away but the struggle of Southern families during reconstruction under adverse political, social and commercial circumstances was the most remarkable feature in those dark days.

NELSON G. WEST 1832-1915

Forsaking his practice in Frederick County he followed his convictions of rightness and justice as he was lead to the Southern Confederacy. On February 5, 1862, he was ordained an assistant surgeon and saw field duty with the 1st Virginia Battalion of Cavalry. Upon reorganization on March 18, 1862, they became the 9th Regiment Virginia Cavalry. By that fall, Assistant Surgeon West was with the 7th Georgia Infantry, then transferred to the 2nd Georgia Infantry Regiment. He was stationed successively at Warrenton Hospital and Lovington Hospital. On July 21, 1864, he was administering in General Hospital No. 2 at Danville where on November 4 he was advanced to a surgeon. He was then assigned to the capital city in General Hospital No. 10 after a short term of field service in Longstreet's Corps. There was no immigration into the Southland, it had been looted after reconstruction and was in a prostrated condition, offering no invitation to capital which promised a prospective return. There were but few banks and Southern men had few friends among the great financiers anywhere. Spared of better times the people of the South had immigrated westward. The social fabric of the people had been uprooted and turned upside down. The great crime of slavery had been conquered but the deep Southland had before them the lamentable failure of their conquerors. The north maintained their bad blood by putting negro governments over the populace. The Anglo-Saxon people of the South began to realize again that their destinies had fallen into their own hands. They recalled the terrible ordeal through which they had passed, a fiery furnace as it were of devastating war, reconstruction and destruction of over fifteen years. Every true citizen realized the fearful conditions surrounding them to begin social, political and material life anew. A condition without a precedent in history confronted them. The people of the North were still hostile, suspicous, distrustful and watched them with vigilant eyes. They faced the future to apply their wisdom and statesmanship to the upbuilding of a new civilization, having to accept the thirteenth, fourteenth and fifteenth amendments to the Constitution.

THOMAS J. WHEEDEN -1888

Dr. Wheeden of Baltimore, accompanied a group of Confederate naval officers aboard the C.S. *Alar*. Off the Ushant French coast in April of 1863, the *Alar* approached a Scottish, iron screw steamer of 600 tons, burdened with a 200 horse power motor, at an appointed time. Here this new ship received her guns, ordnance stores and supplies. The Confederate flag was hoisted and she was formally put in commission as a C.S.S. man-of-war. The officers of the newly named *Georgia* came off the *Alar*, the ship's medical officer was Dr. Wheeden. On October 18, 1864, he was reexamined by the medical board, his appointment was from the state of Maryland and he was promoted to passed assistant surgeon. Later he can be found serving on the iron-clad *Richmond*, then with the James River batteries. After the cause could no longer be maintained he was performing his profession in Baltimore. After the war, he practiced in Brooklyn, New York. The period from 1885 to 1895 was the period of readjustment to normal conditions for the entire South; the people were really too busy in restoration and in making permanent their new born self-government to take any great interest in national affairs. The year 1895 was really the year when the North and South were again permanently cemented together in a broad national spirit. Feelings had been growing steadily since the inauguration of President Cleveland but now it bore substantial fruit. There were three prominent events of that year to emphasize fraternal feeling that encouraged and broadened the people below the Mason-Dixon Line in their attachment to the government. The first was the dedication of a monument at Chicago to the Confederate soldiers who died during the war in that prison. The money to build the monument was raised in that city, showing that they were again in heart and spirit one people. The dedication of the battlefield of Chickamauga had monuments erected out of the national treasury that were similar in every respect, equally honoring the valor of both armies as Americans rather than former foes. The Atlanta exposition demonstrated with what vigor the Southern people had progressed in material and industrial development.

WILLIAM McNIEL WHISTLER

A son of the late Major George W. Whistler of the old army, his uncle was the late general William Gitts McNiel. He was appointed an assistant surgeon in the Confederate Army on October 7, 1862. Until there was a dire need for medical officers many times it was extremely difficult for Maryland physicians to obtain an appointment. There were various high ranking officers from our state that were repeatedly recommended for promotion to general and were capable and deserving. Due to the fact that most "Free Staters" were absorbed into commands of other states and there were no Maryland divisions for them to command, the already seventeen flag ranked men were presiding over troops from other states. President Davis and Congress received protests that there were already two many generals from Maryland and their state troops should be presided over by their own flag ranked officers. In a letter of November 6, 1861, Dr. Whistler states that he left his home in Baltimore in May with his wife and came to Virginia to join the C.S.A. "Being a physician by profession I requested a medical position as the want of any military education disqualified me for any other office except to go into the ranks. All my attempts have been unsuccessful." Finally after seventeen months he was commissioned and assigned to Libby Prison Hospital, then at the Small Pox Hospital at Howard Grove. In January of 1863 he was transferred from General Hospital No. 25 at Richmond to the 22nd South Carolina Regiment. On July 21 he was ordered to Jackson Infirmary until February 7, 1864, when he was sent to administer to the local defense troops of Richmond.

ZEPHANIAH K. WILEY 1843-

He was born in North Carolina and was graduated from the University of Mississippi. On November 1, 1861, he enlisted as a private in Company C 1st Mississippi Cavalry. In May of 1863, he became a corporal and the following May a sergeant. By that fall in 1864 he was commissioned an acting assistant surgeon and sent to Punola County, Mississippi. He surrendered at Citronelle, Alabama, on May 19, 1865. Settling in Texas he became a clerk in the Williamson County Court House. Dr. Wiley attended medical lectures in St. Louis, then coming to Baltimore in 1872 he graduated from the College of Physicians and Surgeons in 1874. He turned around and started to teach at the above school; later he lectured at the Baltimore Medical College and Baltimore University where he became dean. The wonderful Maryland Southern women who were fabulous during the hostilities and afterward worked so feverishly to relieve the suffering of the Southern people now erected monuments. They were assisted by elderly and young men, maidens and children who acknowledged the valor and virtues of the Confederates' deathless fame. All shades of religion and politics were represented in the bazaars by the noble women of our state in 1885 and 1895 which collected $50,000. A third bazaar yielded $10,000 which was 1/3 the cost needed for the monument on Mt. Royal Street in Baltimore to the soldiers and sailors of this state in the C.S.A. which was erected in February of 1903. Also in this city is the large monument to the Confederate women of Maryland who in difficulty and danger regardless of self, fed the hungry, clothed the needy, nursed the wounded and comforted the dying. Monuments can be seen through the state that we may not forget the love for the thin gray line: two at Rockville, another in Montgomery County, in Easton, at Ellicott City, several in Frederick County and the massive Maryland's Tribute to Lee and Jackson in Wyman Park in Baltimore. In various cemeteries throughout the state Confederate monuments have been erected. Even outside of the state, in 1880 a life-size statue of a Maryland Confederate Infantryman was dedicated in the Maryland lot in the Stonewall Cemetery at Winchester and in 1886 a granite block on Culp's Hill at Gettysburg was erected.

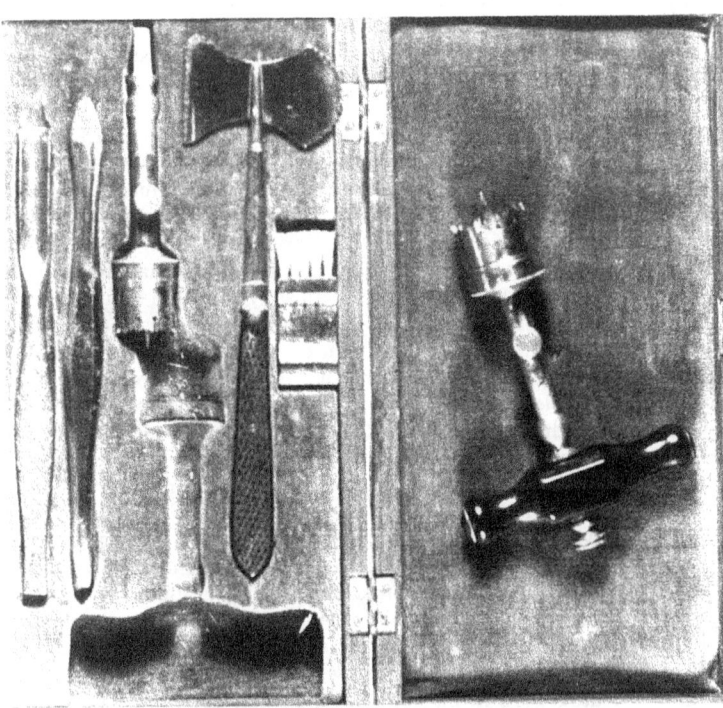

Walnut cased 5 1/2" x 9 3/4" red velvet lined treptin kit for operating on the cranium. The six instruments, 1" drill and handle in lid, brush, saw, 3/4" drill are all stamped "Lentz Phila."

G. Craig Caba collection

THOMAS H. WILLIAMS 1829-

Thomas was born in Dorchester County, and went to school at Washington Academy in Princess Anne and the University of Maryland Medical College, class of 1848. On March 2, 1849, he was commissioned assistant surgeon in the army and by 1857 Surgeon Williams was medical director of the army in Utah. When his state could not respond to the Union bayonets that held her he resigned on June 1, 1861; without selfish ambition he joined the C.S.A. On June 22 he was appointed a surgeon and ordered to report to General Beauregard at Manassas as medical director. As the first medical director of the Army of the Potomac he was busy in establishing the field medical corps. Upon reorganization of the army he continued his present duty as medical director of the Army of Northern Virginia. On June 6, 1862, Surgeon Williams was inspector of general hospitals at Petersburg, Danville, Farmville, Lynchburg, and Charlottesville. He established many of the large hospitals in Virginia except those at Richmond and Petersburg. By December 15, he was relieved and assigned to temporary duty as medical director of General G. W. Smith's command. On January 14, 1863, he was ordered to the surgeon general's office in Richmond where he was in charge of the Medical Purveyors Department until the city was evacuated. After engagements ended he returned to the Eastern Shore practicing in Cambridge and in 1898 Dr. Williams became a staff member of the United Charities Hospital.

Surgeon Thomas H. Williams
Daniel D. Hartzler collection

WILLIAM G. WILLIAMS 1837-1912

William was a spirited young man who was reared and educated in luxury just beginning his practice of medicine. He was diverted from absorption in this pursuit by throwing himself into the thick of the fray as an enlisted man. Dr. Williams sought out state friends and in the spring of 1862 joined the 12th Virginia Cavalry in Company F which was composed entirely of Marylanders. He fought with this conspicuous company until September 8 when his previous knowledge was required and he was made acting assistant surgeon. On June 13, 1863, he was officially appointed assistant surgeon of the 12th Virginia Cavalry. In the fall of 1864 Assistant Surgeon Williams was assigned to Washington Hospital at Abingdon where he labored valiantly for his fellow soldiers for the cause in which they believed. As soon as practical after the war, at the insistence of surviving Maryland Confederates, they removed the remains of their fellow soldiers in scattered graves from fence corners and hedge rows. They were properly buried in the state where they fell or returned to their known mother earth. This was done by private funds. In 1874 the Society Of The Army and Navy Of The Confederate States In The State Of Maryland spent $5,000 to remove the remains of Marylanders to the Confederate plot established in Baltimore's Loudon Park Cemetery. In 1870 the state legislature appropriated $3,000 to purchase two acres of land at Point Lookout to re-inter the prisoners who died there. In 1874 an additional $1,000 was provided to complete the cemetery. Again in 1870 $2,000 was used to remove the remains of Confederate dead in Frederick County to a section of Mount Olivet Cemetery. Also in the same year $5,000 was appropriated to remove the remains of Southerners who fell in the battles of South Mountain, Crampton's Gap, and Sharpsburg. Ten acres was purchased in Rose Hill Cemetery in Hagerstown.

PIERCE BUTLER WILSON, SR. 1836-1902

Educated at the Philadelphia College of Pharmacy, he received a doctor of medicine degree from the University of Pennsylvania and the University of Heidelburg in Germany and a Ph.D. from Princeton. He studied chemistry under Baron von Liebig and Bunsen in Germany. During the early part of the war he entered the Confederate Navy as an acting assistant surgeon. He was seriously wounded at the fall of New Orleans and received a discharge. On September 18, 1863, Dr. Wilson enlisted as a private in the Augusta Sharp Shooters which was Company G of the 1st Georgia Reserve Troops. In March of 1864, he was detailed to the Nitre and Mining Bureau where he continued to serve as a chemist in ordnance duty, superintending the making of gunpowder with the rank of major. After the war Dr. Wilson can be found working as a general practitioner in Baltimore and a chemical manufacturer. He was a member of the Society Of The Army And Navy Of The Confederate States In The State Of Maryland. The years had rolled by since the comrades in medicine, bound together by victory and defeat, by hardship and trial, pleasures and suffering, had made new lives for themselves. The stars that long ago looked down wonderingly upon fields bathed in blood now smiled upon hospitals where there were no wounded from man's weapons. The blazing sun that then hid his face in clouds of smoke cast up by booming cannons went down sorrowfully in the night where thousands lay torn by shot and shell. In this setting was a surgeon with only one candle and little medicine. Now the sun unfolded its rays over hill and valley and blue and gray physicians worked together for the glory of a reunited country. The prejudices and passions born and fostered by the War Between The States were turned into motivations in the fight against the recrudescence of disease.

Surgeon's brown leather bag 8" x 11" bottom is stamped "I.O.C.E." with outer and inner pockets. The top brass lock has a relief military eagle with shield which moves to release the lock and is surrounded by 32 stars.

G. Craig Caba collection

RICHARD H. WOODWARD -1865

Born in Middlesex County in Virginia and graduating from Georgetown University in 1844, he hung out his shingle in Carroll County until he offered his professional skill to those who bore the "Bonnie blue flag." On April 30, 1862, he was appointed an assistant surgeon and on August 8 he was to report to Surgeon William Hay at Staunton. He obtained a leave of forty days on September 8, 1864; however, twenty days later his furlough was cancelled and he was relieved from Staunton and ordered immediately to Charleston for duty at the prison hospital. The cherished ties of comradeship of those who survived in the state gathered to help those veterans who stood in need. The Society Of The Army And Navy Of The Confederate States In The State Of Maryland was organized in 1871 and numbered over a thousand veterans. There was also an auxiliary membership for those who were sympathetic to the cause but not in the Confederate service. The Association Of The Maryland Line was formed in 1880. The United Confederate Veterans was organized in 1895 in Nashville, Tennessee, with camps through the states. They credited Maryland with thirty-one organized United Confederate Veteran Camps and two in the District of Columbia. The author has been able to document fifteen of these camps and locations plus the two in Washington. He has also established eighteen chapters of the United Daughters Of The Confederacy. They were founded in 1894, also in Nashville, with headquarters in Richmond and the first in our area was the Baltimore Chapter No. 8 formed in 1895 which at one time had over eight hundred members and was the largest chapter in the country. Today the Maryland Division contains eight active chapters whose object is historical, educational, benevolent, and patriotic. They bestow Southern crosses of honor to military men of linteal Confederate descendants. They have various scholarship funds, one is for two of the state's medical schools. Confederate Memorial Day in Maryland is celebrated the closest Saturday to June 3, which is Jefferson Davis's birthday and the following day, Sunday, memorial services are commemorated at Arlington National Cemetery in Washington. Seven Sons Of Confederate Veterans organizations have been located and three chapters of Children Of The Confederacy, but only one is still active. The Society Of Confederate Mothers and Widows Of Baltimore was formed in 1876 and a Confederate Womens Home was established. In 1925 the organization moved the home from Baltimore to Catonsville. In 1879 the Frederick County Confederate Monumental and Memorial Association was organized and in 1895 The Baltimore Southern Exposition Management was established.

A. M. WOOLFOLK

This physician was the son of Austin Woolfolk, a well known slave dealer of Baltimore, but was reared on Bayou Grosse Tete in Talbot County. He entered heartily into the movement for Southern independence inspired by the illustrious services rendered by his ancestors in the cause of self-government. Dr. Woolfolk was commissioned surgeon of the 2nd Maryland Cavalry when it was formed in June of 1863. Under the leadership of Lieutenant Colonel Harry Gilmor "the band," as they were affectionately known, became distinguished for their daring and audacious ventures. Medical Officer Woolfolk did not trail the battalion in a wagon but armed with saddle bags of medicines and dressings and a colt revolver on his hip he could be found in the midst of the troopers ready as a coadjutant in combat or medical treatment. During the Baltimore-Washington campaign, as the Maryland cavaliers returned from their ride around Baltimore, Surgeon Woolfolk stopped to see his family. As he was trying to catch up to the battalion he was captured in Prince George's County on July 12, 1864. Being sent to the Old Capital Prison, then to Fort Delaware, he was exchanged with other Confederate surgeons on August 7. He returned to the troop of the 2nd Maryland Cavalry until amidst confusion and dismay the veil of silence was drawn and the most sanguine lost all hope for it was finished. As the calendars changed, the matured hearts of those who wore the gray turned in memory to those who struggled and fought together. With serene confidence they awaited the verdict of the Judge Of Nations. The motives of their hearts were actuated by the high sense of duty that sustained the Southerners. For they were led by the immortal Lee, peerless as a soldier and stainless as a gentleman, and enthusiastic Christians in Jackson and Stuart. Even now they had no excuses to make, no regrets to offer for the part the Maryland Confederates took in the great struggle.

EDWARD WOOTTON 1839-

Edward was the son of Dr. Turner Wootton, a well-known practitioner and legislator of Montgomery County. Young Wootton, after graduating from Georgetown University in 1858, was a pupil of his cousin, Dr. William Turner Wootton, in Frederick. He then started his doctoring in Rockville where his deceased father had been. In the fall of 1862 young Dr. Wootton enlisted as a private in Elijah V. White's Border Rangers, where he was acting assistant surgeon of the many Marylanders in the 35th Virginia Cavalry. He was detailed for a short time at the General Receiving Infirmary at Gordonsville which was known as Charity Hospital. Assistant Surgeon Wootton returned to the "comanches" of the Laurel Brigade and shared the splendid garlands of glory that wreathe the brows of this battalion. He was captured on February 3, 1865, in Loudoun County and incarcerated in Fort McHenry, sent to the West's Building Hospital, then rapidly exchanged. He was paroled on May 8 at Winchester and returned to his state making Poolesville his homestead. Dr. Wootton continued his medical practice until 1878 when he and his former commander, Lieutenant Colonel White, formed a partnership dealing in grain. In 1887 he was elected to the House of Delegates, then to the Senate for two terms. Exconfederates in this state were prominent in all types of civil society. Not only were there important contributions in modern military medicine, operative surgery, hospitalization and public health which came from those who had been in the Confederate Medical Departments, but they also turned to education, as editors, in universities as administrators and faculty staff, in elective positions, in medical associations and surgical societies. Other Southern medical officers turned to business, law and politics. By the 1880's the distribution of those who returned from the war defeated with rags on their backs, barely shoes on their feet and nothing to put in their bellies, had been converted to success. They were once again prosperous, socially prominent and held the high esteem of their fellow Marylanders as they did prior to the rebellion.

WILLIAM TURNER WOOTTON 1828-1896

William was born in Montgomery County, son of Dr. John Wootton. Receiving his M.D. from the University of Pennsylvania in 1846 he practiced at Clarksburg until 1850 when he moved to Frederick. Dr. Wootton never married. He was active in politics and was known as an avid aversionist toward Federal authority. After the Battle of the Monocacy he was again in trouble for showing aid and comfort to the Confederate soldiers by using his professional knowledge to reduce the pain and anxiety of the boys in butternut. Dr. Wootton was arrested and on August 1, 1864, he was sent by authorities within the Southern lines. Going to the lower portion of the Shenandoah Valley he worked as a civilian contract physician, at Ladies Relief Hospital at Lynchburg. After the conclusion of the conflict he returned to his office in Frederick and continued his professional business. Although the bugle call of eternity has called many veterans, yet those whose hair has turned gray and whose faces are marked with the cares and trials of those intervening years are still struggling, not with sword and carbine, but together both blue and gray labor under the cross that binds up the wounds of carnal warfare and can be victorious from sin to righteousness.

JOHN B. WORTHAN 1840-

Dr. Worthan was commissioned assistant surgeon of the 2nd Maryland Artillery on June 19, 1862. The Baltimore Light Artillery was organized on September 17, 1861, and by the time he joined them they were in the artillery battalion of Richard Snowden Andrews. On February 25, 1863, Assistant Surgeon Worthan was ordered to proceed to Fredericksburg and report to General J.E.B. Stuart for trial before court martial. The proceeding from this inquiry cannot be found but he must have been acquitted because he was restored to his command. On June 13, 1863, the 2nd Maryland Artillery received severe fire but by a vigorous response drove the enemy beyond Kernstown. The next afternoon the guns of the Baltimore Light Artillery were posted on a commanding hill a little to the left of the pike and dropped their first shell into the very center of the Star Fort just north of Winchester. With the exact range the gunners commenced a furious fire which threw the enemy into confusion. Their fire was soon spiritedly returned by Alexander's Federal Baltimore Battery and continued until night fall, when Milroy evacuated his fortifications and attempted to escape. The precision and effect with which the cannon of the Baltimore Light Artillery whipped their state adversaries elicited

Pocket watch engraved "Dr. J. B. Wortham Surgeon Balto. Light. Arty." The outside of the gold is engraved with the Baltimore Battle Monument.
William A. Albaugh III collection

the highest praise from General Gordon and as a mark of esteem, the battery was given first selection of the captured guns. In the desperate fight at Yellow Tavern the battery lost many men, horses and two guns. Private John Hayden was struck by a piece of shell and would have bled to death if not for the devotion of Assistant Surgeon Worthan who carried him on his back into the woods and stanched the hemorrhage. The enemy acquired possession of the woods but the physician concealed himself and young Hayden until night came when he carried him back to the withdrawn Confederate lines. In the late spring of 1864 Dr. Worthan was promoted to surgeon and assigned to the care of his brother "Free Staters" in Steuart's Horse Artillery. On May 8, 1865, he received his parole at Winchester and, finding the door closed to practice in his native state, he settled in Huntsville, Alabama. During the war many friendships were formed which had existed over all these years. Although the paths of these comrades lay in diverse ways they would meet from time to time and enjoy the stories of old that time could never erase. But now one more time, for the last time, the long gray line was thinned by death.

WILLIAM E. WYSHAM

Resigning as a passed assistant surgeon from the U.S. Navy on April 25, 1861, this Baltimorean returned to his home. Seeing his state shackled and not being allowed to secede, Dr. Wysham gave four terrible but glorious years of unequaled strife to the Confederacy. Proceeding to Richmond he was ordinated as surgeon in the Provincial Navy on June 10. He was sent to Gosport Navy Yard and then to duty on the defenses of the North Carolina shore line. In the summer of 1862 he was transferred to the Mobile Naval Hospital. Surgeon Wysham faithfully continued his treatment at this post until the tattered flag was furled. Going to New Orleans he took the oath on May 11, 1865. After several years Dr. Wysham returned to this state; making Catonsville his residence he was active as a general practitioner and as a member of the C.S.A. veteran societies. In 1885 the Society Of The Army And Navy Of The Confederate States In The State Of Maryland had a most successful bazaar; the proceeds of $31,000 was devoted to the care of indigent veterans and the reinterment of those buried in battlefield graves. A number of the gallant older veterans were finding refuge in the alms house of the state and some were being buried in potter's field. The Union soldiers had various Federal government benefits so an appeal was made to the General Assembly for the Confederates. An affirmative action was taken by an annual appropriation of $5,000 and they were granted the Pikesville Arsenal which had been abandoned for twenty years and in a sad plight. On June 27, 1880, the Maryland Line Confederate Soldiers Home was dedicated and formally operated. Ten separate buildings, named after distinguished state soldiers, were furnished by generous friends at an estimated cost of $10,000 which usually housed over one hundred veterans. The administration of the home was by the board of governors of the Association of the Maryland Line under the supervision of a board of managers. They were largely aided by ladies of the board of visitors. Supplements were needed to meet the yearly budget and they were made by veterans whose experiences in life were more fortunate. It was a comfort to the old veterans when adversities proved too strong for them in their declining years to have a haven of rest in which they could retire and find refuge.

HENRY P. P. YEATES

He received his M.D. from the University of Maryland in 1845. Dr. Yeates established his occupational training in Baltimore, the city of his birth, where he was a member of the state Medical and Chirurgical Faculty in 1853. During the second year of the war he broke the cords of family and friends to take up arms against the Union Government. He apparently did not apply for a commission in the Confederacy but entered into an agreement with the medical department as a contract medicine man. His treatment was to those experiencing pain or grief in the hospitals of Virginia where the greatest concentration of general hospitals can be found. After the war, Dr. Yeates returned to his former clientele. These veterans did not forget the dead on the field of honor. They continued to pay tributes of homage to those heroes and the sacrifices they cheerfully made for a cause that was dearer than life itself. Imprinted in their memory is the unselfish devotion, giving the ultimate of which human nature is capable. For they came not for fame or reward, not for place or rank, not lured by ambition or goaded by necessity, but in simple obedience to duty as they understood it. Most fill unmarked graves, no stately abbey will ever cover their remains. Their dust will never repose beneath fretted or frescoed roof. No costly bronze will blazon their names for posterity to honor them but the Monocacy and the Rappahannock, the James and the Chickahominy, the Cumberland and the Tennessee, the Mississippi and the Rio Grande could sing of their prowess. The mountain peaks from the Catoctin to the Blue Ridge, from the Appalachian to the Cumberland, and from the Ozarks to the Smokies stand as eternal witnesses of the valor of the half-fed, half-clad magnificent legions of the Confederacy.

WILLIAM PROBY YOUNG, JR.

Dr. Young was practicing in Frederick County at Middletown. With a large hostile army holding the state in subjection it was apparent to Dr. Young that her sons that were ready to protest for her could only defend her by removing the seat of war south of the Potomac. In July of 1861 when he entered the 116th Virginia Militia he was destined for four long dreary years of trials and hardships unequaled in the annals of free America. After his twelve months enlistment as a private had expired he appeared before the army examining board and being successful he received a commission. Assistant Surgeon Young on July 15, 1862, was assigned to the 4th Georgia Infantry. Returning that fall to his native country, during the Antietam campaign he was wounded where a year and a half before he was treating patients. Returning to this regiment they continued to serve in the Army of Northern Virginia. On June 9, 1863, he was promoted to surgeon, then later transferred to hospital service. The funeral of Major General Joseph E. Johnston was on March 24, 1891, from St. John's Church in Washington and he was interred in Greenmount Cemetery in Baltimore. The active pallbearers were selected from the Confederate

Veterans Association and Dr. Young was chosen. The gallant defenders of the stainless Confederate banner have gone to their heavenly eternal rewards, but they did not die in vain. They marched, camped, and battled side by side in the sacred bond of a common consecration to a cause that was holy. With cheerful endurance of unaccustomed hardship, heroic steadfastness in danger, they gave up their lives with magnificent courage in the deadly trenches or while charging at the flaming cannon's mouth. Those who survived to limp away from the disaster at Appomatox had only tears in their eyes. They were broken in fortune, body and spirit but they turned the defeat of war into the victory of peace. Out of the depth of the bitter flood of reconstruction, through fortitude, patience and courage they emerged more beautiful than ever. Their deeds have cast a halo of glory over our Southern land which will only grow brighter. Their remembrance and legacy is a priceless heritage that we must transmit to our children and their great grandchildren untarnished. They have all heard the last great reveille and those who are born again in Christ are reunited with those brothers whom the fortunes of battle had divided, in a far far better land.

Assistant Surgeon
William Proby Young
William A. Albaugh III collection

JOHN FORNEY ZACHARIAS

John was born and raised in Frederick, son of Dr. Daniel Zacharias, receiving his educational discipline at the Frederick Academy and the Jefferson Medical College, class of 1860. Young Dr. Zacharias was working in the office with his father until the sentiment of the revolution led him into the C.S.A. On January 5, 1863, the resources of his training were utilized as he became an acting assistant surgeon at Danville General Hospital No. 2. By that summer, he was an assistant surgeon. He was captured on May 13, 1864, and was exchanged at Rough and Ready on September 28. Assistant Surgeon Zacharias was assigned to General Hospital No. 1 in Danville; writing of his experiences here he relates, "I first used maggots to remove the decayed tissue in hospital gangrene and with eminent satisfaction. In a single day they would clean a wound much better than any agent we had at our command. I used them afterwards at various places. I am sure I saved many lives by their use, escaped septicaemia, and had rapid recoveries." In that fall his service was at Shipp Hospital with the Army of Tennessee. Dr. Zacharias returned immediately after the war to Frederick and reported to the provost marshal. Not being allowed to practice he again crossed the Potomac to Leesburg and after five years settled in Cumberland. In 1903 he was commander of the United Confederate Veterans

Assistant Surgeon
John Forney Zacharias
Maryland Historical Society,
Baltimore collection

in the State of Maryland. The fact that the Confederate soldier and the people of the South made their superb struggle and their enormous sacrifice for the right of local self-government has gained strength. The conquered banner triumphs in defeat; the lost cause is lost no longer, God denied success in the way of their choosing but granted it in another and better way. The North saved the Union from dissolution, the South saved the rights of the States within the Confederation. Thus victor and vanquished today are both adjudged victorious, for it was due to the Federal soldier that the Union is henceforth indissoluble, it is equally due to the Confederate soldier that this indissoluble Union is composed and shall forever be composed of indestructible States. Indeed God has blessed America.

Veterans of the Maryland Line Confederate Soldiers Home
Daniel D. Hartzler collection

Walnut, green velvet-lined surgeon's kit with brass inlay engraved "Dr. J. F. Zacharias". Top tray contains three amputation knives, forceps, elevator, aneurism hook, tenotome; the bottom has lifting metacarpal saw, tourniquet, Key's saw and in the small compartment with an ivory knob is a small curved needle with wire and cloth sutures, all instruments are marked "Gemrig Phila. Pa."
Maryland Historical Society, Baltimore collection

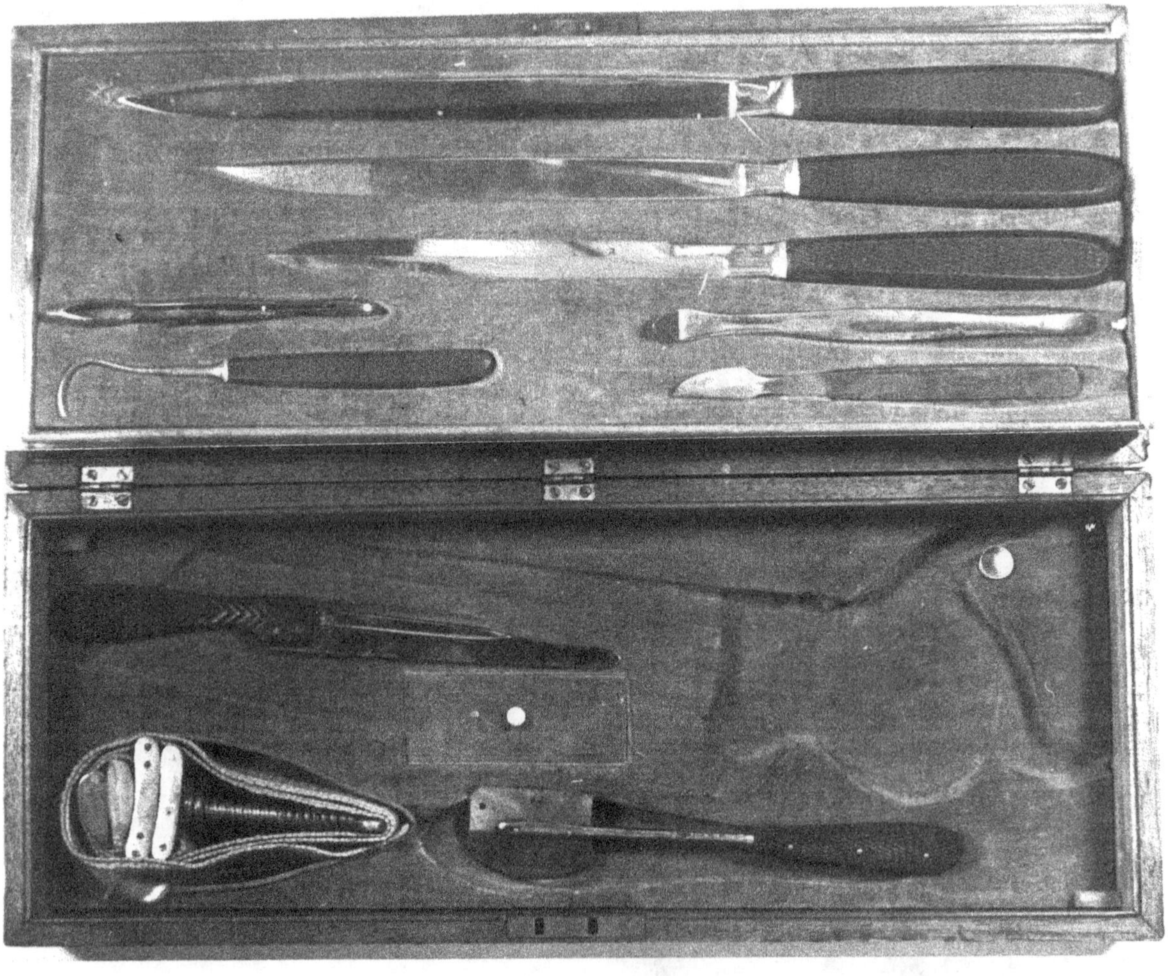

MARYLAND CONFEDERATE VETERANS WHO, AFTER THE WAR, PURSUED THE MEDICAL CURRICULUM AND BECAME LICENSED PRACTITIONERS WITHIN THE STATE

Baker, Newton D., Private
   1st Virginia Cavalry Company F, Washington County
Beale, James Shields, Private
   1st Maryland Artillery
Bean, Hezekiah Henry, Lieutenant
   1st Maryland Infantry Company, Charles County
Blodget, William, Private
   Davis's Maryland Cavalry Company A
Booker, William D., 1844/1921, Private
   3rd Virginia Cavalry Company K. Baltimore
Boyle, Charles Brooke, Private
   1st Maryland Cavalry Company D, Taneytown
Browne, Bennet Bernard, 1842/1922, Private
   7th Virginia Cavalry Company G, Queen Anne's County
Bussey, Bennett F., Sergeant
   General John H. Winder's Detectives.
Campbell, William H. H., Hospital Steward
   Owings Mills
Chapman, Nathaniel, 1842/ , Lieutenant
   1st Maryland Cavalry Company E, Charles County
Christian, John H., 1845/1902
   43rd Virginia Cavalry Company D, Baltimore County
Clewell, Augustus A., Private
   21st North Carolina Infantry Company E, Baltimore
Cordell, Eugene Fauntleroy, 1843/ , Captain,
   Assistant Adjutant General
   51st Virginia Infantry, Baltimore
Coyner, Samuel Fulton, Private
   Lomax's Cavalry, Baltimore
Dawson, Robert Morris, 1839/ , Private
   2nd Maryland Infantry Company C, Talbot County
Dorsey, Nicholas W., Lieutenant
   35th Viriginia Cavalry Company B, Urbana
Duvall, Samuel F., Private
   Hampton Legion Artillery Company B, Anne Arundel County
Edwards, Alexander G., Private
   1st Virginia Cavalry Company K, Brownsville
Eyster, George Hupp, 1845/ , Major
   General J. A. Early staff, Baltimore
Forward, R., Private
   5th Louisiana Infantry Desota Rifles, Harford County
Gough, Benjamin, Private
   4th Virginia Cavalry Company I, Leonardtown
Grimes, John H., Private
   1st Virginia Cavalry, Company A, New Windsor
Hambleton, James P., 1841/ , Sergeant
   35th Georgia Infantry, Talbot County
Harding, Charles A., Private
   2nd Maryland Cavalry Company C
Hatton, J. W. F., Private
   1st Maryland Artillery
Howard, James McHenry, 1839/1916, Captain
   Engineer Corps, Baltimore
Knight, Louis W., Private
   2nd Maryland Cavalry Company D, Baltimore
Lickle, John D., /1900, Private
   1st Maryland Cavalry Company D, New Market
Lynch, John Stevens, Lieutenant
   6th Alabama Infantry Company C, St. Mary's County
Martin, Hugh, Private
   2nd Maryland Cavalry Company C, Baltimore
McLeod, Wilford M., Private
   1st Maryland Cavalry, Company B, Georgetown
McSherry, Edward Coale, 1849/1900, Private
   1st Maryland Cavalry Company D, Frederick
Meire, Julius Ernest, 1833/1905, Captain
   Marine Corps, Talbot County
Mobberly, Bradley, Private
   1st Missouri Cavalry, Frederick County
Morgan, William L., Sergeant
   31st Virginia Infantry, Company A, Baltimore
Mullen, William H., Private
   1st Virginia Infantry Company B, Pikesville
Nelson, Hugh, Private
   2nd Virginia Cavalry, Company K, Baltimore
Nouse, Charles H., Jr., Private
   35th Virginia Cavalry, Company B, Darnestown
Regester, Wilson Gray, 1845/1882, Private
   2nd Maryland Artillery, Montgomery County
Riddlemoser, Joseph, Private
   2nd Maryland Infantry Company H, Emmitsburg
Russell, Charles F., Private
   7th Virginia Cavalry Company G
Schell, Joseph, Private
   1st Virginia Cavalry Company G, Frederick
Shower, George T., 1841/1923, Private
   1st Maryland Cavalry Company D, Manchester
Steinback, John M., Private
   56th Virginia Infantry Company E, Baltimore
Stuart, Fred, Lieutenant
   General C. Lee staff
Thomas, Charles Byron, Private
   35th Virginia Cavalry Company B, Furnace Ford
Thomas, Samuel Franklin, Private
   35th Virginia Cavalry Company B, Adamstown
Ward, Thomas J., Private
   2nd Maryland Artillery. Baltimore
Warfield, Milton W., Lieutenant
   General John H. Winder Detectives, Lisbon
Waring, William Worthington, Private
   1st Maryland Cavalry Company B, Upper Marlboro
Wilhelm, James T., 1839/ , Lieutenant
   2nd Maryland Artillery, Leonardtown
Wilkerson, Basil M., Sergeant
   8th Alabama Cavalry Company K, Baltimore
Williams, Edward Jones, 1841/ , Lieutenant
   31st North Carolina Infantry Company I, Baltimore
Wilson, John T., 1843/1910, Private
   1st Maryland Artillery, Prince George's County
Wiltshire, James Gerard, Lieutenant
   43rd Virginia Cavalry, Company H, Funkstown
Wyman, Edward, Sergeant
   3rd Maryland Artillery

Daniel D. Hartzler

When the author completed "Arms Makers of Maryland" that was published in 1977, he pursued a list of Marylanders in the Confederacy which has surpassed 12,000 names. Through the research of over 1,500 sources he knew there were a number of physicians who had voluntarily gone into exile to serve in the Southern forces. Six months ago he extracted them from his register and was astounded at the number. Feeling that each of these practitioners deserved a biographical sketch, which he could not include in the forthcoming "Marylanders in the Confederacy," and being involved in the medical sphere himself, brought to fruition this little volume.

INDEX

Adams, Edward T. 11
Adams, J. P. 36
Addison, W. John 11, 41
Anderson, P. 38
Allison, Richard Taylor 38
Andrews, Richard Snowden 47, 88
Annan, Andrew 11
Annan, Samuel 11
Archer, George W. 11, 12
Archer, James J. 11, 56
Archer, Robert Harris, Jr. 11
Archer, Robert Harris, Sr. 11
Arnold, W. H. 53
Ashby, Turner 37, 54
Atkinson, Archibald, Jr. 12

Baden, Joseph Abell 12
Baer, Caleb Dorsey 12
Baer, Charles J. 12
Baer, Jacob 12
Baker, Newton D. 93
Baldwin, Joseph 13
Baldwin, Thomas S. 14
Baltimore Heavy Artillery 14
Baltimore Light Artillery 73, 88
Baltimore Southern Exposition Management 87
Barber, Charles 14
Barney, Joseph N. 35
Barry, Arthur R. 14, 26
Barry, William J. 14
Beale, James Shields 93
Beall, Lloyd James 38
Bean, Hezekiah Henry 93
Bean, James Baxter 25, 43
Bear, Alexander 14
Beard, John W. 36
Beauregard, P. G. T. 19, 44, 68, 73, 85
Beck, Samuel 14, 15
Bell, Alexander T. 15, 16
Bell, John 35
Belvin, James W. 16
Best, J. W. F. 16, 17
Blada, V. 43
Bland, John 43
Bledsoe, Powhatan 17
Blodget, William 93
Bond, Frank A. 23
Booker, William D. 93
Booth, John Wilkes 17
Booth, Joseph Adrian 17
Boswell, Lewis A. 17
Boteler, Robert H. E. 17, 18, 49, 77
Boyd, John Mason 18
Boyd, Samuel Beckett 18
Boykin, Thomas Jackson 19
Boyle, Charles Brooke 93
Boyle, Cornelius 19, 20
Bradford, Charles H. 36
Bradford, J. P. 36
Bragg, B. 63, 68
Braxton, Tomlin 20, 21
Breathed, James 16, 21, 22, 61
Breckenridge, John C. 34
Brengle, William D. 22
Brent, Joseph Lancaster 26, 29
Brewer, Charles Mrs. 22
Brewer, William 22
Brice, Carroll 14, 17, 23
Briscoe, Henry 22
Brogden, Arthur 22, 23
Brooks, John W. 36
Brown, George William 26, 33, 74
Brown, John W. 23
Browne, Bennet Bernard 93
Bruns, John Dickson 23
Buchanan Battery 47
Buchanan, Franklin 16, 19, 38, 47, 55, 57, 64

Burns, Arthur P. 23
Bussey, Bennett F. 93
Butler, Benjamin F. 30, 43
Byrd, Harvey Leonidas 23, 24

Cadwallader, G. 41
Campbell, Alexander Mills 24, 25
Campbell, William H. H. 93
Caperton, George Henry 25
Carmichael, Richard Bennett 53
Carr, Richard Wilson 36
Carrington W. A. 72
Carter, Thomas H. 25
Cary, Constance 73
Cary, Hettie 73
Cary, Jennie 73
Chancellor, Charles William 25
Chapman, Nathaniel 93
Chapan, William 43
Chesapeake Artillery 47
Chew, Samuel C. 36
Chisolm, Julian J. 26
Christian, John H. 93
Church, Dr. 36
Clagett, James Hawkins 26
Clagett, Joseph Edward 26
Clarke, J. Lyle 21
Clarke, Powhatan 26, 27
Clendenin, Alexander F. 26, 36, 74
Cleveland, Grover 83
Clewell, Augustus A. 93
Cochran, Henry King 26
Cochran, Robert M. 26
Cockerville, Samuel John 43
Coechling, C. W. 36
Cole, William H. 27
Commanches 87
Conrad, John Summerfield 28, 29
Cook, Theodore 36
Cooke, James Philip 29
Coonan, John N. 36
Cordell, Eugene Fauntleroy 93
Correll, John William 29
Costen, Isaac Napoleon 29
Covey, Edward Napoleon 29
Covington, W. A. 43
Coyner, Samuel Fulton 93
Cromwell, Benjamin Mellicamp 30

Dailey, Robert Wood 30
Daniel, J. 41
Dashiell, Jeremiah Yellott 30
Davis, Benjamin 31
Davis, James 31, 63
Davis, Jefferson 11, 26, 36, 37, 42, 44, 45, 56, 59, 62, 77, 84, 87
Davis, John J. 30, 31
Davis's Maryland Cavalry 93
Davis, Surgeon 43
Davis, T. Sturgis 39, 54
Dawson, Robert Morris 93
Dea's Maryland Artillery 37
Dickson, John Hamilton 43
Dorsey, Harry Woodward, Jr. 32
Dorsey, Ignatius Waters 32
Dorsey, Nicholas W. 93
Douglas, Stephen A. 35
Dryden, Robert H. 33
Dunbar, J. R. W. 49
Duvall, Philip Barton 33
Duvall, Samuel F. 93

Early, Jubal A. 25, 73, 93
Echols, J. 25
Edwards, Alexander G. 93
Edwards, J. H. 34
Eliason, Talcott 34
Elzey, Arnold 44, 54

Emory, Richard 35, 36, 74
Emory, Thomas Hall, Sr. 35, 38
Erich, Augustus 36
Everett, Edward 35
Everett, William 35, 36, 74
Ewell, Richard 79
Eyster, George Hupp 93

Farandis, George G. 36
Floyd, John B. 58
Flying Artillery 75
Foreman, Arthur L. 36, 74
Forrest, French 40
Forward, R. 93
Franklin, Joel W. 36
Frederick County Confederate Monumental and Memorial Association 87
Freeman, Robert J. 36, 37, 74
Frick, Charles 46

Gaillard, Edwin Samuel 37, 40
Gaines, John M. 37
Gaither, George Ridgely 23, 40
Gale, Frank 38
Gamble, Cary Breckenride 38
Garretson, Frederick 38
Geddings, Eli 39
Gibbes, Robert R. 39
Gibson, Charles Bell 37, 38, 39
Gibson, R. 35
Gilmor, Harry W. 39, 41, 54, 73, 75, 87
Gilmor's Battalion 40, 41
Glisan, Rodney 40
Glocker, Albert Campbell 40
Glocker, Theodore W. 40
Goldsborough, Edmund K. 40
Goldsborough, W. W. 54
Goolrick, Peter 39, 40
Gordon, John B. 89
Gough, Benjamin 93
Green, Daniel Smith 40, 41
Green, William 41
Gregg, Maxcy 42
Grimes, John H. 93
Grove, Philip D. 41
Grover, Leonard 26
Guild, Lafayette 30, 76, 80
Gwynn, Charles L. 41

Hahnemann, Samuel 47
Hambleton, James P. 93
Hamlin, Hannibal 34
Hammond, Alexander 42
Hammond, George B. 42
Hammond, Harry 42
Hammond, William A. 42, 46, 59
Hampton, W. 37
Hancock, F. W. 83
Handy, William 30
Hardcastle, Aaron Bascom 23
Hardcastle, Jerome Humphrey 42, 43
Harding, Charles A. 93
Harding, Hiram W. 43
Harman, A. W. 41
Harris, Chapin A. 43
Harris, James Howard 43
Hatton, J. W. F. 93
Hay, William 87
Hayden, John 89
Hayward, William H. 26
Healey, Thomas A. 43, 44
Heath, Horace M. 44
Hebb, Herbert J. 44
Hebb, John Wise 44
Hebb, Thomas A. 44
Herbert, James R. 48, 58
Hicks, Thomas H. 26, 29, 30

Hill, D. H. 25
Hilliary, Washington M. 33, 44, 45
Hodges, James 45, 46
Hodges, William Ringgold 45
Holden, Robert Randolph 46
Hollins, George Nichols 74
Hood, John B. 30
Hooker, Joseph 71
Howard, Charles Jr. 46
Howard, Charles Sr. 46
Howard Dragoons 40
Howard, Edward Lloyd 46
Howard, Frank Key 46
Howard, James McHenry 93
Howard, John Eager 46
Howard, McHenry 46
Hoxton, Leewellyn G. 57
Huger, Benjamin 22
Hughes, Alfred 46, 47
Hughes, George W. 26
Hughes, James Fritz 47
Hunter, Frederick 47
Hunter, J. A. 25

Inglehart, Osborn S. 47

Jackson, J. K. 38
Jackson, Thomas J. 37, 46, 47, 49, 54, 58, 71, 82, 84, 87
Jarrett, James H. 48
Jarrett, Martin L. 48
Jenkins, Thomas 73
Johnson, Andrew 35
Johnson, Bradley Tyler 23, 37, 49, 54, 73
Johnson, Claudia Saunders 37
Johnson, J. Newman 49
Johnson, James Thomas, Jr. 49
Johnson, Otis 49
Johnson, Richard Potts 49
Johnson, William Hilleary 18, 49, 77
Johnston, Albert Sidney 29, 46
Johnston, John R. 26
Johnston, Joseph E. 19, 36, 64, 77, 89
Jones, Henry M. 49, 50
Jones, Joseph H. 58
Joynes, Levin Smith 38, 50

Kane, George Proctor 23, 33
Keats, John Thomas 50
Kent, Joseph, Jr. 50, 51
Ker, John 51
Key, Francis Scott 46
Key, Henry J. 51
Kinlock, R. A. 83
Kirkland, William C. 51
Kleinschmidt, Karl H. A. 51, 52
Kloman, William C. 52
Knight, Louis W. 93

Lane, Joseph 35
Lanier, George 41
Lanier Guards 41
Latimer, Thomas Sargent 53
Lawrence, George Washington 53
Lee, C. 93
Lee, Richard C. 36
Lee, Robert E. 20, 42, 44, 47, 54, 56, 64, 66, 68, 77, 82, 84, 87
Leeman, William M. 53
Letcher, John 36
Lewis, G. T. 53
Lewis, George W. 53
Lewis, Greenville R. 53
Lickle, John D. 93
Lincoln, Abraham 14, 16, 17, 30, 33, 34
Lindsay, Alexander 53
Lister, Joseph 11
Little, Lewis Henry 58
Locke, Leonard E. 53, 54
Longstreet, J. 47
Lovell, Mansfield 18

Lownes, Lloyd 40
Lublock, Frank R. 30
Lucas's South Carolina Artillery 20
Lynch, John Stevens 93

Macgill, Charles 56, 57
Macgill, Charles G. W. 57
Macgill, David 57
Macgill, James 21, 57
Macgill, William D. 57
Mackall, William Whann 47
MacKenzie, John C. 36
MacKenzie, Thomas G. 36
Maddox, Thomas Clay 54
Maney, Thomas F. 54
Martin, Hugh 93
Maryland Children of the Confederacy 87
Maryland Division United Daughters of the Confederacy 87
Maryland Flying Artillery 38, 47
Maryland Guard 21, 35, 36, 59
Maryland Guerilla Zouaves 11
Maryland Line 49, 68
Maryland Line, Association of the 87
Maryland Line Confederate Soldiers Home 14, 16, 44, 50, 60, 72, 79, 89
Maryland Sons of Confederate Veterans 87
Maryland United Confederate Veterans 87
Maryland Zouaves 35
Mason, Augustus Smith 54
Mason, Frank J. 23, 39, 54, 55
Mason, John Thompson O. 55
Mason's Maryland Cavalry 41
Maury, Richard B. 57
Maximillian 14
McCausland, John 58
McCaw, James Brown 43
McDonald, Edward Hitchcock 27
McDowell, Irvin 44
McGill, Charles B. 58
McGill, Samuel 58
McGill, Thomas J. 58
McGill, Wardlaw 58
McGowan, S. 42
McGuire, H. 29
McIntosh, David G. 64
McLane, Robert Milligan 26, 64
McLeod, Wilford M. 93
McKnew, Wilberforce Richard 32, 50, 58
McManus, Felix R. 36
McNeil's Rangers 75
McNiel, William Gitts 84
McPherson, William Smith 58
McSherry, Edward Coale 93
McSherry, James W. 58
Meire, Julius Ernest 93
Merryman, John 41
Middleton, Alexius L. 58, 59
Miles, Francis Turguand 59
Miller, J. H. 53
Mobberly, Bradley 93
Moberly, Eldred W. 49
Monmonier, John Francis 59
Monmonier, John N. K. 59
Montgomery, James 60
Montgomery, William T. 60
Moore, Samuel Preston 62, 68
Morfit, Charles McL. 59, 60
Morfit, Clarence 59
Morfit, Henry Mason 59
Morfit, Mason 59
Morgan, Gerald E. 36
Morgan, William L. 93
Mosby's Rangers 18, 43
Mott, A. R. 68
Mullen, William H. 93
Murdock, Russell 61
Murphy, Samuel W. 61
Murray, William H. 61
Myrick, John D. 39

National Volunteers 27
Nelson, H. C. 36
Nelson, Hugh 93
Newell, Analanah Ritchie 61
Newell, D. 60
Newell, William Henry 61, 62
Newman, Harry Wright 40, 53
Nicholas, Wilson Carr 23
Nickerson, Charles E. V. 36, 62, 74
Noel, Henry Reginald 62
Norcom, James 62
Norcom, William Augustus Blount 62
Norris, William H. 36
Northrop, Lucius Bellinger 62, 63
Nott, Josiah Clark 63
Nouse, Charles H., Jr. 93

Offutt, Thomas Zadac 63, 64
Opie, Thomas 64
Ordeman, Charles 64
Ordeman, John H. 64

Page, Isham Randolph 64, 65
Page, John Randolp 65, 66, 82
Palmer, John Williamson 66
Parker, John Thomas 66
Parker, William Harwar 16
Pasteur, Louis 11
Patterson, Francis W. 66
Patterson, R. J. 66
Pelham, John 21
Pendleton, W. N. 64, 65
Perry, M. C. 55
Peters, George P. 22
Pettit, Henry McEwen 66, 67
Pettigrew, J. J. 47
Piggot, Aaron Snowden 67
Pitts, John William 68
Polignac, C. J. 26
Polk, Leonidas 68
Poole, Ephraim Howard 49
Porcher, F. Peyre 26
Potts, Richard 49, 68
Powell, Alfred H. 68
Price, Abram H. 36
Price, S. 58, 71
Pue, William H. 68, 69
Pugh, Thomas Cloman 69

Raborg, Samuel A. 36, 70, 74
Randall, James Ryder 73
Read, N. M. 70
Regester, Wilson Gray 93
Rhett's South Carolina Artillery 20
Richardson, John Summerfield 71
Riddick, Joseph Henry 71
Riddlemoser, Joseph 93
Ringgold, R. Samuel 71
Robbins, William H. 71
Robertson, Fenwick 71, 72
Rogers, Frank 71
Rogers, Thomas J. 72
Rosser, Thomas 31
Russell, Charles F. 93
Rutledge, Charles A. 72

Sappington, Thomas 36
Schaffer, Francis B. 14
Schell, Joseph 93
Schwartz, Edward 25
Scott, Henry C. 73
Scott, W. 26
Semmes, Alexander Ignatius Jenkins 73
Semmes, Raphael 38, 40, 48, 79
Shower, George T. 93
Shutt, Augustus P. 22
Sibley, H. H. 30
Simpson, Edward B. 73, 74
Simpson, George R. 74
Sinclair, Arthur 74
Sinclair, William Beverley 74

Smith, Allen P. 36, 74
Smith, E. Kirby 18, 36, 44, 50, 77
Smith, G. W. 37, 40, 54, 85
Smith, Lewis H. 58
Smith, Nathan R. 29, 35, 59, 74
Smith, Otho J. 38
Snowden, Arthur Monteith 74
Snowden, DeWilton 74, 75
Snowden, Nicholas 23
Society of the Army and Navy of the Confederate States in the State of Maryland 38, 50, 52, 53, 54, 57, 58, 63, 64, 72, 77, 86, 87, 89
Society of Confederate Mothers and Widows of Baltimore 87
Spalding, Basil William 75
Spalding, Samuel E. 75
Steinback, John M. 93
Steiner, Harry H. 75
Stephens, A. H. 77
Steuart, George Hume, Jr. 49, 75
Steuart, George H., Sr. 27, 35
Steuart, Harry A. 76
Steuart, William Frederick, Jr. 76
Steuart, William Frederick, Sr. 46, 76
Stout, S. H. 47
Strange, John Bowie 63
Stuart, Fred 93
Stuart, J. E. B. 21, 22, 35, 68, 87, 88
Stuart's Horse Artillery 16, 22, 31, 61, 89
Sutherland, Joel B. 69
Sutherland, Samuel 69
Swan, Robert 56

Taney, Roger Brooke 41
Tarr, B. A. 77
Tarr, Charles E. 77
Tarr, William H. 77
Taylor, Algernon Sidney 38
Taylor, Calvin B. 68
Taylor, Milton N. 36
Taylor, R. 72, 77
Temple, Thomas Price 77
Thom, J. Pembroke 77
Thomas, Allen 18
Thomas, Charles Byron 93
Thomas, Francis J. 36
Thomas, Jacob G. 18, 49, 77
Thomas, John Hanson 36, 77
Thomas, Richard 66
Thomas, Robert L. 77
Thomas, Samuel Franklin 93
Thomas, Thomas H. 77, 78
Thompson, Ignatius Davis 36, 74, 78
Thompson, Meredith 79
Tilghman, Lloyd 55
Tinsley, Alexander 79
Trimble, Isaac Ridgeway 16, 19, 26, 27, 49, 58
Turner, William Mason 79
Turpin, Henry W. 79
Tyler, Robert Charles 66
Tyler, William 36

Van Bibber, Frederick Garretson 38
Van Bibber, W. C. 38
Van Buren, Martin 56
Vance, Zebulon B. 19
Virdin, William Ward, Jr. 80
Volck, Adalbert Johann 43

Walker, Edmund Rhett 80, 81
Walker, Hiram H. 81
Walker, Samuel T. 26
Walls, J. William 82
Ward, Thomas J. 93
Warfield, James H. H. 82
Warfield, Milton W. 93
Waring, William Worthington 93
Warner, Joseph P. 22
Warren, Edward 36, 45, 46, 74, 82

Washington, George 71
Weems, Julius B. 82, 83
West, Nelson G. 83
Weston Guard 36, 46, 53, 60, 68, 73
Weston, J. Alden 36
Weston's Battalion 37, 46, 49, 53, 59, 60, 68, 73
Wheedan, Thomas J. 83
Whistler, George W. 84
Whistler, William McNiel 84
White, Elijah V. 39, 54, 73, 87
White's Border Rangers 87
Whitridge, John 36
Wiley, Zephaniah K. 84
Wilhelm, James T. 93
Wilkerson, Basil M. 93
Williams, Edward Jones 93
Williams, Thomas H. 35, 85
Williams, William G. 86
Wilshire, James Garrard 18
Wilson, Dr. 36
Wilson, John T. 93
Wilson, Pierce Butler, Sr. 86
Wiltshire, James Gerard 93
Winder, Charles S. 82
Winder, John Henry 15, 93
Winder, Sidney 40
Winter, Charles S. 47
Wise, James A. 44
Withers, J. M. 63
Woodward, Richard H. 87
Woolfolk, A. M. 87
Wootton, Edward 87, 88
Wootton, John 88
Wootton, Turner 87
Wootton, William Turner 58, 87, 88
Worthan, John B. 88, 89
Worthington, Charles G. 56
Wyman, Edward 93
Wysham, William E. 89

Yeates, Henry P. P. 89
Yellott, Dr. 36
Young, William Proby, Jr. 89, 90

Zacharias, Daniel 91
Zacharias, John Forney 91, 92
Zarvona's Maryland Zouaves 66

www.ingramcontent.com/pod-product-compliance
Lightning Source LLC
Chambersburg PA
CBHW080252170426
43192CB00014BA/2652